Jimmy Carter

An Hour
Before Daylight

Memories of a Rural Boyhood

Simon & Schuster

NEW YORK LONDON TORONTO SYDNEY SINGAPORE

SIMON & SCHUSTER
Rockefeller Center
1230 Avenue of the Americas
New York, NY 10020
Copyright © 2001 by Jimmy Carter
All rights reserved,
including the right of reproduction
in whole or in part in any form.
SIMON & SCHUSTER and colophon are registered trademarks
of Simon & Schuster, Inc.
Designed by Brooke Zimmer Koven
Manufactured in the United States of America

1   3   5   7   9   10   8   6   4   2

Library of Congress Cataloging-in-Publication Data
Carter, Jimmy
An hour before daylight : memories of a rural boyhood / Jimmy Carter.
p.   cm.
Includes index
1. Carter, Jimmy—Childhood and youth.   2. Presidents—
United States—Biography.   3. Farmers—Georgia—Plains—
Biography.   4. Plains (Ga.)—Biography.   5. Plains (Ga.)—Social life
and customs—20th century.   6. Country life—Georgia—Plains—History—
20th century.   7. Plains region (Ga.)—Rural conditions—20th century.
8. Carter family.   I. Title.

E873 .C36 2001
973.926'092—dc21
[B]   00-048248

ISBN 0-7432-1193-6

Photo credits appear on page 285.

To my newest grandson, Hugo,
with hopes that this book might someday let him
better comprehend the lives of his ancestors.

Contents

An Hour
Before Daylight

1

Land, Farm, and Place

Main Street of Plains, Georgia, 1905

I F YOU LEAVE Savannah on the coast and travel on the only
U.S. highway that goes almost straight westward across the
state of Georgia, you will cross the Ogeechee, Oconee, and Oc-
mulgee rivers, all of which flow to the south and east and empty into
the Atlantic Ocean. After about three hours you'll cross the Flint
River, the first stream that runs in a different direction, and eventually its often muddy waters empty into the Gulf of Mexico. Unlike
the Continental Divide in the Rocky Mountains, our "divide" is not
noticeable, because the land was all part of the relatively flat bottom
of the sea in the not-too-distant geological past. It is still rich and

productive, thanks to the early ocean sediments and the nutrients it has accumulated from plants and animals since that time.

If you keep on for another thirty miles, still heading toward Columbus, Georgia; Montgomery and Birmingham, Alabama; and points beyond, you'll come to Plains, a small town on land as level as any you will ever see. As people have always said, "When it rains, the water don't know which way to run." Its original name was "Plains of Dura," derived from the place in the Bible where King Nebuchadnezzar set up his great image of gold (Daniel 3:1). Although the land was flat and rich, no one knows why the earliest settlers wanted to commemorate the worship of a false god. It may have been to honor Shadrach, Meshach, and Abednego, who refused to bow down to the idol, and escaped the fiery furnace because of God's protection.

Just beyond the town there is a place called Archery, where the topography begins to change for the first time since Savannah, from flat plains to rolling hills and poorer soils that extend on to the Chattahoochee River, which divides Georgia from Alabama. Archery is no longer there, except on the old maps, but it's where I grew up and lived from when I was four years old in 1928 until the very end of the Great Depression, when I left for college and the United States Navy in 1941.

In addition to being 190 miles west of Savannah, Plains is located exactly 120 miles due south of Atlanta, and the seat of the county—Sumter—lies nine miles to the east. It is named Americus, the Latinized first name of Amerigo Vespucci, an Italian navigator and explorer who claimed to be the first European to land on the North American continent and, as a mapmaker, also gave it his name. The coming of automobiles and tractors has caused most of the small towns in Southwest Georgia to wither away, but Plains is an exception. It is surrounded by productive farms, and seems to have citizens who are exceptionally inclined to resist moving away to distant places.

Archery, on the other hand, was never quite a real town. At the heart of it, a little more than a half-mile west of our farmhouse, were the homes of the Seaboard Airline Railroad section foreman and the six black employees who kept the rail bed in good repair. A half-mile farther west was a strong African Methodist Episcopal church congregation, across the road from the most notable landmark, a small store by the railroad tracks that was sheathed completely in flattened Prince Albert tobacco cans. Except for the church, which is still vibrant and active, all the rest is gone.

Our own farm, just to the east, occupied the last of the good land; otherwise, around Archery the soil was marginally fertile and somewhat hilly, and the surrounding sandy fields were some of the first to be planted in pine-tree seedlings, which now compose an almost monocultural forest, approaching maturity. Back in the 1930s, however, Archery was substantial enough to be the center of my world.

My most persistent impression as a farm boy was of the earth. There was a closeness, almost an immersion, in the sand, loam, and red clay that seemed natural, and constant. The soil caressed my bare feet, and the dust was always boiling up from the dirt road that passed fifty feet from our front door, so that inside our clapboard house the red clay particles, ranging in size from face powder to grits, were ever present, particularly in the summertime, when the wooden doors were kept open and the screens just stopped the trash and some of the less adventurous flies. Until 1938, when a paved highway was cut through the woods a mile north of our house, we were proud that our small crooked dirt road was the official United States Route 280! For those days, it was heavily traveled by automobiles, trucks, and buses, but with few exceptions the local people passing in front of our house walked or rode on mule-drawn wagons. The railroad ran just a few feet on the other side of the dirt road, and we never failed to wave at the conductors, engineers, and passengers, who seemed as remote as travelers from another planet.

It didn't seem that we watched outside all the time, but someone in the house was always aware if a nonstranger was passing by, and we knew a lot about the people and their vehicles. We recog-

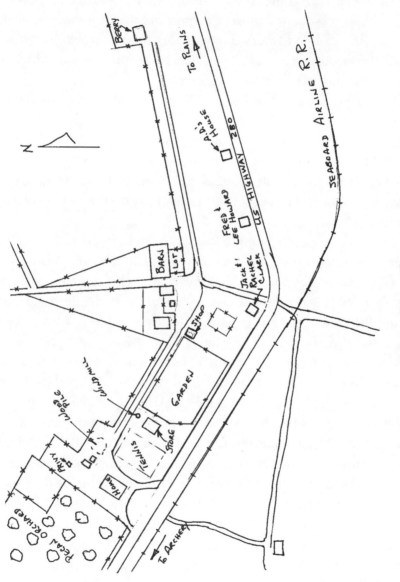

Carter Home Place

nized the make of cars and pickup trucks as far as we could see them and could identify most of the local vehicles by the sound of their engines and rattles. One difference between then and now, I guess, was that there was usually someone out in the yard, the store, the garden, or a nearby field who was watching the passing scene. Really old people, those who were not feeling well, and able-bodied folks on rainy days or on Sundays were most often sitting on their front porches. When we passed someone's house, we felt somewhat uncomfortable if we didn't see anyone there with whom we could exchange a wave or a hello.

Very few farm homes had a telephone, but there was one in our house. It was number 23, and we answered two rings. On the same party line, the Bacons had one ring and the Watsons picked up on three. (In fact, there were usually two other listeners to all our calls.) We seemed to have an omniscient operator in Plains. If we placed a call to Mr. Roy Brannen, Miss Gladys would say, "He left for Americus this morning at about nine-thirty, but he plans to be back before dinner. He'll probably stop by the stable, and I'll try to catch him there." She also had the latest news on any sickness in the community, plus a lot more information that indicated there were maybe three listeners on most calls.

I've often wondered why we were so infatuated with the land, and I think there is a strong tie to the Civil War, or, as we called it, the War Between the States. Although I was born more than half a century after the war was over, it was a living reality in my life. I grew up in one of the families whose people could not forget that we had been conquered, while most of our neighbors were black people whose grandparents had been liberated in the same conflict. Our two races, although inseparable in our daily lives, were kept apart by social custom, misinterpretation of Holy Scriptures, and the unchallenged law of the land as mandated by the United States Supreme Court.

It seemed natural for white folks to cherish our Southern heritage and cling to our way of life, partially because the close ties among many of our local families went back another hundred years before the war, when our Scotch-Irish ancestors had come to Georgia from the British Isles or moved south and west, mostly from Virginia and the Carolinas. We were bound together by blood kinship as well as by lingering resentment against those who had defeated us. A frequent subject of discussion around my grandparents' homes was the damage the "damn Yankees" had done to the South during Reconstruction years.

Many older Georgians still remembered vividly the anger and embarrassment of their parents, who had to live under the domination of carpetbaggers and their Southern allies, who were known as scalawags. My grandfather Gordy was thirteen years old when what he saw as the Northern oppressors finally relinquished political and economic control of the state in 1876, eleven years after the conflict ended. My mother was the only one in her family who ever spoke up to defend Abraham Lincoln. I don't remember ever hearing slavery mentioned, only the unwarranted violation of states' rights and the intrusion of the federal government in the private lives of citizens. Folks never considered that the real tragedy of Reconstruction was its failure to establish social justice for the former slaves. The intense bitterness was mostly confined to our older relatives, who couldn't understand the desire of some of us younger ones to look more into the future—or at least the present—instead of just the past.

Georgia had begun its early colonial existence in 1733 by rejecting fervently the concept of slavery, but this ideal yielded twenty years later to the influence of large landowners along the Atlantic coast who saw their neighbors in the Carolinas getting rich from rice, silk, indigo, and cotton produced by the slave labor they imported from Africa. Within a few decades after being legalized, slaves made up two-thirds of a plantation family's total wealth, with about one-half the remainder coming from the land they worked.

My great-great-grandfather Wiley Carter is an example. He died during the war, in 1864, and in his will he left to his twelve children forty-three slaves, 2,212 acres of land, and other property and cash, or $22,000 for each. Neither he nor his heirs realized at the time that the slaves would soon be free, and that the Confederate money would be worthless. His children ended up with small farms, and they and their descendants retained a deep-seated belief that only the land had any real and lasting value.

Another legacy of the war was the refusal of white people to accept the children of liberated slaves as legal or social equals. Having been effectively disenfranchised themselves if they had been loyal to the Southern side, white leaders considered themselves justified in using every means to control the political system when Northern domination finally ended. Elections quickly came to be decided solely by the Democratic Party primary, from which black citizens were carefully excluded, and rural dominance was guaranteed by basing election results on counties (regardless of their size) instead of on the votes of individual citizens. For more than a century after the war, and even when I first ran for public office in 1962, each vote in some of the smaller counties of Georgia was worth a hundred votes in Atlanta.

Someone had to be blamed when the ravages of the Depression years struck, and many of the smoldering resentments against Yankees and the federal government were given new life in my childhood. Yet, with the racially segregated social system practically unchallenged, it seemed that blacks and whites accepted each other as partners in their shared poverty. So there were negative and positive aspects of our white Southern heritage. Our white families were generally close-knit, relaxed in dealing with black neighbors, deeply wedded to the land, and penurious with our cash holdings, especially as we saw them dwindling away during the hard years of the 1930s.

Despite the legal and social mandate of racial segregation, the personal relationships among black and white families were quite different from those of today, at least in many aspects of life on our farm, because our daily existence was almost totally intertwined. At the same time, throughout the years of my boyhood and youth the political and social dominance of whites was an accepted fact, never challenged or even debated, so far as I knew, by white liberals or black protesters. I recall a few instances when disreputable whites had to appeal to the larger community to confirm their racial superiority by siding with them in a dispute, but their very need to do so confirmed their own low social status. For those who were lazy or dishonest, or had repulsive personal habits, "white trash" was a greater insult than any epithet based on race.

In fact, the final judgment of people I knew was based on their own character and achievements, and not on their race. There is no doubt that black families had to overcome severe and unfair obstacles, but those who were considered to be honest, hardworking, and thrifty had at least a chance to succeed financially and to enjoy general respect, despite the unalterable social distinctions. This was true even though they still came to the back door of a white family's home, rode in a separate part of the passenger train, sat upstairs in the Americus movie theater and in the county courthouse, and attended their separate schools and churches. They were not allowed to vote, serve on juries, or participate in any political affairs. Their spokespersons could make appeals to the local school board, the city council, or in various ways to the system of justice, but they could not participate in the final decisions made, and their appeals were often ignored if they were contending with prominent whites.

All white children around the Plains community, including Archery, attended Plains High School, from the first grade through the eleventh. Black children in our part of the county had classes in more than a dozen churches or private homes, often with all grades crowded into a single room. They were usually furnished with chairs of various sizes, a blackboard, and textbooks considered too dilapidated for use by white students. The County School Board was strict on mandatory attendance for white children, but quite flexible for blacks, assuming that their education above an elementary level was not important. This division of the two races was supposed to meet the U.S. Supreme Court's mandate of "separate but equal."

In Archery, a black man enjoyed the highest social and, our community believed, financial status. He was African Methodist Episcopal Bishop William Decker Johnson, whose primary religious responsibilities encompassed five Midwestern states. His home base was a combination private school, insurance company, and publishing company located across the railroad from St. Mark African Methodist Episcopal Church. The entire Plains community knew when Bishop Johnson was at home, and about once a year he invited our family and perhaps the Watsons to come to the worship service at St. Mark AME Church. In honor of his presence, a choir from Spelman College, or one of the other black institutions in Atlanta, would come down to sing, and the bishop would preach.

In addition to St. Mark AME Church and one still-occupied tenant house, the most important landmark in Archery now is one of the few historical markers erected in Georgia to commemorate important events or the lives of outstanding citizens. This one, in a couple of hundred words, recounts the notable contributions of a famous son, William Decker Johnson. (In one phrase, it also mentions that the thirty-ninth president of the United States was his neighbor.)

As a little boy, I was accustomed to the relatively sedate and time-constrained services of our own congregation at Plains Baptist Church, so our family's visits to St. Mark were strange experiences. The small white clapboard building was always overflowing with worshipers and would rock with music and with religious spirit far exceeding anything we ever experienced. We knew the words to many of the hymns, but we had to struggle to keep proper time with

Bishop William Decker Johnson

the strange, slow rhythms, with syllables often stretched into words, and words into entire verses. Soon, however, we would be rocking back and forth in harmony with the swaying bodies of the beautifully dressed choir behind the altar.

Bishop Johnson would preach, and his character seemed to change during his sermon. He was well educated and a master of the English language, but would shift to the vernacular of a semiliterate sharecropper when he wanted to emphasize a key point. His voice would sometimes become so soft that the congregation would lean forward to hear, and then he would erupt with a startling volume of sound. He used a singsong rhythm on occasion, even when quoting scripture, so that long-familiar words assumed a different meaning. There was no doubt that he dominated the consciousness of everyone in the church, and, at least during the sermon, the sense of being brothers and sisters in Christ wiped away any thoughts of racial differences. To me, he seemed the epitome of success and power.

At some time during the seemingly interminable service, when emotion was at a high point, everyone would line up and pass by the offering plates placed on a table immediately in front of the pulpit, and the church stewards would call out the amount of each offering. Daddy would always make a generous gift, acknowledged with clapping and "amen"s from the congregation.

Bishop Johnson was certainly aware of the racial customs of the day, but he did not consider it appropriate to comply with all of them. It was understood, for instance, that he would not come to our front door when he wished to talk to my father—but neither would he deign to come to the back. After ascertaining through a messenger that we were at home, he would arrive in his chauffeured black Packard or Cadillac, park in our front yard, and sound the horn. My father would go outside to the automobile for a conversation, while Bishop Johnson either stayed in the car or came out so the two men could stand together under the shade of a large magnolia tree. I don't remember that he ever came closer to our house. We could see them talking and laughing together, and afterward

Daddy always said that they just exchanged ideas about the bishop's work and the farming situation around home.

Like their father, the bishop's children were quite successful. His daughter, Fannie Hill, lived in Oklahoma, and her husband was the first black legislator in the state. (They supported me strongly when I ran for president.) One of his sons, Alvan, was a special friend of my mother, and attended one of the Ivy League universities—Harvard, I think. In any case, on his visits home he always came to call on Mama. Representing a younger and more liberated generation, Alvan came to our front door, where Mother would welcome him and invite him onto the front porch or into the living room. Since it was not possible for my father to acknowledge this breach of Southern etiquette, he would just ignore the event altogether. So far as I know, he never confronted Mama about it.

Even before I was an adult and able to understand the difficulty of overcoming racial barriers, I looked on Bishop Johnson as an extraordinary example of success in life. He had come from a tiny rural place, set his sights high, obtained a good education, and then risen to the top of his chosen profession. Of no less importance to me, he retained his close ties with Archery and the people who lived there. I still go by his relatively modest grave on occasion, and wonder how much my own ambitions were kindled by these early impressions.

There were gross abuses of the "separate but equal" principles laid down by the U.S. Supreme Court in 1896 that prevailed at the time, but most people chose to ignore them. In the mid-1950s, almost two decades after I left home, the Atlanta newspapers and civil-rights leaders began to challenge these discriminatory practices, but most of the distinguished lawyers and respected religious leaders in the South defended them as justified under the U.S. Constitution and the mandates of God Almighty.

Despite some early New Deal efforts to provide "farm relief," the Depression years were marked by a sense of frustration and even despair in our region. Cotton sales were slow, even at the government-supported price of eight cents a pound. Uncertainties about the impending war in Europe had reduced this most important export market for our basic cash crop, and there was at least a full year's carryover stored in Southern warehouses. Furthermore, cotton production was moving to the Western states, where boll weevils were less prevalent, yields were greater, and mechanization and irrigation were much more advanced.

There was a rapid shift toward dependence on peanuts while I was growing up, and this was the crop that made the greatest impact on my life, both when I was a child and much later, when I returned home with a wife and family. At first, we had to depend for cash income on the small Spanish varieties, used as salted nuts and in candy bars, while growing the more prolific Runner type for hog feed on the farm. But the demand for both kinds increased when a third of all peanuts began to go into peanut butter as a popular food for urban consumers. This took place because of the innovative work of George Washington Carver, a black agricultural scientist who taught at Tuskegee Institute in Alabama and began a career with the U.S. Department of Agriculture in 1935.

Some basic and unalterable circumstances perpetuated our farm problems. From the time of the Civil War until after I became an adult, too many people struggled to make a living on the limited amount of productive farmland in our region. Despite the extreme rural poverty that prevailed at the time, Southern farm population increased by 1.3 million between 1930 and 1935, as desperate people lost their jobs in failing factories, left their urban homes, and eventually wound up in places like our community. The farm families I knew had to divide the available cropland into ever-smaller plots on which a husband, a wife, and their children could barely subsist, then averaging about thirty-five acres. (With more advanced machinery, grain farms in Kansas were then four times as large.)

Throughout the South, and particularly in Southwest Georgia, there had long been a growing dependence by landowners on destitute families who owned little other than their clothes and some cooking utensils and who were eager to occupy any vacant shack and to work as day laborers or "on shares" under almost any arrangement. By 1935, families who owned no land worked more than half of Southern farms. As I grew older, I came to understand the personal consequences of this self-destructive scramble for a few small fields on which a family could work as sharecroppers.

Some foreign journalists who toured the South during those years reported that nowhere in Czarist Russia or in Europe under serfdom had families lived in such abject poverty or with so few basic rights as did the tenant families, black and white, of the South. Despite their abominable living conditions, neither my neighbors nor the economic or political powers in America were able to devise a better alternative.

There was a lot of ballyhoo in the Northern press about industrial progress, but not much change had taken place in farming techniques since colonial times. As late as 1942, *Fortune* magazine honored an outstanding Georgia farmer whose agricultural practices were described as "revolutionary." He did not have a tractor, and relied on five black sharecroppers, two other black tenants who worked by the day, and fifteen mules to work his six hundred acres, and the net annual income of his entire family was $1,500. The most admirable accomplishments mentioned were the diversification of crops and the annual production of $500 worth of food for his family. On the farm I knew as my home, the achievements of my father were much more remarkable, but even when I left home in 1941 to go to college, the absence of mechanized power, the almost total dependence on manual labor, and the basic agricultural techniques employed were relatively unchanged since colonial times. One commentator said that Jesus and even Moses would have felt at home on a farm in the Deep South during the first third of the twentieth century.

Even as a boy, I could see a profound difference between my

father's practices and those of other farmers, especially the share-croppers among whom I lived and worked. A logical option for all farmers was to diversify their agricultural practices, but this choice was available in inverse proportion to the income of the families. It took extra money to expand a rudimentary farming operation. Daddy could afford to take a chance on new ideas; he could buy superior milk cows, brood sows, and beef cattle, and we were able to produce the feed for them. He could also pay the costs of labor, seed, and equipment needed to produce noncash food crops that would be used for our family's own consumption. This was certainly better than having to pay retail prices for meal, flour, syrup, pork, and other basic commodities. However, such choices were almost impossible for the more destitute and dependent sharecroppers, and particularly when their landowners also had a store or commissary and wanted maximum sales of these items, often at grossly inflated prices and exorbitant credit charges.

Perhaps family incomes are the best indication of living standards in those days. Under average conditions, with cotton selling for about ten cents and peanuts three cents a pound, what income could our farm families expect? Although growers always anticipated much more at planting time, it usually took about three acres of land to produce a bale of cotton ($50) or a ton of peanuts ($60). My father was pleased in a good year when he produced this much on two acres. For most tenant farmers, permanent poverty was inevitable. Even with high yields, a one-horse family with fifteen acres of cotton would have a *gross* income of $300 to $400 for the year, and after paying the landlord his share for land use and often the rent of mules and equipment, the tenant would be lucky to keep half of this for a year's labor for himself, his wife, and their children. The cash "draw" from the landowner for the eight or nine months from preparing land to harvest would be from $100 to $200, not counting interest. So net indebtedness was almost inevitable for marginal farmers on the poorer land, and the chance for a profitable year was remote. Day laborers didn't have even this rare chance for a good year, but with their weekly wage they could at least pay cash for groceries and clothing and avoid some of the credit and interest charges.

I knew a number of small farmers who owned their own land. Most of them were white, of course, and it was their children who came to our church and were my classmates in school. Many of them were as poor as black day laborers, but they were expected to maintain better houses, wear mostly store-bought clothes, and keep their children in school more days each year. The income of small landowners, who cultivated about forty acres, was approximately the same as that of tenants with an operation of the same size. Paying taxes and the full cost of livestock, seed, fertilizer, and other supplies ate up the advantage of not paying rent. Even those who owned enough land to work their own crops and to support a few sharecropper families quite often made very little profit. They bore the full risk of low harvest prices, and nonpayment of the tenants' debts was their loss. In fact, with very few exceptions, everyone in our rural community was in the same economic boat. All of us had a chance to prosper when the weather was good, particularly when the cotton price was high. Obviously, local merchants welcomed good years, which brought a chance to collect old debts and to sell new shoes, overalls, and perhaps even a sewing machine to their usually destitute customers. Such years were rare.

Although I was born in Plains and actually lived next door to my future wife, Rosalynn, when she was a baby, the first thing I remember clearly was when I was four years old and my father took us out to show us our new home on the farm. There were four of us, including my sister, Gloria, who was two years younger than I. The front door was locked when we got there, and Daddy realized that he had forgotten the key. He tried to raise one of the windows that opened onto the front porch, but a wooden bar on the inside let it come up only about six inches. So he slid me through the crack and I came around to unlock the door from the inside. The approval of my father for my first useful act has always been one of my most vivid memories.

Our house was typical of those occupied by middle-income landowners of the time. Set back about fifty feet from the dirt road, it was square, painted tan to match the dust, and had a broad front porch and split-shingle roof. The rooms were laid out in "shotgun" style, with a hall that went down the middle of the house dividing the living room, dining room, and kitchen on the left side from three bedrooms on the right. We also had a screened porch that extended across the back of the house, where we worked and stored things such as well water, corn for the chickens, and extra wood to keep it dry. The front porch was where our family congregated in warm weather, which was about nine months of the year. We had a swing suspended from the ceiling and some rocking chairs out there, and Daddy often used the slightly sloping floor for a quick nap after dinner and before going back to work in the afternoon. I relished lying beside him as a little boy, long before I could do useful work in the fields.

There is little doubt that I now recall those days with more fondness than they deserve. We drew water from a well in the yard, and every day of the year we had the chore of keeping extra bucketfuls in the kitchen and on the back porch, combined with the constant wood-sawing and chopping to supply the cooking stove and fireplaces. In every bedroom was a slop jar (chamber pot) that was emptied each morning into the outdoor privy, about twenty yards from our back door. This small shack had a large hole for adults and a lower and smaller one for children; we wiped with old newspapers or pages torn from Sears, Roebuck catalogues. These were much better facilities than those I knew when I was with the other families on the place, who squatted behind bushes and wiped with corncobs or leaves.

Gloria and me

My boyhood home

It was a great day for our family in 1935 when Daddy purchased from a mail-order catalogue and erected a windmill with a high wooden tank and pipes that provided running water for the kitchen and a bathroom with toilet. We even had a rudimentary shower made from a large tin can with its bottom perforated by nail holes. One extra benefit was that the top platform of the windmill, up near the fan blades, gave a good view of the nearby fields.

Our house was surrounded by a white-sanded yard, which we had to sweep frequently to remove fowl and animal droppings and leaves from our pecan, magnolia, mulberry, and chinaberry trees. Most of our brush brooms were made of small saplings or limbs of dogwood, which were resilient and long lasting. Several times a year we took a two-mule wagon about three miles to a pit and loaded it with fresh sand, which was scattered on the yard to give it a new white surface. Behind our house and surrounded by fenced fields were a small garage (never used for a car), a smokehouse, a chicken house, and a large woodpile.

Our artificial light came from kerosene lamps, and it was considered almost sinful to leave one burning in an unoccupied room. The only exception was in the front living room, where we had an Aladdin lamp about five feet high whose asbestos wick miraculously provided illumination bright enough for reading in a wide area. We turned this flame way down when we went to eat a meal, both to conserve fuel and to avoid the lamp's tendency to flame up and blacken the fragile wick with thick soot. When this happened—a mishap for which someone always had to be identified as the culprit—we had to endure an extended period of careful flame control while we waited in near darkness for the soot to burn off enough for us to read again.

One significant difference between my parents was their reading habits. Daddy mostly limited his reading to the daily and weekly newspapers and farm journals, but he also owned a small library, which I still have, that included Halliburton's *Royal Road to Romance*, a collection of A. Conan Doyle's Sherlock Holmes stories, and a complete set of Edgar Rice Burroughs's Tarzan books, each carefully signed and numbered by my father to indicate their proper sequence. By contrast, my mother read constantly and encouraged us children to do the same. Since we stayed busy most of the time, Mama and I always had a magazine or book to read while eating our meals, and this became a lifetime habit for my own family and me. The only exception was Sunday dinner, which, for some reason, had too formal an atmosphere for literature at the table. At night, at suppertime, there was no such restraint.

I didn't know of any rural families that had electric lights until the rural-electrification program came along in the late 1930s. We had a large battery-powered radio in the front room that we used sparingly, and only at night, as we all sat around looking at it during "Amos and Andy," "Fibber McGee and Molly," "Jack Benny," or "Little Orphan Annie." When its power failed, we would sometimes bring in the battery from the pickup truck to keep it playing for a special event. I recall some rare baseball games re-created by the announcer from telegraph reports, a few boxing matches, and the late night in 1936 when Alfred Landon was chosen as the Republican nominee for president. The voting went on so long that the battery in our house gave out, and we took the radio outside and set it on the hood of the pickup until the convention made its choice, hours after midnight.

The most memorable radio broadcast was in 1938, the night of the return match between heavyweight boxers Joe Louis and Max Schmeling. The German champion had defeated the black American two years earlier, and the world's attention was focused on the return bout. For our community, this fight had heavy racial overtones, with almost unanimous support at our all-white school for the European over the American. A delegation of our black neighbors came to ask Daddy if they could listen to the broadcast, and we put the radio in the window so the assembled crowd in the yard could hear it. The fight ended abruptly, in the first round, with Louis almost killing Schmeling. There was no sound from outside—or inside—the house. We heard a quiet "Thank you, Mr. Earl," and then our visitors walked silently out of the yard, crossed the road and the railroad tracks, entered the tenant house, and closed the door. Then all hell broke loose, and their celebration lasted all night. Daddy was tight-lipped, but all the mores of our segregated society had been honored.

I don't remember much about the summer heat, but I have vivid memories of how cold it was in winter. The worst job was getting up in the morning to start a fire going somewhere in the frigid house. We kept a good supply of pine kindling, which we called "lighterd," to start the blaze that would eventually ignite the long-burning hickory and oak, but I always hoped that some live coals were still smoldering under the ashes so the fire would start quickly. There was an open fireplace in the living room that we lit only late in the afternoon, when the family would gather there, but the fire (later a wood-burning heater) in the bedroom where Mama and Daddy slept was made at dawn, so we shivering children would rush there in the mornings to put on our clothes. I had the northeast corner room, which had no source of heat. We never thought about pajamas, which would have been warmer than the BVDs that Daddy and I wore on cold days under our shirts and trousers, and then slept in at night.

Almost all our food was produced in our pasture, fields, garden, and yard. My mother did not enjoy cooking, but was good at preparing a few basic dishes, and Daddy liked to cook special meals such as batter cakes, all-too-rare waffles, and fried fish. At hog-killing time, he fixed souse meat, a conglomeration of meat from heads, feet, and other animal parts that were boiled to a thick, soft mush, heavily spiced, and then congealed into a loaf that could be sliced for later consumption. He also assumed the responsibility of preparing homemade mayonnaise throughout the year and eggnog at Christmas. Whichever farm woman who came in to cook for us when Mama was working as a nurse just embellished the basic meals of her own family with a few of our fancier foods, like rice, cheese, peanut butter, macaroni, and canned goods. Nothing went to waste around our house, and we were expected to eat whatever was prepared and to clean our plates before leaving the table.

Corn was our staple grain, and rarely would we have a meal without grits, lye hominy, roasting ears, or one of the half-dozen recipes for corn bread. We always had chickens available, either hens or fryers, and it was usually my job to catch and kill them so they could be dressed and then baked, fried, or made into a pie for dinner or supper. (We never heard the word "lunch" applied to sitting down at a table.) Chicken was standard for Sunday dinner after church, when we also had fresh vegetables: peas, potatoes, string beans, butter beans, okra, rutabagas, and all kinds of greens, with collards our favorite, but never any spinach. We also had mashed Irish potatoes or rice and gravy, biscuits, and a pie made from seasonal fruit or sweet potatoes. Cured pork products were available most of the year, and it was surprising how often we ate seafood that Daddy bought from two local men who made regular truck trips from Plains to the Gulf and brought back mullet, mackerel, shrimp, and oysters. Canned salmon, which sold for either a nickel or a dime depending on the quality or size of the can, was usually transformed into fried croquettes and eaten with gobs of catsup. Another staple was kit fish, which was dried mackerel packed with salt in small wooden kegs. We soaked the pieces in clear water overnight to reduce the saltiness, and fried them for breakfast to go with our grits and biscuits.

I still have vivid memories of the home place where I spent my boyhood. There was a dirt tennis court next to our house, unknown on any other farm in our area, which Daddy laid out as soon as we moved there and kept clean and relatively smooth with a piece of angle iron nailed to a pine log that a mule could drag over it every week or so. Next was my father's commissary store, with the windmill in back, and then a large fenced-in garden. A two-rut wagon road ran from our back yard to the barn, which would become the center of my life as I matured and eagerly assumed increasing responsibilities for the work of a man.

Beyond the garden and alongside this small road was a combination blacksmith and carpenter shop surrounded by piles of all kinds of scrap metal, where everyone on the farm knew that rattlesnakes loved to breed. This is where we shod mules and horses, sharpened plow points, repaired machinery, made simple iron implements, and did woodwork, with Daddy providing the overall supervision. He was skilled with the forge and anvil, and did fairly advanced blacksmith work. This is one of the first places I was able to work alongside him. I could turn the hand crank on the forge blower fast enough to keep the charcoal fire ablaze, and to hold some of the red-hot pieces on the anvil with tongs while Daddy shaped them with a hammer and then plunged them, hissing, into water or oil for tempering. It required some skill to keep a plow point completely flat on the steel surface; otherwise a hammer blow would bring a violent and painful twisting, with the tongs and red-hot metal sometimes flying out of my hands. There was almost always something broken around the farm, and only rarely would anything be taken to town for welding. I learned a lot from Daddy, and also from Jack Clark, a middle-aged black man who was something of a supervisor on our farm and did most of the mule- and horse-shoeing.

In front of the shop was a large Sears, Roebuck grinding stone, and we would sit on a wooden seat and pedal to keep the thick disc spinning, with the bottom of the stone running in half an automobile tire filled with water. This was a busy place where we sharpened hoes, axes, scythes, knives, and scissors. Daddy didn't believe in paying for something we could do ourselves, so he also had an iron shoemaker's last in the shop that he used for replacing worn-out heels and soles for the family's shoes. As I got older, I helped with all the jobs in the shop, but was always most interested in working with wood, especially in shaping pieces with froe, plane, drawknife, and spokeshave.

The centerpiece of our farm life, and a place of constant exploration for me, was our large, perfectly symmetrical barn. It had been built by an itinerant Scottish carpenter named Mr. Valentine, whose basic design was well known in our farming region. Daddy was very proud of its appearance and its practical arrangement, which minimized labor in handling the large quantities of feed needed for our livestock. There were special cribs, bins, and tanks for storing oats, ear corn, velvet beans, hay, fodder, and store-bought supplements, including molasses, a bran called "shorts," and cottonseed meal. The sheep, goats, and cattle were usually kept in stalls separate from each other and from the mules and horses, and animals requiring veterinary care could also be isolated while being treated. Hogs had their own pens, and were not permitted inside the barn.

Before I was big enough for real fieldwork, Daddy encouraged me to spend time with Jack Clark, knowing that it was the best way for me to be educated about farm life, as Jack kept up a constant stream of comments about the world as he knew or envisioned it.

Jack was very black, of medium height, and strongly built. He had surprisingly long arms, and invariably wore clean overalls, knee-high rubber boots, and a straw hat. Knowing (or at least claiming) that he spoke for my father, he issued orders or directions to the other hands in a somewhat gruff voice, always acting as the final arbiter over which field each hand would plow and which mule he would harness. He ignored the grumbled complaints. When all the other workers were off to their assigned duties, Jack was the sole occupant of the barn and the adjacent lots—except when I was following behind him like a puppy dog and bombarding him with questions. We became close friends, but there was always some restraint as to intimacy between us. For instance, although my daddy would pick me up on occasion to give me a hug or let me ride on his shoulders, this would have been inconceivable with Jack, except when he might lift me over a barbed-wire fence or onto the back of a mule or horse.

Radiating from the barn was a maze of fences and gates that let us move livestock from one place to another with minimal risk of their escape. This was one of my earliest tasks, requiring only a modicum of skill and the ability to open and close the swinging gates. Within the first array of enclosures was a milking shed that would hold four cows at a time, adequate to accommodate our usual herd of eight to a dozen Jerseys and Guernseys that we milked in two shifts, twice a day. Later, we had a dozen A-frame hog-farrowing structures, which I helped my daddy build after bringing the innovative design home from my Future Farmer class in school. One shelter was assigned to each sow when birthing time approached, and the design kept the animals dry, provided a convenient place for feed and water, and minimized the inadvertent crushing of the baby pigs by their heavy mamas. Except during extended dry seasons, the constantly used lots for hogs and milk cows were always ankle deep in mud and manure, which made bare feet much superior to brogans.

A little open shed near the barn enclosed a pump that lifted about two cups of water from our shallow well with each stroke. It was driven by a small two-cycle gasoline engine that we cranked up and let run once or twice a day, just long enough to fill several watering troughs around the barn and sheds. This was the only motor-driven device on the farm, and was always viewed with a mixture of suspicion and trepidation. We were justifiably doubtful that it would crank when we needed it most, dreading the hour or two of hand pumping as the only alternative source of water for all the animals. Between the pump house and barn was a harness shed, an open-ended building where we stored a buggy, two wagons, and all the saddles, bridles, and other harness needed for an operating farm. Also near the barn was a concrete dipping-vat about four feet deep, filled with a pungent mixture containing creosote, through which we would drive our cattle, goats, and newly sheared sheep to protect them, at least temporarily, from flies and screwworms.

The farm operation always seemed to me a fascinating system, like a huge clock, with each of its many parts depending on all the rest. Daddy was the one who designed, owned, and operated the complicated mechanism, and Jack Clark wound it daily and kept it on time. I had dreams that one day I would be master of this machine, with its wonderful intricacies.

The workers on our place, all black, lived in five small clapboard houses, three right on the highway, one set farther back from the road, and another across the railroad tracks directly in front of our house. This was the community in which I grew up, all within a stone's throw of the barn.

Except for Jack Clark, who received monthly wages and worked seven days a week, rain or shine, all the other hands worked and were paid by the day, as the weather permitted and as they were needed. To be more accurate, Daddy and Jack kept accounts in increments of one-fourth of a day, with a full day being from before daybreak until after sundown. For this amount of work, grown men dependable enough to plow a mule received a dollar, women got seventy-five cents, competent teenagers a half-dollar, and younger children a quarter. The exception to this was during harvest time, when each person was paid for the pounds of cotton picked or the quantity of peanuts pulled out of the ground and stacked up to dry. Day workers were paid on Saturday, when they were expected to repay any loans and settle up for purchases made during the week at my father's commissary. For too long, I thought, I was given a child's wage, and I was always eager to be promoted.

Although I respected and admired Bishop Johnson as the most successful and widely traveled man I knew, my own life was affected most profoundly by Jack and Rachel Clark. Without young children of their own to care for, they seemed to enjoy having me with them. Jack Clark knew more than anyone about work around the home site. He was in charge of the barn, the mules and horses, the equipment and harness, and all the other livestock. He rarely worked in the field but usually plowed our family garden and the community sweet-potato patch. It was Jack who rang the big farm bell each morning of a working day, at four o'clock "sun time," and again at "noon." This was not at any precise time as measured by our clocks, but was always about an hour before daylight and then when the sun reached its highest point in the sky. Jack worked directly under Daddy, and seemed to us boys to have ultimate authority over the farm's life, an illusion he was careful not to dispel.

The Clarks' house was the one I knew most intimately, because I spent a lot of time with them. Only about a third the size of ours, it followed the standard design of the other tenant houses on the place. There was a small private bedroom where Jack and Rachel slept, one end almost completely filled by a bed frame on which was a tick that could be stuffed with either corn shucks or wheat straw. A large pine chifforobe in the corner held some clothes and the Clarks' other personal belongings; with no closets in the house, most of their clothing and other possessions were hung on nails or placed on shelves along the walls. The main room, much larger, contained a rough-hewn four-foot-long table with a bench on each side, and two straight chairs that could be moved near the fireplace or out on the front porch. Next to one wall was a pallet on the floor, which consisted of a narrower mattress similar to that in the bedroom. This is where I always slept when my parents were away, dragging it near the fire on cold nights. Jack and Rachel had a kerosene lantern that hung from the ceiling over the table, and a lamp that could be moved around the house.

Sometimes Rachel's mother, Tamar, or her grown daughter, Bertha Mae, came to stay with them for a few days, and there were often other farm workers visiting in the Clarks' house. As in the

Rachel Clark, 1976

Jack Clark, 1976

Rachel Clark,
c. 1935

fields or woods when no white adults were around, the place would be filled with a natural exuberance, loud talk and arguments, and subtle jokes that I enjoyed even though I didn't always understand them. Except in my own room in our house, this is where I felt most at home. At the table, three or four of us played a card game called Seven-Up; it was similar to rummy, but every card could be played with emotion. There was also a checkerboard, used for playing "pool," a fast-moving form of checkers where even the uncrowned pieces could be moved forward to the limit of the unoccupied diagonals instead of just one space at a time. Crowned pieces could move both forward and backward, of course.

An enclosed shed on the back of the house served as the kitchen and held a woodstove, a wood box, a wide shelf against the wall, and a churn. A back door opened onto a tiny back porch, where the major item was a washbasin on a shelf, with a towel hanging on a nail. Just below was Rachel's bait bed, where the red wiggler worms were fed discarded water, coffee grounds, and any food scraps available from the kitchen. The house also had a narrow porch extending across the entire front, very close to the road, where we sat on the steps or on the chairs and benches that were moved back and forth from inside.

A different kind of special family lived in the smallest cabin on the farm, also facing the main road and next door to the Clarks. Fred Howard was relatively young, quiet, and one of the most dependable workers on the farm. He minded his own business, settled his accounts on time, barely made a living, and every now and then mentioned how much he wanted children. His wife, Lee, was some kin to Rachel Clark, and extraordinarily beautiful. She was light-colored, small, and slender, and wore her long, silky-looking hair under a flower-printed bonnet and pulled back from her ears, either in a bun or a long ponytail. It never mattered that her dresses were made of printed flour- or guano-sacks. Lee always seemed timid to me, glancing downward whenever she talked to another person. It was difficult for other eyes not to follow her as she walked or worked in her graceful manner. For some reason, I was rather uncomfortable in her presence, and resented the comments I heard from both black and white men insinuating that they would be glad to help if she decided to earn a little extra money with her beauty. Lee's Aunt Rosa was widely known as an expert in tatting, and my mother helped her sell her beautiful lace to supplement the family's budget.

One of the most interesting men on the place was called Tump (he said he didn't have another name). He lived by himself, claimed to eat rats, and was even less educated than the other workers. It was especially difficult to understand what Tump was saying, because he used the intonations of the Gullah dialect of the Georgia coast. He eliminated all "unnecessary" words, such as prepositions, adjectives, and adverbs, and spoke in a strange rhythm with varying tones and pitches to express his meaning. Respected as by far the strongest man on the place, he was called on to do special jobs that were beyond the capability of others. For some reason, Daddy had a big iron weight under the windmill, with an eyebolt on top and "500 pounds" stamped on it. Tump was the only one who could pick it up and walk with it. He seemed to be a special friend of my Uncle Lem, Mama's brother, who helped Daddy one or two seasons at the peanut picker and the sugarcane mill.

One night, as we shut down the mill and headed home, Uncle Lem said, "Tump, I've noticed that you don't usually get to work as early as I do."

Tump responded, " 'T'ain't so, Mr. Lem, I'm there time everybody is."

Uncle Lem, following up, said, "I'll bet you a quarter I'm at work before you in the morning."

With wages a dollar a day, this was a good-sized bet, but Tump didn't hesitate. "Yes, sir, I bet."

When I asked Uncle Lem what was going on, he laughed and said, "Well, Tump don't know it, but I'm going coon hunting tonight, and will just come back by the cane mill long before daylight and pick up my quarter."

It didn't seem fair to me, but I didn't say anything.

The next morning, even before the farm bell rang at the barn, Uncle Lem arrived at the cane mill. Tump sat up from some cane pummlings where he had spent the night and asked, "Dat you, Mr. Lem?"

Both in our house and in those of tenants, the long workdays and the high price of store-bought kerosene prevented much staying up after dark, except perhaps on weekends. All the workers' cabins were constructed with rough boards produced by one of the traveling sawmills that came to our farm every now and then to harvest our pine trees. The clapboard siding was the only barrier to the outside heat, cold, wind, and rain, so occupants covered the inside of the boards with old newspapers pasted on with a mixture of flour and water. The wooden windows were kept closed during cold weather, making it necessary to depend on the lamp and fireplace to illuminate the cabin. There were no screens on the doors or windows, so flies and other insects had unimpeded access. It was impossible to seal the floor, and I could see the ground underneath through the cracks between boards. Except for these design limitations inherent in any simple clapboard structure, Daddy made sure that we kept our tenant houses in good shape, with necessary repairs made during the winter months between harvest and land-breaking time. This added to the skills I learned in the workshop.

The only other buildings, far from our house, were the syrup mill, located on a small stream, and two sheds where seed cotton, fertilizer, and workers could find shelter from a sudden rain shower.

All our fields were fenced with woven hog wire about three feet high nailed to wooden posts, and topped with two strands of barbed wire to hold the larger cattle, mules, and horses. Daddy also bought some steel rods with corkscrew bottoms that were used as temporary fenceposts. The fence corners were well braced, and the gates were level, swung easily, and were strong enough for little boys to ride on them. Daddy always said that the condition of tenant houses and fences was a good indication of the pride and industry of a landowner.

A lane from the barn extended north to connect all our lots, fields, pastures, and woods. Most of our woodlands were also fenced, having some value as forage areas for the livestock. Acorns, hickory nuts, walnuts, a few chestnuts and chinkapins, and leaves from bushes and trees supplemented the pastures and feed grown in the fields. Almost all the leaves and even pine needles were eaten as high as cows could reach, giving the woods and swamps an openness that was convenient for us boys to explore, for hunters to follow dogs, and for finding and observing the domestic animals. There was a big black-cherry tree down the lane, and we boys used to see and sometimes catch floundering blue jays that were intoxicated from eating too much of the ripe fruit.

My playmates were mostly the sons of tenant families on our farm, but a few others would join us from houses farther down the road. We used to claim the most remote shed, not too far from the creek, as our clubhouse, and slept in it when we couldn't stay awake all night on the creek bank. I don't remember that my parents ever put any limits on my explorations around the farm, even including the more remote woods and swamps. They expected me to perform my assigned tasks, know basic safety rules, and be on time for meals, but otherwise I was completely free to roam throughout the 350 acres of our home place.

Just to the west of our house, and extending to the boundary of our land, was a pecan orchard. I vividly recall helping my daddy plant the grafted seedlings in precisely straight rows when I was nine years old. The trees are still there, but not as well groomed as when my mother tended them; harvesting the nuts was her special moneymaking project. On a hill beyond our land and back from the road was a large house with a windmill in back. The soil on this neighboring farm was comparatively thin and sandy, and a series of white families moved in for a crop or two before abandoning the effort. One of them had children about my age, who joined my permanent black playmates and me for a few months. Toward the end of the 1930s, not long before I left home, my mother's parents moved in and lived there for several years.

Just before getting to our house, the rather crooked westbound dirt road from Plains ran into the straight railroad tracks of the Seaboard Airline Railroad and had to make a very sharp turn to the right so that the two could run almost exactly parallel for about a mile. Since there was no warning sign, the deep ruts in the soft sand on the curve caused a regular procession of wrecks, one every week or so. Luckily, the quality of the road approaching the curve precluded high speeds, so not much damage was done. Usually the vehicles just rolled over naturally toward the outside of the curve, slid along on the soft sand, and came to rest on their sides. We children were alert to these accidents, and would respond to the characteristic sounds by shouting, "A wreck! A wreck!" and running to the scene. There were always interesting people and conversations and, on occasion, some vivid language. Unless something exceptional occurred, such as an injury, our parents didn't bother to go out to see them.

The bad curve was right in front of Jack Clark's house, and he assumed the responsibility of attending to the distressed travelers. Since he was the "lot man" and in charge of all the mules and harness, it was natural for him to perform this service. After examining the situation, making sure everyone was all right, and having a brief discussion with the driver, he was always able to figure out what to do. Using two mules and a plow hitch, and hooking a chain to the vehicle's frame, he could soon have it righted. For larger, loaded trucks, he would have to get some help from others on the farm—first to unload the cargo, then to set the truck upright before reloading it. He kept under his front porch a large block and tackle (which he called a "tickle") that could be rigged between the truck and one of the trees in his yard to help with the heavier jobs. Jack never charged more than a dollar for this service, and my father didn't demand anything for the use of the mules and harness. Most of the time, for a small car or pickup, Jack let any contribution be voluntary, since he knew that some of the families didn't have much for themselves.

For some reason I have never understood, places along the dirt road would develop a corrugated surface, with shallow indentations running crosswise about every two feet along the way. When this happened, there was an optimum speed for each stretch of roadway. Driving too slow gave a teeth-jarring ride, with the wheels dropping to the bottom of each groove. Faster was usually better, with the wheels just hitting the tops of the bumps, but could be deadly at higher speeds or on a curve, because the tires had no grip on the surface. The county road-scraper would smooth the roads every few weeks, usually after a good rain, but the washboards would soon return.

It was an exciting event for us boys when one of the big motor-driven "road scrapes" arrived on the road in front of our house. We viewed the operators as some of the most exalted and fortunate of men, and each attempted to demonstrate to us and to the community that his handiwork was superior. They had to make at least four passes along the road, first to pull the ditches clean of sand and other sediment, and then to smooth the surface in both directions, leaving a slight crown so water wouldn't stand on the driving surface. Reducing the washboard effect and ensuring that drainage paths were maintained out of yards and fields, down through the ditches, and then into the branches and creeks was a notable engineering feat.

We had one problem with the location of our home: there were a cemetery and a haunted house between Plains and Archery. Neither my parents nor my sisters ever had to walk down this road, so they were not concerned, but there were many times, especially during the winter, when I returned home after dark from work in town or from a late school activity. None of my black friends would dream of passing this way at night, and their fear had a great effect on me. The graveyard was bad enough, but the haunted house was much worse. There were frequent reports of a woman who could be seen through the attic windows, wearing a long white flowing dress and carrying a candle, apparently looking for something or someone she had lost. The local newspapers ran a number of articles about this house, quoting people who had lived there in the past. One temporary occupant, Sonny Faircloth, claimed to be familiar with a large black dog, which could be seen in the yard among his several coonhounds. I heard Sonny tell many times how he finally got up the nerve to go close to the animal and tried to touch it, but the hair stood up on his head when his hand penetrated the dog's body without feeling anything.

I really tried to discount these kinds of tales, but I sometimes thought I had glimpses of the searching woman, which may have been a reflection of the setting sun or Venus in the western window. In the end, I was able to add my own horror tale to the others. When I was in high school, Dr. Thad Wise bought the house and lived in it with Mrs. Gussie Abrams Howell, who was the supervising nurse at Wise Sanitarium, a much-respected local hospital. When he became desperately ill, Miss Abrams (as she was always called) asked me to spend some nights with them to help care for Dr. Thad. Late one night, as she and I were preparing some food in the kitchen, we heard all three of his dogs begin a weird howling, unlike anything we had ever heard before. Miss Abrams rushed into the bedroom and found that Dr. Thad had just died. We assumed that the dogs had seen his spirit leaving the house.

Luckily for my friends and me, the railroad gave us an alternate path home, and we usually used it instead of the road, balancing on one of the iron rails. After years of practice, all of us could walk the two and a half miles back and forth to Plains without falling.

This was Archery, the small farming community where I lived, worked, and played for fourteen years, with my greatest ambition to be valuable around the farm and to please my father.

2

Sharecropping as a Way of Life

. . . cursed is the ground for thy sake; in sorrow shalt thou eat of it all the days of thy life; thorns also and thistles shall it bring forth to thee. . . . —Genesis 3:17,18

I'm sure that many farmers during the Depression felt that God's harsh words to Adam were a continuing curse, and no one bore a heavier burden than those who owned no land but worked the fields with increasing hopelessness and despair.

There is now a general condemnation of the system of farming that we knew as sharecropping. The very word suggests powerful and ruthless landlords perpetrating something like a system of peonage on innocent and long-suffering serfs. There were certainly abuses of the system, and I saw some of them during my youthful days on the farm. But it would have been difficult if not impossible to devise a reasonable alternative. Sharecropping was an old system and in some ways a natural one. From the time when Georgia was still a British colony, landowners would assign a portion of their cropland to white farm families who owned no land but had enough

livestock and equipment to produce a crop, with a mutual understanding about how the harvest would be divided. Good or bad fortune for owners of smaller farms would inevitably be shared by their
tenants.

When the slaves were freed, many of them were skilled farmers
who had no means of earning a livelihood, while their previous owners had more land than they could work themselves. There were two
basic options for those who chose to continue living in the same
neighborhood: either for workers to be hired by the day, with all the
crop to be kept by the landowner, or for the two to "share" the
"crop" along with the risks involved in its production in some mutually agreed fashion. The essence of sharecropping, during the Great
Depression as it had been a century earlier, was the freedom of both
parties to accept or reject any proposed arrangement. There were
almost limitless options in how available land was to be worked, and
my early days were spent within the various systems that had
evolved.

Many white farmers didn't own land and had to rent or work on
shares, but I don't usually think of white sharecroppers, because
none of them lived on our place and my personal involvement was
with the black families that I knew. The tenancy arrangements depended on the type of crops grown, the amount of manual labor required, the fertilizer used, the availability of competing day
laborers, and the personal preferences of the landowners and tenants. Workers were plentiful, and there were enough experienced
farmers who did not own any land to provide a reservoir of eager
tenant families. I was familiar with two basic arrangements that
formed a framework for our economic system.

Those who did not own land, mules, equipment, or tools other
than a hoe and an ax had almost the same lowly status as day laborers and usually worked "on halves." The landowner would allot the
family as much land as they could work, and usually furnish two
mules, a wagon, necessary equipment for plowing, fertilizer, and
seed, plus a cabin and a garden plot. Depending on the size of the

family, they were expected to work from twenty to forty acres of land, relying almost entirely for income on cotton and peanuts. They had the right to cut firewood as well. When the harvest came in, the owner received half of everything produced on the farm, and collected what the cropper had borrowed, or "drawn," to meet the needs of his family during the year. A typical draw might be $3 or $4 a week, as mutually agreed in advance of the planting season. It was expected, of course, that almost all of this would be spent at the owner's commissary. These stores were an important source of income for landowners, who could abuse their tenants by charging unscrupulously high prices and credit charges for the loans and supplies. One study in the South showed that credit and interest charges averaged about 25 percent. I presume that these rates prevailed in our area.

Unlike most other landowners around Plains, Daddy disliked this arrangement of working on halves, and traded with more dependable and competent families to work our land. They had their own livestock and equipment and worked on "thirds and fourths." In exchange for use of the land, the family allotted one-third of the cash crops and one-fourth of the corn to the landowner. Various formulas were used to decide who furnished how much of the seed and fertilizer. Where the tenants were able to furnish all of it, a common agreement was for a specific amount of the cash crop, in bales of cotton or tons of peanuts or some combination of the two, to go to the owner as "straight rent."

In all too many cases, the poorer sharecroppers failed to produce an adequate cash crop to pay their accumulated debts. They would go from one year to the next seeing their obligation to the landowner increase each time, or, at best, stay the same. For all practical purposes, their negotiating freedom was lost. The planters kept the books, and in some cases the landowner's year-end settlement was unfair. Even if a barely literate tenant kept rudimentary records or carried the owner's records to someone else for analysis and found them to be in error, there was little he could do. The influence and legal presumption lay with the owner of land, and to question his honesty was a serious matter indeed. If the tenant was black (about 80 percent in our area) and the owner white, such an accusation was almost inconceivable. In some cases, an owner was known by his white peers to be harsh or unfair, and commiseration was felt with the unfortunate families who came under his financial domination. But nothing was done to help them.

One of the old stories told around the filling stations and stables was about the landlord who finished settling up with his sharecropper and said, "Well, Jim, you almost broke even again this year. You just owe me twenty dollars." Jim replied, "Boss, I thank the Lord for this good year! I have one more bale of cotton in the storehouse not ginned yet." The landlord said, "Well, I think I forgot about the interest charges. We'll have to figure your account one more time."

On Saturdays, Daddy always paid the field hands and gave credit or cash loans to tenants at the commissary store, where he kept careful records of all advances and sales. The poorer farmers who had minimum weekly draws never bought the more costly items. Instead of streak-of-lean bacon, they bought only fatback; instead of syrup, only molasses; instead of flour, only meal; and they bought no patent medicines except castor oil. They used secondhand flour- or guano-sacks covered with printed designs for men's shirts and women's dresses, and chose the cheapest overalls or a pair of work shoes for a dollar. These would last several years if worn only when older clothes and bare feet would not do. High quality Wolverine shoes cost three times as much, but would last for years.

I once made a summary of Daddy's old store accounts for 1929 and 1930 and found that the average customer spent fifty-two cents of every dollar on food, of which twenty-four cents went for flour or meal, eleven cents for lard, ten cents for meat, five cents for coffee, and two cents for molasses. For an entire family with an expenditure of less than a dollar a day, this was all they could afford, because they also had to buy kerosene, matches, salt, turpentine and castor oil for medicine, and *always* the snuff and tobacco. Even the poorest bought a can of Prince Albert or Sir Walter Raleigh smoking to-bacco, Brown's Mule chewing tobacco, or some CC, Buttercup, or Maccoboy snuff almost every time they came in the store. Only the more affluent customers who traded with my father bought such luxuries as ready-made cigarettes, cheese, macaroni, peanut butter, grits, canned salmon, tea, starch, socks, or gloves.

More than anyone else in my family, perhaps even including my father, I could understand the plight of the black families, because I lived so much among them. During most of the year they ate only two meals a day, usually cornmeal, fatback, molasses, and perhaps sweet potatoes from our common field. The more industrious fami-lies also had small gardens that provided some seasonal corn, Irish potatoes, collards, turnips, and cabbage, with a few rows of running peas and beans planted alongside the garden fence. The combina-tion of constant and heavy work, inadequate diet, and excessive use of tobacco was devastating to the health of our poorer neighbors. With the exception of a few very old women who could no longer do fieldwork, I don't remember any of the tenant-family members' being the slightest bit overweight.

The life expectancy of black men and women was less than fifty years. My mama was strongly influenced by Dr. Thad Wise, who was the oldest of three brothers who founded Wise Sanitarium in Plains. During his career, Dr. Thad concentrated his energies more and more on diet as the cause of debilitating diseases, especially pella-gra. There was quite a debate within the medical community, but Mama had no doubt that the lack of fresh vegetables was the cause of lassitude, mouth lesions, and other symptoms that showed up in the winter months. So she encouraged small gardens for the families she nurtured, and shared our vegetables with them in season. The black women must have inherited information about mineral sup-plements from their ancestors, because our work wagon never passed an excavated roadside that revealed a chalk deposit without stopping. They would eat chunks of the white mineral and fill empty flour-sacks to carry home to their families. It didn't taste bad, except for the grit particles embedded in the soft and almost pure calcium carbonate.

According to the 1930 U.S. Census, the average value of all equipment and machinery on a Georgia farm was $134. Only the larger farmers like my father could afford hay rakes, harrows, seed planters, fertilizer distributors, stalk cutters, and multi-plow cultivators, and I was in my high-school years before I managed any of these.

Although everyone in a farm family had to work long hours, the heaviest burden fell on the women. In addition to their fieldwork, often more onerous than the men's plowing, all the cooking, churning, other housework, and care for the family garden were their responsibility. Most workdays began at daybreak, and the morning meal had to be prepared before the men or the entire family went to the field. The chopping and toting of firewood for the stove was a constant chore, as was the feeding of chickens, pigs, or other livestock in pens or around the yard. Most of the families were not blessed with a dug well near the house, and water had to be toted from a sometimes distant spring for drinking and washing clothes. Of course, women were also responsible for the bearing and care of the children, and, with no form of birth control except continence, the babies arrived on a regular schedule in many families. The tenant families each worked an average of thirty acres of field land in rural areas that were mostly woodland, making the homes about a half-mile apart, so, except for their own children, the women usually lived and worked in solitude.

I never knew of a tenant or sharecropper who was a woman, but it was a common practice for the widows of landowners to continue operating their family farms. They were highly respected and had the full support of neighbors in the community. A black or white foreman usually supervised the fieldwork, but the woman made the overall management decisions and financial arrangements. Later, as a warehouseman myself, I had a number of highly valued female customers, some of whom operated very large farms.

The busiest time of the year, and the most nerve-racking, was when we were gathering peanuts and cotton, our cash crops. Wheat, oats, and rye were cut, shocked, and threshed in late spring for food and feed, but they played a relatively small role in our farm economy. The labor crunch came when all farmers were harvesting peanuts and cotton simultaneously. Our parents always kept us in school, and we envied our classmates who stayed on the farm to help their families with gathering the crops. It was not much compensation that Daddy was eager for me to work in the fields every possible moment—after school hours and even all day on Saturday.

"Shaking" peanuts was especially difficult, because of the heat, dirt, and the constant stooping all the way to the ground. We had to erect pine-sapling stackpoles, nail on cross-strips to keep the crop at least a foot off the ground, plow up the peanuts, shake each plant to remove the clinging dirt, and place the root and nuts adjacent to the pole. We put bunches of grass on top of the stack to help shed the rain during the succeeding six weeks or more, while the vines and nuts slowly dried. If stacked properly, the peanuts could wait even into late fall or early winter to be threshed and taken to market. Once the cotton bolls burst open, the white lint would also stay in the burrs without much damage from a few weeks of weather, but it was crucial to begin marketing these crops to get some money and satisfy impatient creditors.

Beginning in mid-August, every able-bodied person in the community was needed for harvest, and Daddy stayed busy hauling hands to and from the fields to work each day from long before daybreak until after dark. The key to peanut harvest was the threshing machine, which we called a "picker" because it picked the nuts from the vines. It was most often driven by a flat belt from the rear axle or wheel of a truck, and the dried stacks of peanuts were hauled to it on wooden sleds, each pulled by a mule. The nuts were collected in a basket or washtub and dumped into a pickup truck or wagon; the nutritious dried vines were baled for animal feed. This was a big and important operation, and involved all the men on the place.

To the consternation of my father and every other landowner in the area, on one Monday morning late in September of 1940 none of the hands showed up for work. Even the day laborers who were living on our farm sent their wives to report that they were too sick to leave their cabins. By eight o'clock, Daddy and the other employ-ers learned that a decision had been made at all the black churches to demand an increase in pay from $1 to $1.25 a day for labor at the peanut pickers.

As their machines sat idle and the mules and horses remained in the barns, the white community leaders reached a unanimous deci-sion not to make any public acknowledgment of the problem, and certainly not to yield to this "anarchic" and "destructive" ultimatum. I didn't hear about the crisis until that afternoon, when I returned from school, and I was afraid of what my father would do when he came back to the farm. He had a brief whispered conversation with Mama, but refused to say anything to the rest of us.

After supper, he walked to each of the tenant houses in succes-sion (except for the Clark home) and told all of them either to be at the peanut picker or to have all their families and belongings off our place by sunrise. They were all back at work the next morning, and there was no subsequent reference to the event, as if nothing had occurred.

The story doesn't end here, however. Daddy decided to obtain advice from his best possible source. That weekend he drove over to Webster County and had a long discussion with Willis Wright, the pre-eminent black leader who lived and worked on our family's largest and most distant farm. Willis convinced him that the workers were loyal and had confidence in him, but felt that they could no longer survive without an increase in pay. Daddy told Willis that, beginning on the first day of the new year, there would be a twenty-five-cent daily raise for both men and women and a proportional increase for picking a hundred pounds of cotton or shaking a stack of peanuts. He wanted it clearly understood, though, that this was *not* being done under pressure from the workers. All the other landowners implemented the same change.

Peanut harvest

3

Hard Times, and Politics

D URING SOME of the worst years of the Depression, the
most frequent travelers we saw in front of our house were
tramps, some looking out of open boxcar doors as the
trains passed, and a far greater number walking down the road, toward either Columbus or Savannah. They were usually men traveling singly or in small groups, but every now and then an entire
family would go by. Even as late as 1938, almost one-fourth of
American workers were unemployed, many put out of jobs by newly
mechanized assembly lines in factories.

When Mama was home we never turned away anyone who
came to our back door asking for food or a drink of water. Those who
showed up were invariably polite, and most of them offered to cut
wood or do other yard work in return for a sandwich or some left-
over fried chicken or biscuits. We enjoyed talking to them, and
learned that many were relatively well educated and searching for
jobs of any kind.

One day the lady from the next farm came to visit, and Mama
commented on how many tramps she had helped that week.

Mrs. Bacon said, "Well, I'm thankful that they never come in *my* yard."

The next time we had some of the vagrant visitors, Mama asked why they had stopped at our house and not the others. After some hesitation, one of them said, "Ma'am, we have a set of symbols that we use, to show the attitude of each family along the road. The post on your mailbox is marked to say that you don't turn people away or mistreat us." After they were gone, we went out and found some unobtrusive scratches; Mama told us not to change them.

In addition to the tramps, we were always intrigued by the chain gangs that came to work on the road near our house. It seemed strange then that black and white men worked side by side, all chained together, but it seems even more curious in retrospect that most of the prisoners were white men. There are some obvious reasons. Except when a death was involved, crimes by one black person against another were not considered very important, and crimes by a black person against a white were very rare. Then, too, whites were more inclined to take legal cases to the authorities, and were more likely to be guilty of fraud, bad checks, and thefts. Another factor was that landowners did not like to see able-bodied black field hands removed from their service, and would intercede with the sheriff and judge to minimize the lost time of a good worker. Compared with modern times, few people were incarcerated, and only those with longer sentences were put on the gangs.

We boys were fascinated with criminals and their punishment, and would observe the chained men from a distance, imagining them to be mysterious gangsters and discussing Pretty Boy Floyd, Baby Face Nelson, Al Capone, or John Dillinger, who were all very famous and whose exploits we followed closely. In our rubber-gun battles, we preferred to play the gangsters instead of the FBI agents or the local sheriff. It was common knowledge that, after a prisoner was sentenced and assigned to a prison camp, a blacksmith permanently riveted shackles to each ankle and wrist, and connected them with heavy chains. We could see that each ankle chain was too short to permit a full step, and to its center was riveted a three-foot "strad" chain that had an iron ring on the end. This was used to secure the men together when being transported, or when they lay in their bunks at night. The prisoners in their barracks could move only far enough to reach the toilet, which was an open ditch down the center of the bunkhouse. Each man wore a leather pouch around his waist that held the strad chain while he worked. Georgia law permitted the chain gangs to be contracted out to private employers, so they helped with road construction, railroad maintenance, and other such jobs. They wore identical trousers and shirts with broad black-and-white horizontal stripes, and were watched closely by guards who carried double-barreled or pump shotguns loaded with buck-shot.

One day, Mama stopped her car near one of the chain gangs. She spoke briefly to the guard, and after a few minutes called me and one of my playmates to the kitchen and had us take a bucketful of lemonade to the guard and then to the chained men. It was quite an adventure being this close to them, and we were somewhat dis-appointed to find that they resembled the older boys and young men who went to church with our families on Sundays. Most of them were guilty of crimes such as theft that resulted from abject poverty, and most of the folks in Archery felt some sympathy for them as they swung their axes, bush hooks, mattocks, or scythes, not singing a lyrical song, as in the movies, but keeping time to a funda-mental rhythm that they hummed or chanted in unison.

The best music came not from prisoners but from the railroad sec-tion gang, a half-dozen black men who worked under the super-vision of Mr. Watson. He and the workers would leave their homes in the center of Archery and ride to their work site on a little car that they propelled down the track by pumping up and down on both ends of a wooden shaft. After setting their vehicle aside so the trains could go by, the workers would begin the task of method-

Mr. Watson and crew

ically checking each wooden crosstie, replacing those that had deteriorated and driving spikes to hold the rail in place. Theirs were the most cherished jobs in the community, and they wore their work clothes with pride—all issued by and bearing the insignia of the Seaboard Airline Railroad. These fortunate men had worked together all their adult lives, and knew that their best sons could someday inherit their jobs. They all attended St. Mark AME Church, near their homes in Archery, and we would recognize them in the choir when we attended services there. It was a pleasure to be near them as they sang and worked in perfect harmony.

· · ·

Although at the time we knew no other communities to compare with ours, statistics reveal the extent of the poverty and helplessness that prevailed at the time when Franklin D. Roosevelt was elected president. A precipitous drop in family income occurred at the beginning of the decade. According to the 1932 *Yearbook of Agriculture,* total farm earnings in the South decreased by more than 60 percent between 1929 and 1932. The value of a bale of cotton was cut in half, while the prices farmers had to pay for machinery and supplies remained almost the same. Although the land was already overloaded with farmers, many people moved back from cities and towns as factories closed or sharply reduced their labor forces. The Red Cross reported widespread starvation among both white and black families. I didn't know of anyone actually starving, but malnutrition and other ravages of poverty were prevalent in our community. Our shared concern brought us closer together while, paradoxically, the intensity of our competition for jobs and income increased the suffering of the weaker and more helpless among us.

All of us on the farm were familiar with unexpected disappointments resulting from weather and uncontrollable market prices, and we believed that things would soon have to get better. We were wrong. Prices for farm products continued to fall, far below the cost of production. Although much of the South had supported Herbert Hoover in 1928 (not Georgia, however), even as an eight-year-old I knew that it was the growing sense of economic desperation that brought Roosevelt an overwhelming victory four years later. He promised a New Deal, with an emphasis on farm relief, and, knowing that powerful Southerners controlled many of the committees in Congress, my father and most Georgians had confidence that he would fulfill his campaign promises. However, Roosevelt's inauguration in March 1933 did not affect the willingness of cotton farmers to respond to market conditions. Beginning that same month, with cotton at its record low price, farmers increased the acreage they planted by more than 10 percent.

Furthermore, it was an excellent spring season, so that, by the time the Congress had rushed through the Agricultural Adjustment Act in May 1933, a fine harvest was in prospect. The decision in Washington was that a substantial part of the crop would have to be destroyed! Most Southern farmers approved the offer of cash payments at harvest time, equivalent to the expected net profit from each acre, to those who would plow up as much as half their crop. The law was implemented over the vehement and sustained opposition of my father and many others around home.

We have a friend named Curtis Jackson, who lived on Rosalynn's grandfather's farm at the time and later lost one of his legs in a sawmill accident. Recently, he and I were discussing this farming crisis, which he remembered vividly. "It was bad times on Captain Murray's farm," he said. "Mr. Captain thought it was wrong before God to plow up a crop, but we had to do it. I couldn't keep my mule up on the row, where she had never been before without being whipped. I had to let her walk near the middle, and hold the plow way over sidewise to reach the cotton stalks. It was hard work, and I almost cried." Most farmers had similar feelings. *The New York Times* quoted one farmer who proposed to his neighbor, "Let's swap work. You plow up my cotton, and I'll plow up yours."

Despite these wrenching experiences, the federal cotton program seemed at first to be successful. More than ten million acres of cotton were destroyed, about one-fourth of the total crop, and by fall the price had jumped back up to ten cents a pound. There was still an excess of cotton on hand, but it was assumed that the government was permanently committed to stabilizing prices. In addition to plowing up cotton, farmers were required to slaughter and burn two hundred thousand young hogs, or shoats. For some, including my father, these were sacrilegious acts, and a totally unacceptable invasion by the federal government into the private affairs of free Americans. Despite being an otherwise loyal Democrat, he never forgave Roosevelt, nor did he ever vote for him again. Within two years, the cotton-control program was mandatory for all farmers, and peanuts were added to the list of commodities that had acreage controls, along with tobacco and sugarcane. Facing unbearable financial penalties, Daddy was forced to comply.

Regardless of these government efforts, the blight in Southern agriculture was too deeply ingrained to be eliminated. Too many farmers were still attempting to work farms that were too small to support a family. Capital was not available to expand operations or to buy new equipment that would permit diversified operations on their land. The tenancy system remained, with more than half the farms still worked by those who owned none of the land. By 1934, the New Deal programs had increased total farm income in the South, but income from cotton was still only 45 percent of what it had been in 1929, and few government benefits went to the most needy.

A sharecropper with twenty acres of cotton could earn as little as $35 a year for reducing this by five acres, of which the landlord received half. A federal Works Progress Administration (WPA) study showed that average per-capita income for sharecropper families was $28 a year, and only $44 even for tenants who owned their mules and equipment!

Even as a boy, I could see how these catastrophic developments were harming individual families and also straining relations between black and white citizens. I heard on the streets of Plains a steady stream of racist condemnations of the federal government's programs that "paid the worthless niggers not to work." But I also learned from the tenant farmers themselves how little help the New Deal assistance programs provided, and how they often created additional problems. Government compensation in exchange for reduced plantings was, almost of necessity, made through the owners of land. Despite legal requirements that payments were to be shared in the same proportion as specified by the rental or lease agreements, a landlord could legally withhold government payments for what the tenant owed him, which was often more than the size of the federal check. Thus, all the money would go to the owner of the land. Furthermore, it was easy for unscrupulous proprietors to force the tenant families from the farm and subsequently receive payment for the portion of the total crop that would not be planted. For many of the poorest farmers, the New Deal had become a curse, not a blessing.

There were other, intermittent federal relief programs designed to assist the most destitute families, and these, too, were only of marginal help, especially for blacks. The programs were administered through committees of influential citizens, many of whom strongly opposed relief payments as an incentive for recipients to reject available farm work. The prescribed payments, although minuscule by national standards, were more than many tenant families drew each month. According to another government study in 1932, rural families in our region received about $12 monthly—if they were white. By law, the average black family got only $8, because the presumption was that they could live more cheaply. When government funds arriving in a county were scarce, it is not difficult to guess who received the first chance at relief.

Even honest landlords like my father, who treated tenant farmers with scrupulous fairness, found it impossible to alleviate their plight. Money was simply not available to advance during the year to the families on the farms, and there was no advantage in doing so if the loans could never be repaid. Instead of sharecropping, day labor with payments for actual work performed was the most efficient way to use farm help.

For small landowners, there were great pressures to reduce farm operations to the point where their own family members could be used most beneficially. Still, they were also devastated during these years; more than a third of farmers with less than three hundred acres lost their property through foreclosure by banks and insurance companies. I well remember those times. For a number of years, absentee owners controlled most of the land surrounding Plains. My Uncle Wade Lowery had never done well before, but now he had what seemed a great job as an overseer of some of these large insurance-company plantations. We could readily identify them while riding down the road, because their managers minimized risks by growing only small grains, mostly wheat, which required the least possible expenditures for seed, land tillage, and labor. There was also an adverse effect on the Plains community. For the former day laborers, tenant farmers, merchants, equipment dealers, cotton ginners, warehousemen, and local bankers, it was almost as though a substantial portion of our county had been wiped off the map. This was my first picture of the difference between political programs as envisioned in Washington and their impact on the human beings I knew.

With Daddy so opposed to the New Deal and President Roosevelt, the dominant political force in our lives became Governor Eugene Talmadge, who was able to combine an intimate knowledge of agriculture and a flamboyant campaigning style with, according to a Southern encyclopedia, "the populism of Tom Watson (Populist candidate for president in 1904 and 1908) and parsimony of Thomas Jefferson." He strongly opposed the interference of New Deal policies in the private lives of farmers and business leaders, and advocated clear and simple programs such as $3 automobile license plates and breaking up the "fertilizer trust" that he claimed robbed the dirt farmers of Georgia.

All these characteristics aroused my daddy's enthusiastic support, and he would put a bed of straw in our two-ton flatbed truck and carry a load of men to Gene's political rallies. One of the most memorable was in 1934, when Talmadge was running for re-election as governor. Daddy let me go along. Although we arrived in Albany early (according to Daddy's habit), we had to park the truck at least a half-mile from the site because of the huge crowd. Everyone there was in a state of great excitement as we went first to examine the long lines of foot-deep pits in which hundreds of hog carcasses were cooking on beds of smoldering embers. The barbecuers were careful to tell everyone that the meat had been cooking since the previous midnight but would be ready to serve as soon as the political speeches were over. There were also two bread-slicing machines in operation that attracted attention, roped off to prevent the onlookers from crowding too close. Soft-drink stands were doing a flourishing business, with Coca-Colas outselling everything else. There were several souvenir stands, mostly selling campaign items for Talmadge, the most popular being pairs of the wide red galluses that were the candidate's trademark. There was hardly a man in the entire crowd who wasn't wearing a hat, and we could tell the dirt farmers by their overalls or the uncomfortable way they wore their Sunday clothes.

Fiddlin' John Carson's band from North Georgia and a men's gospel quartet alternated appearances, with the music booming from loudspeakers lashed up in the surrounding pine trees. Our group from Plains gathered under a tree about thirty yards from the stage, and Daddy boosted me up onto one of the tree limbs for a clearer view. About noon, the master of ceremonies began introducing local politicians of increasing importance, each of whom spoke a few minutes to a largely inattentive audience. About an hour later, there was a furor on the edge of the crowd and the news swept through the expectant assembly, "Old Gene's a-coming!" Everyone struggled to watch as several state patrolmen on motorcycles led a procession of closed and open cars past us, and finally one stopped and the great man emerged, dressed in a dark suit and fedora. He raised his hand and then his hat in response to the sustained cheers and moved slowly toward the speakers' platform, shaking a few hands on the way. After the mayor and our congressman spoke, the Democratic Party chairman stood and introduced Governor Talmadge.

The governor took off his hat when he approached the lectern, and his black forelock fell across his forehead, almost touching his horn-rimmed glasses. After the applause died down, he began to speak, going through a litany of brief paragraphs that some of his more fervent supporters could almost recite by heart. He talked first about a $3 automobile tag and then lower power rates, and new schoolbooks for classrooms. He recited voluminous criticisms of the New Deal, and how the federal government was trying to control the lives of every free American. Everyone awaited and cheered his declared policy of not campaigning in any county with a town large enough for a streetcar. At the end of each brief paragraph, his inflection and demeanor made it clear that applause was appropriate, and he was never disappointed. Like all his opponents, Talmadge advocated strict racial segregation, but he would always point out a number of black farmers in prominent locations in the crowd who were also his supporters.

As he neared the end of his speech, one of his key supporters started shouting, "Take off your coat, Gene!" and this cry was quickly taken up throughout the assembly. At first he seemed to be startled, but then he grinned and played his familiar role in the often repeated drama. A tremendous cheer went up when we could see that he was wearing the same red galluses that many of his supporters had already bought. He snapped them against his chest, thanked everyone for coming, asked them all to maintain their loyal support, said he had another rally to attend, and soon departed. Only then was dinner served, with an unprecedented limit (because the crowd exceeded expectations) of just one plateful of pork barbecue, Brunswick stew, coleslaw, sweet pickles, and the newly sliced lightbread, all washed down with free glasses of sweet iced tea.

Our group from Plains was ready to go home after eating, never to forget one of the most memorable events of our lives. It had been an extraordinary assembly; even the opposition Atlanta newspapers admitted that there were thirty thousand people there. In the Democratic primary that year (in those days, "tantamount to election"), Gene Talmadge carried 156 of Georgia's 159 counties, including all of those without streetcars. I never dreamed that someday I would be following in old Gene's political path to the Governor's Mansion.

· · ·

The event that transformed our family's lives most profoundly came in 1938, when the Rural Electrification Administration brought electricity to some of the most conveniently located farms in the community. Although many of the lucky families installed only a single bulb in one room, we had lights in all our rooms, and even installed an electric refrigerator and stove. Perhaps because of our extraordinary consumption of power, sometimes as much as $10 worth per month, Daddy was soon elected a member of the governing board of the Sumter Electric Membership Corporation. This cooperative immediately became one of the most powerful economic and political forces in our region, with the authority to decide where the next power lines would be run, set rate charges, and assume responsibility for protecting the special low-interest government loans that made further expansion possible. Annual meetings of the co-op were the biggest of all social events, with practically every subscriber attending for a barbecue dinner, speeches by top politicians, closely studied financial reports by the directors, heated debates among the members, and a lottery in which subscribers won valuable electrical appliances.

Daddy and the four other officers attended the national REA meetings, and did their share in lobbying efforts to effect beneficial legislation in Congress. This activity expanded Daddy's political horizons from the Plains community to all of America. Regardless of how much he cherished the rural-electrification program, he would never acknowledge that Franklin Roosevelt was responsible for it or its benefits, and he was never able to forget the forced plowing up of cotton and slaying of hogs during the earlier years of the New Deal.

In fact, the government agricultural program affected my life directly. My first (and last) nonfamily employer was the U.S. government. As a sixteen-year-old high-school senior, I was qualified to measure cropland for the Agricultural Adjustment Administration to determine whether farmers were planting cotton and peanuts within their prescribed acreage allotments and meeting government standards designed to reduce erosion. I was delighted to be paid forty cents an hour, the same as a WPA worker, and I could put in as many as seventy hours a week. I had to figure how many acres were planted, which was not a simple geometrical computation for some of the irregular-shaped fields, but it was made somewhat easier because an acre was defined as ten square chains. I had an assistant who was paid half my salary for dragging the sixty-six-foot chain, but he really earned more than I. I had to furnish our transportation, and the gas and oil took a good toll out of my gross earnings. I would have lost money if Mama had not been staying at home with my little brother, Billy, allowing me to use the family's '39 Plymouth without charge.

I was meticulous in my work. My calculations were sometimes at odds with those of the landowners, but there was only one time when a confrontation became serious. I was working in Plains Mercantile Company late one Saturday night when a farmer named Salter came behind the counter, grabbed my shoulder, and shouted, "Why the hell are you trying to cheat me out of my government payments?" I recognized him, of course, and immediately guessed which of my recent decisions had caused the disagreement. He had a small pecan orchard across the road from his house in which he had planted crimson clover. I tried to explain that he didn't have enough surviving trees per acre to qualify for a soil-conservation payment, but instead of listening he threw me down on the floor and began to beat me with his fists. I covered my face with my arms until my uncle and the other clerks pulled him off of me. At closing time, I slipped out the back door, and got home without seeing Mr. Salter again. My supervisor in Americus came over the next week, met the farmer, and confirmed my decision. I was somewhat relieved the next planting season, when Mama was working again and I went to college.

.   .   .

Although I didn't see them clearly as a farm boy, small trends toward modern agriculture were already emerging. The federal government had become a partner in every farm operation, and its intrusion into farm management was increasing. The acreage planted in cash crops was being reduced, and more agricultural benefits were flowing to larger landowners. Increased mechanization was inevitable, although it was slow in coming to South Georgia and often consisted at first of only a walking cultivator or a two-row insecticide applicator, still pulled by mules. The pressures for more rapid improvements were building, but with little effect. Though my father was a successful and innovative farmer, he didn't buy his first tractor until a year after I left for college, and he never owned a mechanical cotton-picker or a peanut combine.

About a fourth of the tenant families were forced off the farms during the 1930s, and even more after we entered the war in 1941. Fewer Southern farm families owned automobiles in 1940 than ten years earlier. The farm population was relatively unchanged, and the basic tenant system would continue for two more decades. With little opportunity for off-farm employment, the rural families had nowhere to go to find a better life.

Looking back on these circumstances, I can now understand why my parents never made any effort to induce me to remain on the farm, or even to return after a few years of advanced education in agriculture. Everyone agreed that a naval career should be my ultimate ambition.

4

My Life as a Young Pup

FROM THE FIRST DAY we moved to the farm in Archery, my primary playmate was Alonzo Davis, always known as A.D., who lived on our farm with his uncle and aunt. During my first four years in Plains I had known only white children, and it must have been quite a change for me to meet this very timid little black boy with kinky hair, big eyes, and a tendency to mumble when he talked. I soon learned that A.D.'s bashfulness evaporated as soon as we were out of the presence of adults and on our own together, and it took me about an hour to forget, once and for all, about any racial differences between us. Since our other playmates on the farm were also black, it was only natural for me to consider myself the outsider and to strive to emulate their habits and language. It never seemed to me that A.D. tried to change, except when one of my parents was present. Then he just became much quieter, watched what was going on with vigilance, and waited until we were alone again to resume his more carefree and exuberant ways.

I was soon spending most of my waking hours on the farm with him, except when I was alongside Daddy or Jack Clark. Although his surrogate parents didn't know exactly when he was born, A.D. was close to my age, and it was not long after we met that he and his aunt adopted my birthday as his own, so we could share whatever celebrations there might be. A.D. was slightly larger and stronger than I, but not quite as fast or agile, so we were almost equal in our constant wrestling, running, and other contests. I was perfectly at ease in his house, and minded his uncle and aunt as though they were my own parents. At least during our younger years, I believe that he felt equally comfortable in our house; he and I didn't think it was anything out of the ordinary in our eating together in the kitchen, rather than at the table where my family assembled for meals.

When I had a choice of companions, I always preferred A.D. We worked, played, fished, trapped, explored, built things, fought, and were punished together if we violated adult rules. Our other regular playmates were A.D.'s cousin Edmund Hollis and Milton and Johnny Raven, two brothers who lived a half-mile down the road. Rembert Forrest was the only white boy who joined our circle of Archery playmates. He was the older of Mr. Estes Forrest's two adopted children. Mrs. Forrest had died, and Rembert, about my age, became desperately ill and was not expected to live. Mr. Forrest, who ran a large farm and also a sawmill, hired my mother to go on twenty-hour nursing duty, which meant that she became both a nurse and a mother to Rembert. As he slowly recovered, Mama would bring him to our house to stay for several days at a time, and he and I became close friends when we were about six years old.

I was very envious because his father bought him a Shetland pony when he recovered from his illness. Sometimes he would ride his pony all the way to our house so we could enjoy riding together. The small stallion was a fast, nervous animal, and would unexpectedly buck and throw us off or run uncontrollably at full speed until he tired. Rembert and I often worked side by side in our fathers' cotton and watermelon fields.

We boys got along well together, but we had our own idiosyncrasies. For instance, whenever a camera appeared, Rembert always insisted on dressing up and combing his hair before posing for a photograph. A.D. refused to be in any pictures, having heard somewhere that cameras "took something out of a body."

Although I began going to school when I was six, the center of my life remained the farm. We got up early enough for an hour or two of work or play before schooltime, and I rushed home after classes to resume my rural activities.

In the frequent and sometimes extended absence of my mother, who was nursing, and my father, who was busy during the day with his varied farming and business pursuits, a young black woman named Annie Mae Hollis, a cousin of Edmund, worked full-time in our house, and she helped to care for me, Gloria (two years younger than I), and our baby sister, Ruth. My childhood world was really shaped by black women. I played with their children, often ate and slept in their homes, and later hunted, fished, plowed, and hoed with their husbands and children. I learned from them how to understand the natural world. In many ways, from birth to death, they were an integral part of our family. (Annie Mae later moved away to work with a rich family who owned Chasen's restaurant in Hollywood, but in 1953, when she heard that Daddy was seriously ill with cancer, she came back to Plains and volunteered to help my mother care for him. I was in the room in July when my father took his last terrible breath, with Annie Mae holding him in her arms.)

Of all the people who lived near us on the farm, Rachel Clark was the most remarkable and made the most significant and lasting impact on me. She was a small woman, quiet, her skin lighter than that of her husband, Jack. Although she was modest in her demeanor, there was a special aura about her, and I believe that, if Rachel's ancestors in Africa could be traced, they would be found to be a royal family. This was not just my own opinion, but was shared by others who knew her. Although my parents and other white people frequently employed black women as servants in their homes, it would

From left, top row: me, Fred Foster, Rembert;
bottom row: Gloria, Annie Mae, Ruth.

have seemed inappropriate to ask Rachel to assume such duties. Rachel was famous in the community for her natural ability in the field. She was capable of picking an extraordinary amount of cotton, half again as much as any fieldworker who, at sundown, had a day's work weighed alongside hers.

Rachel was the one who taught me how to fish in the creeks that drained our land, and on our long walks together, sometimes as much as five miles from our home, she would tell me about the flora and fauna around us and let me know that God expected us to take good care of His creation. Much more than my parents, she talked to me about the religious and moral values that shaped a person's life, and I listened to her with acute attention. Without seeming to preach, she taught me how I should behave.

As the senior couple on the farm, Jack and Rachel Clark were the ultimate arbiters of all disputes that did not warrant my parents' personal attention. I felt naturally at ease in the homes of the other black families on the farm, especially that of Jack and Rachel Clark. The only thing I didn't like was the bedbug bites that came from sleeping or just sitting on the mattresses or pallets in their houses. This was a problem with all farm families, but Mama, as a nurse, seemed obsessed with keeping our place free of these pests. We put the legs of our beds in saucers of kerosene, and we carried our mattresses outdoors regularly to be beaten and sunned on both sides. We also scoured our house floors at least twice a year with a mixture of Octagon soap and the caustic Red Devil lye, to make sure that cracks between the boards didn't harbor insect eggs.

The families on our home place were all dependable, hardworking day laborers, and any of them would have been qualified to work their own crop under a sharecropping arrangement. However, they would have had to move to another, more remote farm, go into debt to purchase their own mules and equipment, and forgo the regular wages they received each week.

Daddy knew how much each family earned, how much they owed, what equipment or tools they had, their past record as fieldworkers or sharecroppers, the degree of their industry and ambition, and, of course, their misbehavior on weekends if it involved an encounter with law-enforcement officials. Unlike my father, Mama was often inside the tenant houses performing her nursing duties, and she knew about their families, the general status of their health, and their personal sanitary and grooming habits. But I was the one who lived with them, ate at their tables, and participated in their private family conversations. The black parents, and especially the women, would sometimes talk directly to me about their concerns, and I realized as I grew older that these were messages they hoped I would pass on without their having to speak directly to my parents. I usually found a way to bring up these issues at home when I thought it might help.

Food in the tenant houses was usually disappointing—just corn bread, fatback, and maybe some greens. Sometimes, though, they tried to accommodate my presence with a more diverse diet than was customary for them. Molasses and bread were always good; the vegetables were cooked the same way (and often by the same women) as in our house, and we all loved sweet potatoes when they were available. One thing that we never had at home that I particularly liked after a successful hunt was what they called "purloo." I never knew where the word came from and I can't find it in a dictionary, but it is still used in the Plains community. Purloo is a thick stew built around the meat of some wild animal, most usually squirrel, rabbit, or raccoon. In what was a rare banquet, the flavor of the meat was preserved and greatly magnified by cooking it to pieces in a big pot that contained corn, meal, onions, Irish potatoes, squash, okra, peppers, and almost anything else available that didn't have too strong a flavor of its own. Sometimes several families would assemble and contribute ingredients. Whenever anyone asked the hosts what was in their particular concoction, they brought an expected round of laughter by responding, "If I tell you, you might not eat it!"

We farm boys led an active life outdoors, spending our days in the fields and woods, either at work with mules, plows, and hoes or, on off days, fishing, riding horses and bikes, hunting, climbing trees and windmills, wading or playing in creeks and muddy ditches, or fighting and wrestling with each other.

From as early in March until as late in October as weather and my parents permitted, I never wore shoes. The first warm days of the year brought not only a season of freshness and rebirth, but also a time of renewed freedom for me, when running, sliding, walking through mud puddles, and sinking up to my ankles in the plowed fields gave life a new dimension. I enjoyed this sense of liberation on the farm until we boys began wearing shoes to church and school when we were thirteen years old and entered the seventh grade. Many of the men who lived and worked on the farms went barefoot all their lives, except on cold winter days. There is no doubt that this habit alone helped to create a sense of intimacy with the earth.

Although briars were a problem—particularly in early spring when our feet were tender—what I remember most unpleasantly was the hot topsoil. It was enjoyable to walk behind a plow in a cool, newly opened furrow, but when we were pruning watermelons, fertilizing growing crops, or poisoning boll weevils, our feet were in direct contact with the earth's sun-baked surface. The balls of our feet were thick and tough, but it was painful when hot sand and friable earth would spill over onto the more tender tops of our bare feet. On the hottest days, from noon to midafternoon, we had to resort to a kind of shuffling dance, with brief pauses under watermelon leaves or in other small shaded areas. In the barn lots and animal stalls, there was no way we could avoid walking in the accumulated manure, and, in fact, we never tried to do so. I had to help catch and harness the mules and horses, feed the chickens and hogs, and help milk the cows each day; through it all, going barefoot was still preferable to wearing shoes.

There were some disadvantages to bare feet. There was always the possibility of stepping on old barbed wire or a rusty nail, with the danger of tetanus. Another problem was at school. The pine floors were not sanded and polished but rough, the dust kept down by regular applications of used motor oil. We soon learned to pick up our feet with each step, because splinters were prevalent and a threat to bare feet that slid for even an inch across the surface.

Our most common ailments were the endemic ground itch, ringworm, boils and carbuncles, and sties on our eyes, plus the self-inflicted splinters, cuts, abrasions, bruises, wasp or bee stings, and what we called stumped toes. We didn't worry much about red bugs, or chiggers, but Mama made us check for ticks after we'd spent time in the woods and swamps. She knew how to remove them with tweezers, so the aftermath of their bites was never serious. There was no insect repellent available to us except citronella, which was so ineffective that we rarely used it, despite the persistent yellow flies and the swarms of mosquitoes that emerged a few hours after a rain. We quickly developed a lifetime ability to ignore completely the tiny black gnats that were always so annoying to visitors.

Ringworm was more troublesome. The tiny, closely spaced spirals, occurring mostly around the crotch, itched terribly, and we believed they were caused by some demonic little circling creature. Later, to my surprise, I learned that no worm or bug was within these patterns, but something like a fungus. There was sometimes a competition for our scratching between them and the red bugs, which we always expected to pick up when we sat on the banks of a creek to fish.

Almost everyone was afflicted from time to time with hookworm, which we called ground itch. My playmates and I suffered the first stages of it. A study of black and white rural schoolchildren during the 1930s revealed a hookworm infection rate of between 26 and 49 percent. The difference between me and some of the others was that Mama always put medicine between my toes, which prevented the parasites from migrating over time into my lungs, then my throat, and from there into my small intestines. Untreated, the millions of tiny worms consumed a major portion of the scarce nutrients within the bodies of our poorest neighbors. More significantly, I guess, we avoided hookworm by having a fairly sanitary outdoor toilet and didn't habitually walk in soil that included human excrement.

On different occasions, I had both arms and three ribs broken, but my most memorable injury was just a small splinter in my wrist. One morning, as was customary, Mama told me to get a chicken for dinner. A.D. and I were in the midst of experiments with boomerangs, which we'd learned were used by Australian aborigines for hunting. We had some small ones that would sometimes return to us, and some straighter ones we used to hit targets. I went out with my hunting weapon to get a fryer. The chickens were behind our smokehouse, in a small patch of dog fennel, with straight stems from which the bushy tops had been cut, leaving stubble about two feet high. When I threw my boomerang with an overhand motion, my flailing wrist hit one of the sharp weed tops, the point of which penetrated deeply between the wrist bones and broke off. The wound was not even visible, and only a tiny puncture indicated that I had been injured at all.

I got a chicken for Mama, and told her that my wrist was hurting. She looked at it and applied a little Mercurochrome. But it was difficult to move my hand, and I began to suspect that my problem was more serious than I had thought. After a day or so, my hand and arm were swollen, and Mama took me to the clinic in Plains to let Dr. Boman Wise take a look. He probed around, found nothing, applied a small bandage, and sent me back home.

It was midsummer. We were picking cotton and shaking peanuts on the farm, and everyone needed to be working. My arm was swollen only slightly, but I couldn't bend my wrist or move my fingers without intense pain, so I stayed at home instead of going to the field. One day, after our noon meal, as Daddy was leaving to go to work, he said, "The rest of us will be working while Jimmy lies here in the house and reads a book." I was stricken by his remark, knowing that he was disgusted with me when he called me "Jimmy" instead of "Hot" or "Hot Shot." Both of my parents worked untiringly, and it was an inviolable rule in our family that we children perform our chores well. My good reputation as a worker was important to me, and my father's approval was even more precious.

Not knowing what to do, I went out into the pasture near our home, ashamed of my laziness while my daddy had to work even harder than usual. Desperate for a cure, I finally put my hand against a fencepost with my fingers upward, wrapped my belt tightly around it, and then slowly raised my arm to force my wrist to bend. All of a sudden, to my delight, there was a big eruption of pus, in the midst of which was a half-inch piece of blackened wood. I ran back to the house, got on my bicycle, pedaled it as fast as possible to the cotton field, and reported to Daddy for work. When I showed him the splinter, he smiled and said, "It's good to have you back with us, Hot."

I preferred to plow or hoe during cultivating time, but my job as a boy was often to provide drinking water for the dozens of workers in the field, almost always remote from any wells, with natural free-flowing springs the only source of water. Our best springs were carefully maintained, the sand dug out, the water source protected by a boarded enclosure, a dipper or an enameled cup kept hanging on a nearby tree, the surrounding brush removed to reveal any loitering water moccasins, and the access path clean and packed by the tread of hundreds of feet. Many homes had no dug wells and were located in close proximity to a good spring, and those alongside roadways were well known and regularly visited by travelers who paused in their journey.

Fetching water from these springs was hard work. They were almost always at the bottom of a steep incline, where the ground was usually wet and boggy, and the fields were far away on flat ground. Since Daddy was paying the field hands by the day, he didn't want them to take off every time they needed a drink, so I had to keep them supplied. I carried a two-and-a-half-gallon bucket in each hand. At least, that was the amount of water with which I would leave the spring. Despite some short, flat boards I placed on the surface to reduce sloshing, not all my load survived to be offered to the thirsty field hands after I had climbed the hill and walked to the field.

The job had other frustrations. As a boy I was without any authority, subject to importunities for speed in my round trips, and helpless to impose any kind of restraints on those I served. Some had an apparently unquenchable thirst, and I learned to make them wait until the last few inches in the second bucketful. Some had a habit, perhaps unconscious, of drinking one or two dipperfuls, taking one swallow from another, and then pouring the rest on the ground, which was almost like seeing my own blood spilled. With sometimes as many as thirty workers to satiate under a summer sun, this was as difficult as any task I ever had on the farm. I envied the plowmen and hoe hands, and always thought that my father should have given this job to the biggest and strongest man, not to his only boy, though I was sure he loved me despite this torture.

Thanks to our short hair, one affliction that we boys usually avoided was head lice, but even with the good hygiene that Mama enforced around our house, both my sisters had this problem on occasion. Other than a very short haircut or a shaved head, the standard treatment was a concoction of sulfur and kerosene, held in place with a tight stocking cap. Whenever we saw a schoolmate wearing a hat all during the day, we knew what her problem was.

It seemed that none of the treatments for our ailments were pleasant. We always suspected that the patent-medicine manufacturers had concluded that only evil tastes and smells were effective in combating germs—or perhaps they were simply responding to their customers' beliefs. Castor oil, milk of magnesia, 666, and paregoric all met the test, and hot poultices and iodine burned enough to be respected on croupy chests or open cuts and scratches. I think the most obnoxious medical experience I ever had was when someone convinced Daddy that we children could avoid an outbreak of flu or some other prevalent illness by wearing pieces of asafetida, or devil's dung, around our waists. This horrible-smelling extract from some kind of root undoubtedly earned its reputation as a protector by keeping bearers of germs at a healthy distance from the wearer of the stench. We wore it until we convinced Daddy that the threat had passed.

Despite the lectures in school and from my mother about malaria, typhus and typhoid fever, and other diseases spread by insects and rodents, there was not really much that we could do about the ubiquitous pests. As far as flies were concerned, our screen doors were opened too many times each day to keep them out of our house. Containers of milk or other food had to be kept covered, often with a piece of cheesecloth. We used fly swatters and sticky tapes hanging from the ceiling to reduce the fly population, but there was always a fresh phalanx waiting outside the back door— and new ones breeding on the nearby barn lot. The old joke was that cooking chitterlings was the only thing that would make the flies find ways to get out of a house.

Dogs played a significant role in our lives. Not only were they constant companions on the farm and for hunting, but they also provided the most fearsome nightmares of my childhood. The fear of hydrophobia, or rabies, was even worse than the haunted house or the threat of pneumonia or polio. We were brainwashed from early childhood with horror stories about victims of a mad dog's bite. We heard about a farmer with a good family who was bitten by a dog he knew to be rabid. While the farmer still had control of his senses, he secured himself to a tree with strong chains and a lock, and then threw away the key so that in the final stages of his derangement and convulsions he would not be able to attack his wife and children. Such lurid tales were designed to warn us about the totally incurable, ravaging effects of hydrophobia, and we knew that the threat was not exaggerated.

My worst recurring dream was of confronting a dog—always a small and attractive puppy—that turned out to be mad. When I started to run, the little dog would follow me—stumbling, sometimes going around in circles or even wandering off—but always coming back, and I found myself struggling as though wading through thick molasses, able to move my feet and legs only in slow motion. As the slavering jaws finally opened to bite me, I would wake up in a cold sweat, breathing heavily and almost petrified with fear. Even now, more than sixty years later, I can still remember vividly the surreal howling noises and see the blood streaming down the little dog's hind legs from its self-inflicted bites as it came after me.

During my childhood I saw several mad dogs, not much less repulsive than those in my dreams. If one of our own dogs began to act strangely, we would tie it securely or lock it in a crib, then shoot it unless it resumed its normal ways. I remember seeing some of the rabid animals running erratically on the main road and in the fields near our home, and twice when I was in Plains a mad dog appeared in the streets. The news would spread like wildfire, and we would all go into our homes or stores and shut all the doors and windows. One or two men with rifles or shotguns would approach the dog, in an automobile if possible, and kill it. On one unforgettable occasion when I was downtown selling peanuts, a suspected mad dog had been tied to a light post in front of the stores. As it began to suffer convulsions, our nervous town marshal went as near as possible to the animal and shot his pistol six times, without hitting anything except the ground. One of the salesmen finally shot the dog with a rifle and bullet taken from a display case in Plains Mercantile Company, a store on Main Street owned by my Uncle Alton (whom I always called "Uncle Buddy").

There was no way for a farm boy to avoid being bitten by a dog on occasion, and if its history of inoculation was not known, its bite was a real problem. The dog's head would be cut off and sent to the state laboratory, and if the animal proved to be rabid, the victim had to have a series of twenty-one painful shots in order to escape what was known to be inevitable death. (It was not until 1971 that the first person was known to survive rabies.)

One day, I was riding my bicycle past a house about a mile from ours when a small terrier bitch ran out from under a cottonseed house and bit my heel severely. I saw that she was not wearing a collar with an inoculation tag. Daddy and the dog's owner had never been on very good terms, and now there was a serious confrontation between them. Daddy insisted that the animal's head be sent off for a quick analysis, but the farmer refused, maintaining that there were puppies under the seed house that the bitch was protecting. The crisis was finally resolved when our neighbor went to the county courthouse and brought back an official record proving that the dog was currently vaccinated against rabies. Mama still insisted that I have three painful precautionary shots, with a long needle in my butt.

The annual inoculation day was one of the most exciting events on the streets of Plains and, in fact, a great holiday. All the county's veterinarians would come, and all the people living in our part of the county would bring their dogs to town, secured and held tightly with unfamiliar ropes or chains. There would be dozens of dogfights plus a lot of barking and howling, and the stores would do a booming business. But this citizens' duty was serious, and enforced rigidly, both by county health and law-enforcement officials and by peer pressure. Owners knew that any dog without its metal inoculation tag was subject to being destroyed on sight.

Rats were an even worse and more persistent problem. I'm referring not to mice but to wharf rats, some of which were ten inches long, not counting their tails! We rarely opened a crib door or went into the barn loft to throw hay or fodder down into the feed troughs without meeting one of these monsters, who considered the secret recesses of the barn their own domain. Some of them could fight off the cats that stayed around the buildings, and hold their own in a close place with a slow-moving dog. Nothing except steel and solid concrete seemed impervious to their gnawing teeth, and their extensive burrowing under concrete floors would eventually cause even them to collapse. To thwart the rats, Daddy bought some secondhand steel boxes for one of the cribs in the barn, in which he could store and protect especially valuable seed, medicines, or other chemicals. It was common knowledge that rats were more prolific than rabbits. They were not only filthy carriers of disease, but a constant source of worry and annoyance, probably consuming as much grain as our livestock. The rats were also deadly to baby chicks, poults, goslings, and ducklings.

At that time there was no effective rodenticide except strychnine, which would kill anything on the farm, so for control we had to resort to milder but relatively ineffective poisons, big traps, trained terriers, and some extremely large and almost wild tomcats who frequented our barn area. Despite a few temporary successes, this war against rats was a constant struggle around the barn and storage cribs, which we always seemed to be losing. On a few occasions, Daddy traded with one of the nearby farmers to spend a day or so at our place with their pack of trained feists and rat terriers, which would dig madly into the rat burrows to kill the obnoxious creatures. Everyone who was free of fieldwork would gather around the barn area to watch the bloody conflict, which was waged both above-ground and in the maze of tunnels under our buildings.

The yard around our house was more sanitary than the barn area, and we tried to seal our stores of grains and other foodstuffs that attracted the wharf rats, but there were always a few in the woodpile, the smokehouse, or the crib where I kept feed for my ponies and for the calves for my school projects. Daddy didn't like having cats around our house, so he used a .22-caliber rifle for the protection of our back yard and store buildings. When we spotted one of the big rats, either he or I would sit patiently on the back steps until we could get a good shot. In comparison, we almost ignored the little mice except in the kitchen and pantry, where we set small traps baited with cheese or peanut butter.

We also had a flock of about two dozen geese, primarily used to control insects in the cotton fields. We kept their wing feathers clipped so they wouldn't fly away, but they roamed the farm freely, being able to jump over the fences. Of all the animals I had to confront as a little boy, they were the most fearsome. When the geese were on their nests or after the goslings hatched out, the ganders were particularly aggressive, and I had to give them a wide berth. If I saw them on the narrow lane from our house to the barn, I turned aside and took a long detour.

Twice a year the geese were penned up and, one by one, we caught them and picked the down from their breasts. Even when I was big enough to do my share of the work, this was quite a struggle for me, holding the creature with its back against my chest, my left arm under its left wing and behind its neck, and my hand grasping the right wing. While the goose struggled to bite me or escape and defecated again and again, I had to pluck the breast feathers with my right hand and thrust them through the narrow opening in a bag. This extremely fine down made a superb and almost weightless filler in comforters; some of them we used for bedcovers at home, the extra ones going for a fancy price to stores in Plains and Americus.

For a good portion of my young life, I helped Jack Clark with the milking. In the mornings, Jack first had to get the other workers off to the fields with their mules, equipment, fertilizer, and seed, so he milked the cows after I had gone to school, sometimes with his wife Rachel's help. My job was to do some of the milking in the afternoons, after I came home. I usually took care of about three of the cows while he finished the others. Our herd of eight to twelve cows produced far more milk than our family could consume, but Daddy put it all to good use.

We had all the sweet milk we wanted to drink, and everyone consumed a lot of it except my mother, who never drank milk of any kind. Adjacent to the woodstove in our kitchen was a five-gallon stoneware churn, covered with a loose lid that had a hole in its center, which was always kept at least half full of milk. At regular intervals, when all the cream was on top and the stove's heat had curdled the milk to semisolid clabber, we churned it by moving a wooden dasher up and down for about a half-hour, until the cream turned to butter and floated to the top. We skimmed the butter off, salted it, and pressed it into pretty shapes with wooden molds. The remaining buttermilk was (and still is) one of my favorite beverages.

Daddy had one standing order from the local Suwanee store in Plains for all the pure cream we could produce from our surplus milk. There was a cream separator on our back porch, a large aluminum bowl that could be spun rapidly by turning a handle. It served as a centrifuge, quickly separating the lighter cream from the remainder of the milk. I could understand the basic principle, but am still mystified by a little hinged metal clicker that swung back and forth on the handle. The tone of the click would change when the cream was separated. (Perhaps some reader can explain to me the relationship between what was happening inside the container and the small piece of iron hitting the end of the handle.) When the cream was removed, the remaining skim milk, which we called "blue john," was fed to the small pigs and calves. (This skim milk is what Rosalynn and I now use on cereal and for cooking, to reduce our intake of fat and cholesterol.)

Daddy took several gallons of our whole milk each day and made it into vanilla-, chocolate-, and sometimes strawberry-flavored drinks. These were poured into small wide-mouthed bottles, sealed with waxed pasteboard inserts. He had a regular route from one store or filling station to another in a flexible geographical area large enough to handle our current production. In each place, Daddy would pick up the bottles not yet sold, replace them with fresh milk drinks, and collect for the difference. Again, anything returned was fed to the livestock. One of our worst farm crises was when the milk cows found some bitterweed in a remote corner of the pasture, which created for several days a terrible acrid taste in the milk and sent all of it to the hog pens. We had to move the cows quickly and destroy the noxious plants.

We always had a yard full of chickens, plus some turkeys, guinea fowl, ducks, and a few peacocks, most of which were raised from eggs to adults. Once or twice a year, Daddy would order several hundred baby chicks from Sears, Roebuck or another supply house to supplement our need for broilers and eggs to eat or sell. As already mentioned, when it was time for fried chicken or chicken pie, Mama would say, "Jimmy, go get me a big broiler, or a hen," and my job was to catch the chicken, kill it by wringing its neck, and bring it onto the back porch for cleaning and dressing when it had stopped flopping and bleeding. We ate the dark meat of guineas more often than we liked, because they were so stupid about crossing the road in front of passing cars. The domesticated hens—mostly white leghorns, Plymouth Rocks, and Rhode Island Reds—were inclined to use the nests that we had placed in sheds, alongside the buildings, and in the low crotches of trees. Most of the other nests were hidden, including those of the somewhat wild game chickens.

During all those years, chicken eggs were a readily accepted form of currency. Everyone knew the price of eggs of different sizes at the wholesale and retail level. It was a matter of honor for a seller to assure their freshness, and there was an automatic replacement guarantee. A rotten egg could seriously damage the reputation of anyone who knowingly foisted it off on a merchant, and then ultimately on an unsuspecting housewife. However, despite precautions, a bad egg was inevitable every now and then and could wreak havoc in a mixing of dough for biscuits or a cake. Habitually, we even broke the eggs from our own yard into a separate bowl for a preliminary examination, because some might have remained in one of the more hidden nests for several days before being found.

Although I had a lot of work to do around our house and yard, at the barn and in the fields, my playmates and I found time to do other things. Everyone on the farm was familiar with the ripening of wild fruit and nuts, and we boys were always looking forward to the changing seasons, each one lasting a month or six weeks. First came plums, blackberries, wild cherries, and blueberries late in May, then figs, apples, and peaches throughout July, and in August mayhaws, muscadines, and scuppernongs. By October we were looking for chestnuts, chinkapins, walnuts, hickory nuts, pomegranates, and persimmons, and finally, through November, we had pecans and sugarberries. The only wild fruit that was a source of income for tenant families was blackberries, which the women and children picked through the clinging thorns and sold for ten cents a gallon.

An annual ritual, on my October 1 birthday, was for our family to visit a large chestnut tree growing on the edge of our forest. There were two other, smaller ones on the farm, but they were no longer bearing fruit and seemed to be dying. We would gather the few chestnuts on the ground not already eaten by animals, and then throw short sticks into the tree to knock down fresh ones. We were at the southern limit of its native habitat, and our productive tree was something of a curiosity. When I took a few chestnuts to school with me, I could swap each one for a good marble. Later, when I returned from the navy, our tree had succumbed to the pervasive blight.

I copied A.D. and my other friends in devising playthings that didn't have to be bought. Except for the times when I "pulled" one of the boys in front of me on the bar of my bicycle, I parked it and walked or ran with the others. It would be hard for me to remember all the things we made. One of our favorites was a thick steel hoop from a wooden keg, ten to twelve inches in diameter. We rolled our hoops for miles, even hours at a time, propelling them with a strong, stiff wire that had a loop on one end to provide a handhold and a V-shaped notch on the other to fit behind the hoop.

We would have felt undressed without our rubber-banded flips, or slingshots, and a supply of round rocks in our pockets for ammunition. Other projectiles were also important to us, and they could have been deadly weapons. One of the easiest to make and most enjoyable was a kind of dart made from a large corncob, four or five inches long, with a needle-sharp nail embedded in the pith of one end and two chicken feathers in the other that were set at subtle angles to give the thrown weapon the correct amount of spin before it embedded itself in a target or the side of a building.

We used the same sharp tip on dog-fennel spears, and were surprised at how far we could throw them with the help of spear throwers called "atlatls," which we devised after reading about them in

Boys' Life magazine or one of our Indian books. We haunted Daddy's shop for days as we improved on our basic design of rubber guns. After cutting out shapes of long-barreled pistols, we mounted spring clothespins, wrapped them with rubber bands to increase their grip, and then stretched a cross section of inner tube around the end of the barrel. A squeeze on the clothespin released the loop of inner tube as a projectile. We ultimately devised repeaters that would shoot as many as a dozen rubber bands. We would fight wars until everyone on one side or the other had been "killed" by being hit. We also made popgun barrels by removing the pith from the center of American elder limbs, and used green chinaberries as projectiles.

On my seventh Christmas, Daddy bought me a Shetland pony to match the one owned by my friend Rembert. I named her Lady. She was small in height, phlegmatic and slow compared with Rembert's stallion, but stocky and strong—well able to carry two of us boys. For a few years, A.D. and I took every opportunity to saddle Lady and ride her around the farm or to the creek. Daddy believed that everything on the farm should pay its own way, even a pony, so we took her at proper intervals to spend a few days to breed with Rembert's pony. It was a big event when her colts came, but a sad day when they were sold, for as much as $25, either by Daddy or by his brother Alton or at the county livestock-sale barn. I always received half the money, which I deposited in my own bank account in Plains. Between colts, Daddy still compared how much corn and hay the pony consumed with her hours of productive use as my mount. As I grew older and my interest in the pony waned, I always dreaded Daddy's inevitable inquiry, "When's the last time you rode Lady?"

Everyone I knew in the Plains community could swim. The first year we lived on the Archery farm, Daddy had a small pool excavated in a branch behind our house and lined it with boards. We enjoyed

I'm riding Lady, with her colt, Lady Lee,
and our bird dog, Sue.

swimming there, but so did the venomous water moccasins that frequented the swamp area, and we had to examine the surface carefully before jumping or diving in. One day my cousin Hugh (Uncle Buddy's son) and I stopped by for a swim, and found a large water moccasin in the pool. While trying to strike it with a limb, Hugh fell into the water, but he scrambled out so fast that, as we later said, "he didn't even get his clothes wet." The pool is where Daddy taught my sister Gloria and me to swim, but afterward my country playmates and I swam in the much larger Choctahatchee Creek. Later, with my white schoolmates from Plains, I usually went to Magnolia Springs—the resort where my future parents had gone on their first double date.

. . .

It seemed a shame to let Daddy's goats go to waste, so A.D. and I got Jack Clark to help us rig up a little cart, using the two wheels from an old child's bicycle. The next step was lassoing one of the largest billy goats, struggling to get him haltered and hitched to our cart, and then trying to influence him to go in the general direction that we preferred. It didn't take us long to realize that goats are even more cantankerous than mules, and that small boys were not as good at training these animals as were the experienced men on the farm (let alone the cowboys we saw in the movies). We named the billy goat Old Gene Talmadge after our governor and painted the traces red to match his famous galluses; despite all the problems, our goat-cart rides were at least unpredictable and adventurous. The only serious mishap was when I tried one day to ride Old Gene. He didn't try to buck me off like a wild bronco, just ran head-on at top speed into a barbed-wire fence. He stopped, but I didn't; I still have a two-inch scar on my right thigh as a permanent warning against the dangers of goat riding.

One of our favorite activities was flying kites. We made our own, gluing tissue paper onto frames of split bamboo, first concentrating on the highest kite and later on who could fly the smallest one. Another, much more competitive activity was tree climbing. Even as small boys we mastered all the limbs on the chinaberries, magnolias, and pecans in our yard, and eventually we concentrated on larger ones in the woods. Those with reachable limbs weren't too much of a challenge, so we then experimented with a rope loop that went around our waists and the trunks of tall trees. By clamping the bark with our bare feet, we could lever our bodies up a few inches at a time, until the lower limbs were in reach. My talents as a tree climber paid off in helping Mama with pecan harvests, and also with raccoon and opossum hunting. We had a tree house in our yard, and also a secret one in the woods, but never had much luck trying to illuminate them with jars of lightning bugs.

I could hold my own in all the childhood games with my regular playmates, but the baseball team in Archery was out of my league. There were ten boys on a team, including a "backstop," whose position was behind the catcher to handle the wild pitches. Larger black boys were always the dominant players. The two Watson boys, white sons of the railroad section foreman, were good athletes a few years older than I, and were on the regular Archery team. I was sometimes permitted to play backstop, perhaps because I always had a bat and ball and did well with a glove. I really wasted my time at the plate, too afraid of being struck by the hard-flung and often wild pitches to hit the ball.

Every now and then our family would go to a movie in Americus. I missed several of these family excursions: I refused to return to the theater after seeing Al Jolson in *The Singing Fool,* singing "Sonny Boy" after the tragic loss of his son, Davey Lee. I cut a photograph of Davey from the local newspaper and pasted it inside the chifforobe door in my room. After recovering from my grief, I mostly went to movies on Saturday, when the program always included a western, an episode in a serial designed with a heart-stopping conclusion to bring people back every week, a cartoon, and a Pathé newsreel.

On a few occasions when fieldwork was slack, Daddy let A.D. and me go to Americus to see a movie by ourselves. We had to walk up the railroad to Archery, find the little red leather flag left for the purpose, and stick it upright in a hole in the end of a crosstie. The engineer would see the signal and stop so we could board in front of the section foreman's house. It cost fifteen cents each, and we parted company during the ride to sit in the seats marked "white" and "colored." When we arrived in Americus, we walked together to the Rylander Theater and separated again, A.D. paying his dime at a back entrance and sitting in the high third level while I went in to sit either downstairs or in the first balcony. Afterward, we would go back home, united in friendship though physically divided on the segregated train. Our only strong feeling was one of gratitude for our wonderful excursion; I don't remember ever questioning the mandatory racial separation, which we accepted like breathing or waking up in Archery every morning.

From the time I was five years old, my father and I were fascinated by Indian artifacts and the lives of the Native Americans who had inhabited the western part of Georgia. Knowing that our family's farmland had once been theirs and that our ancestors had confronted and replaced them in this area deepened our interest in their history. Daddy had two books about Indian culture and artifacts, and we learned what we could about the people who had worked or hunted on the same land and fished in the same creeks.

I never walked in a field or along a stream without constantly looking for flint points or pottery fragments. After heavy rains, when fieldwork was impossible, my father and I searched our favorite places, which we knew to be sites of ancient villages because of the proliferation of chipped flint and pottery shards. (In South Georgia there are broad swampy areas alongside the larger creeks that flood during rainy weather, so the best sites for Indian settlements were away from the swamps and on well-drained land near good springs or small streams.) We did our best collecting in the winter, after the land was plowed deep and had lain fallow for several weeks, so that subsequent falling rain exposed the flint and pottery fragments and left them on top of small mounds of earth. We would study the more interesting pieces, and sometimes argue about the origin of the particular kind of flint, the shape and size of an arrowhead or a spear point, and its relationship with the nearby pottery fragments. When we became discouraged after a fruitless search, we would reassure ourselves by computing how many thousands of arrowheads must have been left behind by a tribe that had lived there for perhaps a hundred years, even if they lost only one arrow each day.

Looking for arrowheads has been a lifelong habit, even when I walk in densely populated areas. Rosalynn and I played golf for a few years, and I found several nice points along the heavily traveled paths between greens and tees, overlooked by thousands of golfers. After my father's death and my return home from the navy, our entire family expanded our collection by searching the fields in a much more concerted and organized way. One afternoon, with five of us walking abreast up and down one of our best fields, about ten feet apart, we found twenty-six unbroken arrowheads. We keep every interesting artifact and label it according to who found it and where. The configuration of the base of an arrowhead or larger spear, we've learned, is an accurate indicator of its age. We still have about two thousand of the points that we have found, the earliest dating back more than twelve thousand years, and we can estimate the native population during any historic period by the number of artifacts we have found from that era.

More recently, with the advent of larger and heavier tractors and other farm equipment, the smaller fields on the steeper slopes have tended to be abandoned for cultivation and planted in pine trees. Within a year or two, the surface of the ground is covered with weeds and briars, and later with pine straw from the growing trees. For arrowhead hunters, many of these best sites have been lost—at least for another three or four decades, until the timber is harvested.

Throughout my young life, I was obsessed with hunting and fishing, and I was not alone. It was what my father, most of the men in town, families on the farm, and all of us boys wanted most when we were not working. We read, thought, talked, recalled past experiences, and made future plans, all about hunting and fishing. I had a fishing pole in my hands as early as I can remember, and would go hunting with Daddy long before I could have anything to shoot other than a BB gun.

During dove season, Daddy would wake me sometimes two hours before daybreak. We would usually drive first to Plains, where one of the filling stations would be opened early and have coffee brewed to warm up the hunters before the cold outing. Some of the men might join me in eating a Moon Pie, but I usually let them have the barbecued pork skins, or reach into the big-mouthed jars on the shelf that held a supply of pickled pig's feet or dill pickles. I would just stay as close to the stove as possible and relish being the only little boy permitted to attend the ceremonial gathering.

Then we would proceed to a field where the birds were known to be feeding. All the hunters were assigned places by the landowner, far enough apart to avoid injury from the small pellets with which the sky would soon be filled. Daddy would make a fire if the weather was extremely cold, and in the still-remaining darkness we could hear the barred owls, whippoorwills, and other night birds calling. The doves would begin coming in when it was still too dark to see them, and these first birds would light on the ground unscathed. As dawn brightened, the guns around the field would commence firing, and the birds began to fall. My job was to watch in the opposite direction from my daddy to warn him about an incoming flight, to observe the fall of those he killed, and to run rapidly to retrieve each one.

Daddy was a good shot, and was always one of the first to bag his self-imposed limit and leave the field. I remember that when I was in the first or second grade we would return to the schoolhouse after classes had begun, and I would enter the classroom very proudly, knowing how envious the other boys were. I tried to leave a feather or two on my jacket so there would be no doubt about the reason for my tardiness.

The ultimate outdoor sport around Plains was hunting bobwhite quail. This is a pastime or art of such challenge and complexity that it is not easy to describe to those who have not experienced it. One indication of its value is that many of the most successful families in our nation came to South Georgia during the first half of this century and spent a considerable portion of their wealth to buy enormous plantations, sometimes as large as thirty-five thousand acres, with the single goal of having a place on which they could raise and train hunting dogs to find the fast and elusive quail. A large percentage of the land in many Georgia counties is still occupied by the same hunting preserves.

I didn't know about these fancy places when I was growing up, and it was only after I was elected governor in 1970 that I received my first invitation to hunt on any of them. But, immersed as I was in the culture of my father and the other men of Plains, it was inevitable that quail hunting would become a part of my life. At least during hunting season, from late November to late February, it was a prime topic of conversation, and throughout the other months the men talked about the breeding of good dogs, birthing of pups, analysis of the litters, training of the young dogs, arguments about the innate qualities of pointers versus setters, the different makes and bores of shotguns, the prevalence of predators, enhancement of habitat, sighting of hatched baby quail in the spring, and retelling of hunting exploits.

Daddy always had at least three bird dogs, sometimes well known for good performance in the field. It was the custom of most farmers to release dogs from kennels every day, to run freely in the yards and fields, even though we all knew that a really great hunting dog was worth more than a two-hundred-acre farm. We also knew that hunters from big cities were always eager to acquire them—by any means possible—so everyone on the farm was alert for suspicious strangers.

One of the worst days I remember was when our best pointer turned up missing. Daddy placed an old hunting jacket and a pan of water where the dog had last been seen, hoping during the night that the dog would return, and everyone joined in the search for a day or two. Finally, as a last effort, Daddy went to see one of the local fortune-tellers to see if she could tell him where our dog might be, and he let me come along. She had a sign in front of her house covered with heavenly bodies and a large hand, with lines in the palm indicating issues of importance: life, death, wealth, love. We were invited into the house after a considerable wait, which was quite unusual for prominent white people in a black person's yard. I stayed in the background while Daddy paid a dollar, sat across a small table from the woman, and explained the circumstances of his loss. She seemed to go into a trance for a few minutes, and then said, "Mr. Earl, you ain't never gon' see that dog ag'in." She was right.

By the time I was five or six years old, I had been carefully instructed in the proper use of firearms, beginning with a BB gun, then a Remington .22 semiautomatic rifle, and finally a bolt-action .410-gauge shotgun. Daddy let Jack Clark help in the training of our dogs, and I had walked enough with both of them to know the strict safety rules and proprieties of quail hunting. Finally, I was permitted to take our oldest and slowest dog out alone. I still remember precisely where I was when the dog pointed; I flushed the covey and fired in their general direction, and one fell. I rushed forward and knelt down to examine the bird and then ran all the way home to show the trophy to my father. After the expected congratulations, which I enjoyed, he asked, "Where is your gun?" I didn't know—in my excitement, I'd forgotten all about it. I rushed back to the woods to get it, but I was so agitated that all the trees and brush looked alike, and I couldn't find it anywhere. It took Daddy and a search party several hours to locate the shotgun, half buried in some oak leaves where I had dropped it to pick up my bird. I was really grateful that he didn't tease me about it later, or tell the men in town.

Except for transient day laborers, I don't remember any farm family that didn't own at least one hound dog and a single-barrel shotgun. Even when an entire family was living on a few pennies a day, they still found enough food for their dog. We boys knew every one by sight, and I would report a strange one to my father as a stray that might be rabid or inclined to eat sheep. Hunting was a manly and useful pursuit, but often restricted for sharecroppers by landowners who were also avid hunters and didn't want competition for the game. My daddy reserved only the bobwhite quail and mourning doves for himself, leaving rabbits and squirrels to be hunted by the others who lived or worked on our land. Almost universally permitted for tenants was the use of hounds at night to find raccoons and opossums. Often, particularly in the late fall and the winter, several tenants living on adjacent small plots of land would pool their efforts. Four or five men would follow at least an equal number of hounds through the woods, listening carefully to the distinctive voices of the dogs.

I was often invited, and went hunting a number of times with the farmers living near our house. I was a popular companion even when quite young, because of my willingness and ability to climb high into trees. This was the usual way to capture the game, by shaking the limb on which the coon or possum would be crouched. When it hit the ground, the men would try to seize the creature before it was killed or injured by the hounds. Possums would usually curl up and pretend to be dead, but coons would run or fight, sometimes whipped the dogs, and often had to be chased and treed again. The common arrangement among the hunters was to share game equally, but when few animals were caught they went to the men whose dogs had first struck the trail. It seems surprising to me now that there were not more arguments about this, but the voices of the hounds were distinctive and the changes in tone and spirit so pronounced that the issue of which dog was hottest on the trail was usually decided long before the men arrived at the treed quarry.

My only claim to fame concerning dogs was that I happened to own the best squirrel-hunter in the Plains community. My heart still picks up a beat when I look at the old photographs of me and Bozo, a Boston bulldog. He was a constant playmate of mine from the time he was a little puppy, and everyone was surprised that a dog of this nonsporting breed developed superb hunting instincts. He always accompanied A.D., Rembert, and me when we were in the woods, and learned to tree coons, possums, and squirrels. We never encouraged him with the first two, but would sometimes spend an

With Bozo

hour or so trying to shoot the squirrel with BB guns, flips, or my .22 rifle. Not only was Bozo alert and competent in finding the game, but he soon learned to back away from the trunk of the tree and bark ferociously while we would stand quietly on the other side. The squirrel would ease around on the opposite side of the trunk or limb to hide from the dog, revealing itself to us so we could bring it down.

Daddy never hunted squirrels with us, but he shared my pride in Bozo. One day when I was about twelve years old, he told me that his close friend Mr. Edgar Shipp had some friends down from Atlanta and they wanted to borrow my dog for a weekend. He said they were experienced hunters and would take good care of him. I had confidence in both Mr. Shipp and my father, and I agreed. But the following Monday, Daddy came to the schoolhouse—quite unusual for him—and asked me to come outside. He put his arms around me and reported that the men had put Bozo in the back of their pickup truck, and when they stopped in front of the hotel in Americus he had jumped out into the strange street traffic and was killed by a passing car. I didn't want the other children to see me crying, so Daddy let me go home with him. He helped me bury Bozo in a grave under the pear tree behind the tennis court.

Fishing was our second great love. Underground in our region is a tremendous aquifer, a slow-moving stream of tens of millions of cubic feet of fresh water that originates in Florida and eventually emerges offshore in the Atlantic Ocean. During my boyhood days, there were no large, deep pipes sucking up enormous quantities of water to supply paper mills or to irrigate fields, and artesian wells flowed freely from a number of city squares in Georgia, possibly the reason for the location of those towns. At almost any point on our farms, there was a flowing spring nearby, and a hand pump or open dug well could produce good water at depths of less than thirty feet. The constantly flowing springs merged into small branches and then into large creeks that in many states would be called rivers. A stream was within walking distance of any would-be fisherman, and I never heard of a landowner who restricted access to the creeks on his land. Most of the families who lived in the area were hungry for meat, and loved the sport of fishing. Unlike today, when few people fish in the remote swamp areas, we could walk down a clearly defined path along both sides of every stream large enough to produce fish.

Although it was considered improper by many people to fish on Sunday, and all of Saturday was usually consumed in getting paid, settling accounts, shopping, and socializing, it was still easy to find times when fishing did not interfere with farm work. Since men did all the plowing and were in the fields when almost everything else was going on, women had more time off to catch fish. Between lay-by time, when the crops were too big to plow, and harvest time, even the men were free from fieldwork. Perhaps more important, it was not possible to work in the fields with either hoe or plow for a day or two after a heavy rain, and since the streams were rising this was the best time for catching catfish and Atlantic eels. During dry weather, when the creeks were low, we caught mostly largemouth bass, chain pickerel, and several species of bream or sunfish.

I had several kinds of fishing in the area surrounding our farm: with Plains schoolmates, with my Archery friends, with my daddy, and with Rachel Clark. Each experience was different. There were a couple of my town friends with whom I fished for largemouth bass and chain pickerel, which we called "jack." We would ride our bikes to millponds and the streams that drained them, and use casting rods and reels to place our lures in the best places to catch fish. Creek fishing was a challenge because of the overhanging brush that impeded our casts and the submerged snags that seemed to reach out for our gang hooks. We spent a lot of time in the water, the only way to retrieve the precious plugs that we had bought from Sears, Roebuck, sometimes for as much as a dollar each.

One special event occurred early each spring, usually on the full moon in March, when the word would go around in Plains, "The suckers are running!" Some of us would gather on key streams at night, stand in the water with a powerful flashlight focused under the surface, and harpoon the spotted suckers going up the stream to spawn. It was a difficult and exciting sport that might yield one or two of the big fish if we were lucky. Suckers were filled with tiny bones, so the fillets had to be slashed about every half-inch with a sharp knife to ensure that both the meat and the bones would be cooked and eaten.

The time for fishing with other boys on the farm was when it was too wet to work in the fields and the creek levels were rising. We would often camp out overnight on the stream bank, and fish in the increasingly muddy water for catfish and eels. We cut short limber poles from along the bank, tied a strong line and large hook to each, and placed them all along the stream, with small pieces of liver or fish suspended about a foot deep in the water. Every hour or so we would take a lantern and check the hooks, either rebaiting empty ones or pulling in fish. We'd cook at least one meal—usually the eels, because they had to be eaten when fresh—and take the rest of our catch home. Our biggest problem was water moccasins that lay in the edges of the stream or on overhanging limbs and were sometimes caught on our hooks. They also liked to swim up and eat our fish, which we kept on strings in the creek.

Daddy never wanted to do any fishing in the nearby creeks, but, beginning when I was about ten years old, he would take me with him to fish in Southeast Georgia, usually in the Okefenokee Swamp or the Little Satilla River. These were the times when I felt closest to my father, and I appreciated deeply the fact that I was again the only child permitted to accompany the grown men. We fished with long cane poles throughout the day, and the men usually played poker at night, after I went to bed. I caught a baby alligator on one trip, and Daddy let me bring it home and keep it in a wire cage with a flat pan of water in one corner. When it disappeared a few weeks later, my parents said it probably went to the creek, but we knew one of the dogs had eaten it.

One of the most interesting experiences we had in that part of the state was to see women plowing in the fields as their husbands made a living as fishing guides. Back home, the women's farm work was perhaps even more onerous, but it was always limited to hoeing, picking cotton, shaking peanuts, tending gardens, and sometimes milking cows.

The Little Satilla River in Southeast Georgia was my favorite place for fishing. We'd wade waist deep out into the river, on sandbars, and fish along the undercut opposite banks on the outside of curves in the meandering stream. It was a remote and lonely site, so Daddy and I stayed fairly close together. We fished with pond worms and caught mostly large bream—redbreast, warmouth, and bluegills—all of which we called "copperheads" because of the color engendered by tannin in the water. Since we were always in the stream, we kept our caught fish on stringers tied at our waists.

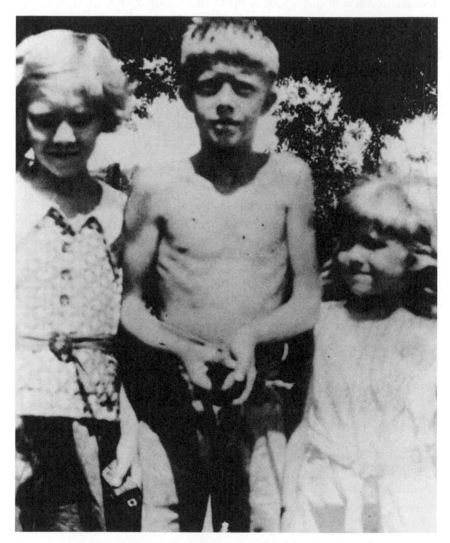

Gloria, me, and Ruth, 1933. (I'm holding a baby alligator.)

Late one afternoon when I was about ten, Daddy asked me to keep his fish while he walked down the river to talk to some of his friends. I tied his stringer with mine on the belt loop on my downstream side while I continued fishing, enjoying the steady pull of the current on our day's catch. It wasn't long before I watched my cork move slowly and steadily up under a snag and knew I had a big one. After a few minutes I saw the copperhead, the largest fish of the day. As I struggled with the sharply bent cane pole, I wondered how I was going to hold the fish while untying the two stringers. Then a cold chill went down my spine as I realized that the tugging of the current on the stringers was gone, as were all our fish! My belt loop had broken.

I threw my pole up on the nearest sandbar, forgot the hooked fish, and began to dive madly into the river below where I had been standing. Then I heard Daddy's voice calling me:

"Hot," he said, "what's wrong?"

"I've lost the fish, Daddy."

"All of them? Mine, too?"

"Yes, sir." I began to cry, even as I continued diving, and the tears and water ran down my face together each time I came up for breath.

Daddy was rarely patient with foolishness or mistakes, but, after a long silence, he said, "Let them go, Hot. There are a lot more fish in the river. We'll get them tomorrow."

I almost worshiped him.

5

My Mama and Daddy

Mama, Ruth, and me, 1933

M Y MOTHER WAS BORN in 1898, four years after my father, and she grew in spirit and influence all her life. When I first remember her she was a very slender, almost gaunt, woman. There was a time when the doctors prescribed iodized salt for a goiter condition and became concerned about her losing too much weight. I remember that she and Daddy joked about her having to drink a bottle of beer each afternoon for medical reasons. Mama was pretty in her own way, with her dark hair parted in the middle and eyes that always seemed to sparkle. At home, she wore loose-fitting dresses and was either barefoot or had on comfortable brown shoes, in which she seemed at ease doing housework or lying on the couch reading a book. Mama seemed to me almost a different person, precise and businesslike, when she was on duty in her starched white nurse's dress and cap and white shoes, of which she was very proud.

Mama was the one who did most of the refereeing at home, and maintained adequate discipline among us three children. (This was long before Billy was born.) She did a lot to protect us from more severe punishment from Daddy, and when one of us had violated a rule or abused another child, she would report the infraction and hasten to add, "Earl, I've already punished them!"

All the time I was growing up, it seemed on the surface that my father made the final decisions in our house. In front of us children or visitors, Daddy's word was law, and it was not until I was older, perhaps in high school, that I realized how strong-willed my mother was and how much influence she had in our family affairs. There were a number of subjects on which Mama prevailed with no discussion, including how the household was managed, what my two sisters could do during the daytime, what food and clothing were purchased, and who paid which bills. She bought what she wanted from one of the grocers in Plains, either in person or more often by telephone, with the supplies to be placed in Daddy's pickup and brought out to our farm. Mama neither knew nor cared about the price of groceries, because Daddy paid those bills—I doubt that she ever saw them.

Mama nursed as much as possible between having children, either in the operating room of our local hospital or on private duty with a patient. She earned $4 a day for twelve hours, or $6 for twenty hours. This was a lot of money during the Depression, especially in the early 1930s when farm prices reached their lowest point. Most of the time we didn't expect Mama to be at home when we returned from school, but she would usually leave us a note on a little black table against the wall in the front room. It would let us know when she would be back home, and contain instructions concerning extra work, in addition to our regular chores. Later, my sister Gloria and I would tease Mama by claiming that we always thought the little black table was our real mother.

Because of Mama's profession, the nurses and doctors in our hospital helped to shape my life. My earliest memories of Wise Sanitarium are of the infrequent occasions when Mother would let me cross the road from the schoolhouse to eat a hot meal with the nurses if she was on duty and not at home to fix my lunch. I didn't realize then what a treasure we had in Plains—a truly outstanding medical center with all the economic and scientific benefits that it brought to the community. Compared with those in other small rural towns, the interests of our citizens were expanded by the stream of doctors and nurses who came to live among us as they trained or practiced their profession.

As "Miss Gordy's little boy" and a pet of the nurses, I had an especially blessed life. The senior nurse, Mrs. DeWitt Howell (always known by her maiden name, Miss Gussie Abrams), was a close friend of my parents and was my godmother. She had high expectations for me, and on my eighth birthday gave me a matched leather-bound set of Victor Hugo's works and a twenty-volume set of *The Outline of Knowledge.* This is still one of my treasured possessions.

When Mama was not nursing she was in charge of the house. She usually had some help with heavy cleaning, and she sent our dirty clothes off in a long square-bottomed white-oak basket to be washed each week by a black family near Plains who specialized in this service. When at home, Mama was up before first light to fix breakfast for us, usually after my father had left the house to get all the farming tasks assigned and under way. (He would awake when

Jack Clark sounded the farm bell an hour before daylight.) On school days she would get us all fed, dressed, and on our way; during the summertime, I would often go to the field with Daddy and, if near home, we might come in later in the morning for breakfast.

Mama had two sources of income: her fees earned as a registered nurse, and proceeds from the sale of pecans. Based on a long-standing agreement between her and Daddy, all the pecan trees on our land belonged to her, and during a couple of weeks late in November she arranged to remove her name from the nurses' call list so she could supervise the harvest. When the crop and prices were good, income from the nuts equaled what she earned all year from nursing. She spent this money as she saw fit, and it covered all the personal items we ordered from Sears, Roebuck and the clothing she bought at local stores for herself and my sisters, Gloria and Ruth.

She was thoroughly familiar with the characteristics of different pecan varieties, including Stuarts, Moneymakers, paper-shelled Schleys, and the ungrafted seedlings. Mama made sure that the trees were kept trimmed and the weeds around them cut, and she followed the recommendations of the county agent on how to control the various diseases and insects. There were a few large pecan-farmers with high-pressure sprayers, and she always bargained with one of them to apply pesticides to the highest limbs on her trees. In November, armed with the longest bamboo poles she could find and with a cadre of hired women and boys, she made certain that every nut was knocked down, picked up, bagged, and then either polished in the hull or carefully shelled. Other farm boys and I climbed the trees to shake the top limbs that the poles couldn't reach; on a few occasions, Mama also climbed the trees. Gathering pecans, she always said, was "like picking up money off the ground."

Daddy never accompanied her when she loaded our pickup with ten to twenty burlap bags of her nuts and drove them to Americus for sale, but I went along whenever possible. I was always somewhat nervous but titillated by the impending pageant, which was repeated during each visit. Her preferred market was in the busy store of Elias Attyah, a Lebanese-American who knew more than anyone else in our region about this important crop. He supervised personally the purchase of each bagful of pecans, dumping them out into a tilting wooden bin adjacent to the big overstuffed chair that accommodated his imposing figure. He would scan the nuts, pick out two or three, shell them, and examine the kernels. When dealing with unsuspecting sellers who brought in small lots from trees growing in their yards, he would examine the outside hull, choose those whose kernels were inferior, shake his head in disappointment at what was revealed, and offer a low price for the lot.

This didn't work with my mother. She would watch impassively, then select a few extra-good nuts from the bin and say, "Now shell these!" Mr. Attyah would smile, look at the superior kernels, and they would then discuss the final price. Mama made a point of knowing what all our neighbors had already received for their pecans, and invariably got the best prevailing prices. She really liked Mr. Attyah, trusting him to treat her fairly; they both knew that all Mama's pecans would come to him regardless of offers she received from other dealers, who sometimes sent eager buyers to our farm when the crop was short and demand was high.

I was born in 1924, Gloria in 1926, and Ruth in 1929. Our brother, Billy, came along in 1937. Except for family outings involving our parents, my two sisters and I had little in common during my earlier years. Gloria and I were competitive and Ruth and I had a loving relationship, but I usually ignored both of them in my daily life. I was outside the house and even away from the yard whenever possible, had my own playmates, and was increasingly employed in the field. Neither Mama nor the girls ever worked in the field, so, while I was becoming familiar with axes, anvils, plow stocks, mules, and guns, they were involved with sewing machines, cooking utensils, dolls, dresses, and other mysterious feminine pursuits. We had meals to-

Daddy, with Gloria, Ruth, and me, Easter Sunday, 1932

gether, and during early-evening hours and rainy days we congregated in the living room. Otherwise, we went our separate ways.

One of our favorite shared pastimes as children was to have Mama tell us about the days before we were born. In the warm months we would sit on the front porch or the steps, and in wintertime we would be near the living-room fire. The routine, which both Mama and we enjoyed, would begin with our chanting, "Tell us a story!" After some friendly delay (and with Daddy aloof from the process, maybe reading his newspaper nearby), we would call out different subjects until a consensus evolved: "How you and Daddy met," "About Grandpa and Grandmama," "When we were born," or "The time you did so-and-so." To us, these accounts were better than fairy tales, and we would press Mama with questions to expand her earlier accounts of the same happenings. When my sisters were young, she usually addressed her remarks to me, and I was the one who probed for more and more information. To some degree, our kinfolks became mythical characters through these tale-telling hours, so that when we met them later we knew a lot more than they could have dreamed, at least about our mother's impressions of them.

My mother, Bessie Lillian Gordy, had moved to Plains in 1920, eager to trade a job in the Richland post office for a career in a hospital. Being accepted as a nurse trainee was an opportunity that she and her parents welcomed. At twenty-two years of age, Mama had already heard other members of her family say, "Lilly, you don't want to be an old maid," so she told us she was not averse to combining marriage with her new career. Her first date in Plains was with George Tanner, a big, rough-looking sawmill man who had a sister named Lucy. They decided to go dancing at Magnolia Springs, a resort near Plains, and Lucy went along with a local grocer named Earl Carter. Lillian had seen Earl once before, swimming in the pool and ostentatiously doing front flips and half-gainers off the springboard into the frigid water. She had considered him a smart aleck and a show-off, and wasn't pleased to have him along for the

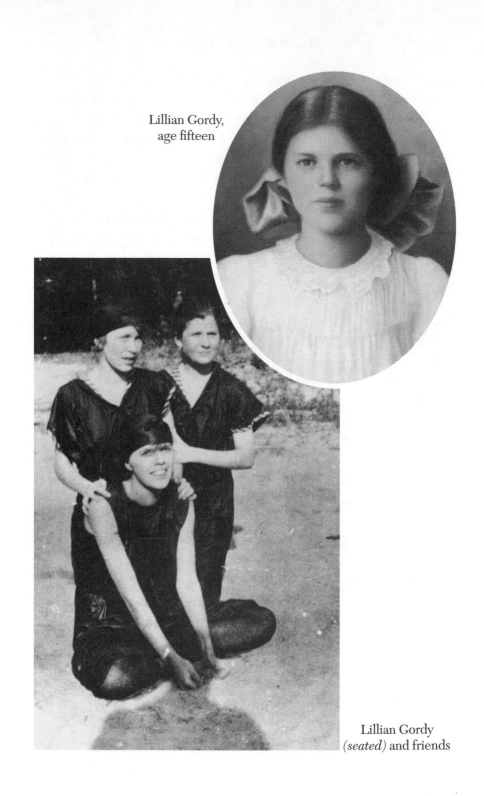

Lillian Gordy,
age fifteen

Lillian Gordy
(*seated*) and friends

dancing. Her dislike was intensified when he asked her to dance just once the entire evening, and then only when urged on by George Tanner and just to be courteous.

The following week, Lillian and some other student nurses were walking from their storefront dormitory toward the drugstore when they passed a group of young men. Earl was among them, and he soon came into the pharmacy and approached the group of trainees at the soda fountain. He tipped his hat and said, "Good morning, Miss Gordy, it's good to see you again." She nodded, and he asked, "May I speak with you for a moment?"

When they stepped aside, he asked if she would like to go for a ride that weekend. She agreed, and they set a time for him to pick her up. She quickly learned that some of the other nurses knew several things about her prospective date. They said he was pretty fast with women, liked to play baseball and poker, and drove an open-topped Model T Ford. In addition to his job at Plains Mercantile Company, he had a small "pressing club" on South Bond Street, where woolen clothes were dry-cleaned by a black man named Robert Jackson, whose wife worked at the hospital.

We always liked to hear Mama describe the situation: "For some reason, I was nervous and excited, and began to worry about what I would wear. I finally borrowed a navy-blue taffeta dress from one of the other nurses. All of us wore uniforms most of the time and swapped our regular clothes with each other when we had a date. I watched from our balcony over the main street when Earl parked his car, and I made him come upstairs to call for me.

"It was a little before sundown, and he said he was going to drive out toward Preston and show me the farmland his family owned. I reckon he wanted to make an impression regarding how well off they were. We hadn't got to Choctahatchee Creek before it started pouring down rain, and the car didn't have a top. He had a real thick wool lap robe, though, and we covered up as best we could and he drove on over to the farm and parked under a wagon shed until it quit raining.

"We were pretty well acquainted by the time we got back to town, and after that we began to date regularly. I could play the piano some, and Earl pretended to like to hear me, especially the 'Twelfth Street Rag.'"

Earl told Lillian that he had sold "flattening irons" in Oklahoma for a few months before giving that up and moving back to Plains, then went off to the army. Later, he became engaged to a woman named Maggie Jenkins, but they "broke it off." Maggie's photograph in an old family album showed a striking brunette; she eventually became a college professor. Mama always described their separation by saying, "He got his ring back."

Mama continued, "I didn't let on that I knew anything about him, and he told me that he was making about a hundred dollars a month, and was planning to open an icehouse near the railroad station. I was impressed with his 'get up and go.'"

After that, the couple drove often to the Carter family farm in Webster County, being especially attracted for some reason to the most remote field, nearest the creek. Sixty years later, when Mama and I went over there to look at some growing peanuts or planted pine trees, she would tell me, "This is where Earl and I did most of our courting."

The nurses' quarters soon moved down the street to some small rooms above the drugstore, where Miss Abrams was their general supervisor and a tough disciplinarian.

Mama continued: "Earl was one of Miss Abrams' favorites, and she would let him come into the doctors' area every now and then to see me even when I was on duty. One day, he came to tell me that his baby sister, Jeannette, had just learned that she was pregnant and had to get married to Wade Lowery, and it almost broke his heart. While we were still sitting there, he asked me to marry him.

"I was ready right then, mainly to get out of training, which was a terrible life, but Earl insisted that I finish and become a registered nurse, which wouldn't be until the following June. I spent six months at Grady Hospital in Atlanta, and didn't have time to go back to Plains.

I almost went crazy, and really hated it when Earl sent my engagement ring to Atlanta by one of the doctors. On graduation, Earl explained to Grady officials that we were to be married, and they let me take the state board examination without the usual waiting period."

We especially liked for Mama to describe the early days of their married life.

My parents first rented a place from the Wellons family—a little room upstairs, with a balcony and some outside stairs going down to the ground. It was on the northeast corner of the house, and Mama called it "the coldest place in the world." The privy was way out in the back yard, so they lived with a slop jar. That room is where they first learned that I would be born, and they stayed there for several more months, until Dr. Sam Wise said Mama couldn't go up and down those stairs anymore. He was concerned about her, but also wanted her to continue working with him in the operating room. That's when they moved to Emmett and Bessie Cook's house, on the ground floor.

When the time came, Mama presumed that I would be born at home, as were all the other babies at that time, but Dr. Sam said there was an empty room in the hospital and she might come back to work quicker if he could deliver the baby there. Mama never failed to mention that Daddy was out at a fish fry and a poker game when she began having labor pains and didn't get home until real late to take her to the hospital.

Someone gave us a little dog after I was born, and after an argument about it, Mrs. Cook made us leave her house. My parents moved two more times, and then Daddy bought the house next door to Edgar Smith's family, where Rosalynn (my future wife) was a baby. That's the house my father later swapped with the Plexico family, who built the home we were to own out in Archery, using plans obtained free from Sears, Roebuck and Company.

Whether Daddy was listening or not, Mama always gave us an

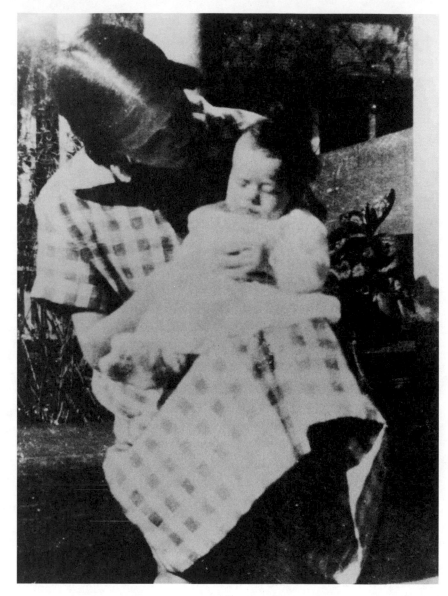

Mama and me, 1924

unvarnished image of their early married life. "Earl was a twenty-nine-year-old bachelor, and he had his own way of doing things. He told me before we were married that he played poker every Friday night, but I figured I could break him of that. The first Friday after we were married, he left right after supper and came home long after midnight. I refused to speak to him and pouted for a day or so, but it didn't do any good—then or later. I always accused him of being kinder to everyone else than he was to me. One time Ethel Wellons and I were both pregnant, and someone sent me some nice grapes. Earl said, 'Ethel is not feeling well, and I'd like to take the grapes to her,' so I threw them at him."

When I was grown, after Daddy died, I asked Mama if they got along all right together. She said, "Sure we did, most of the time. But I must say that we had different ways, and it took us a long time to figure out how much room to give each other. Even after Gloria and Ruth came and I had started to quit nursing and was at home more, we still had our differences. As long as he lived, he still wanted to go out on Saturday night and raise hell, and I got tired of it. As you know, he kind of took over the Elks Club in Americus, and claimed that he had to be there to make sure everything was run right. We would always have a few drinks, and he would dance with most of the pretty women in our crowd. I never was all that keen on dancing, and sometimes we had words afterward, if he seemed to enjoy himself too much."

One characteristic that Mama sometimes deplored but that I inherited from my father—reinforced by my years in the navy—was an obsession with punctuality. He would always be well ahead of time to meet a train, attend a baseball game, or keep an appointment. It was inconceivable that his tardiness would keep anyone waiting, and he expected everyone around him to honor the same standards. When Daddy was scheduled for a physical examination of some kind, Mama would do everything possible both to remind him of the unpredictability of the medical profession and to encourage the doctor to be on time. She knew that if the physician was late Daddy would look at his watch for a very few minutes and then leave. When Mama tried to chastise him, Daddy's reply was, "I'm just as busy as he is."

. . .

Even more than Mama, because I worked with him and observed his daily activities, my father was the center of my life and the focus of my admiration when I was a child. He was a serious and some-times stern businessman, but often lively and full of fun with his friends and with the men and women who lived on our farm. When I joined him on his routes to sell milk, syrup, and other products, I could see how easily he traded with the merchants and filling-station owners who were his customers, but without wasting time at each stop. In addition to taking care of business, he was deeply in-volved in church work, the county school system, and other commu-nity affairs. Also, he was fascinated with sports and the outdoors, and loved to have a good time when his work was done and financial settlements were complete.

Daddy was a relatively small man, about an inch taller than Mama, but stockily built and very strong for his size. He had light-reddish hair—thinning, perhaps, because he was never outdoors without a hat. Despite this, his face was always sunburned, and his body looked surprisingly white whenever he took off his shirt to go swimming. He was one of the best divers at Magnolia Springs and McMath's Millpond, and an outstanding tennis player. He had good control of the ball and a wicked slice that was effective on the dirt courts around Plains. As I've mentioned, one of the first things he built when we moved out to our Archery home was a tennis court between our house and the commissary store. Some of the men would drive out from Plains on Sunday afternoons, and unless there was a big group they usually played singles, with the player who first lost a set dropping out if others were waiting. The winner stayed on the court as long as he wished. Usually that was Daddy.

Daddy was impatient for me to grow up, and began giving me tennis lessons as soon as I was old enough to hold a racket. Although I eventually became the top player in high school, I could never beat him—and he certainly never gave me a point.

Baseball played an even greater role in our family's life. Daddy alternated as a pitcher and catcher for the American Legion team, and enjoyed the sport for the rest of his life as a committed spectator. I remember going to Americus to watch him play, and was very proud of his performance. It was serious baseball, with the teams wearing uniforms and spiked shoes. Once, when Daddy was catching, he blocked the plate as an opposing player slid in with spikes high; he had to spend several weeks on crutches with the resulting injury.

Some of my best days were when I would go to the professional baseball games in Americus with Mama and Daddy. We sat with my Uncle Buddy on the front row along the first-base line, in chairs reserved for him and the other officials of the Georgia-Florida baseball league. It was Class D ball, an integral part of the immense web of farm systems that existed in those days to feed superior players step by step into the major leagues. There were always a few big-league players who began their careers in Americus, Cordele, or Albany, or on one of the other nearby teams. My parents and Uncle Buddy knew every one of them, almost as well as they knew the citizens of Plains. We had a boy from Plains named Charles Sproull who worked his way up and even pitched in the major leagues, winning four games but losing ten for the Phillies in 1945.

Each season began with an exhibition game at the ballpark, and one of the highlights of my boyhood was when the St. Louis Cardinals played in Americus. I was ten years old, and we were at the ballpark when the teams began warming up. Daddy suggested that I go out on the field and ask the legendary Frankie Frisch and Pepper Martin for their autographs. They were standing together not far from home plate when I approached them with a pencil and a clean paper bag that had contained roasted peanuts. Frisch, who was acting as player-manager, signed the bag, but Martin looked down, spat some tobacco juice that almost hit me, and said, "Get your ass off the field, boy!" For years, I kept the peanut bag—with just one autograph—in the safe at our store.

Even during the Depression years, Daddy, Mama, Uncle Buddy, and his wife, Annie Laurie, saved enough money to take at least one trip each summer to Pittsburgh, Cincinnati, St. Louis, Chicago, Philadelphia, Boston, New York, or another major-league city, usually in Uncle Buddy's Chrysler. They planned the trips for after crops were laid by and when they wouldn't miss our Baptist church revival, and so they could see the maximum number of games, with at least one doubleheader. They continued these excursions for years after I left home, until Daddy was too sick to travel.

They had more flexibility on their schedule in those later years, and Mama always considered it to be one of God's special blessings that she and Daddy were present when Jackie Robinson played his first game for the Brooklyn Dodgers in 1947. From then on, Dodgers General Manager Branch Rickey was one of her special heroes for bringing Robinson to the major leagues, and she was a fervent Dodger fan even after they moved to Los Angeles (and the Braves came to Atlanta). She watched or listened to every Dodger game she could, and after our family became famous she would call Dodger manager Tommy Lasorda on the telephone to complain about managerial decisions he had made. When Mama died, we found a complete Dodger uniform in her closet, even including cleats, with a letter signed by the entire team.

My daddy closed his store in Plains two years after we moved to the country, and transferred the unsold stock of basic and durable merchandise out to the little commissary adjacent to our house. This included canned foods and other nonperishable groceries, some hardware, and dry goods. All the workers on the place, men and women, used either chewing tobacco, self-rolled cigarettes, or snuff. Clothing items stocked for male workers were overalls, denim shirts, work shoes, gloves, and straw hats, but a lot of the "hard stock" was long out of style. Though there never was a discount sale as such, Daddy would make sure that the old clothing was sold by lowering the prices to appeal to individual buyers. He had the well-deserved reputation of not wasting anything, so members of our family served as consumers of last resort if there were items that couldn't be sold.

My most vivid memory concerning this policy was a few pairs of high-button dress shoes that had probably been in style both for men and women around the turn of the century. Daddy insisted that I try on the shoes, and finally found a pair that fit my small feet. Despite my protests, he maintained that they were for men, and I had to wear them to school. I tried to cover them up with the longest trousers I had, but the older boys still made me the butt of their jokes. After two days, my suffering was so deep and apparent that Mama interceded and got me a reprieve from the embarrassment. My friend A.D. seemed to be glad to get the ancient footwear.

Another of Daddy's money-saving habits created continuing problems for me. He insisted on cutting my hair, mostly with hand clippers, sometimes supplemented by just a few snips of the scissors. Despite my indirect importunities through Mama as an intermediary, his basic and unalterable design was that of an inverted bowl on top, with no hair below the top of my ears. I really envied the stylish twenty-five-cent haircuts of the other boys in school, who went to the town barber. Once, during the annual springtime clipping of the mules and horses, Daddy decided to save some time and effort on my hair by using the wide hand-cranked clippers at the end of an unwieldy, flexible cable, designed for shearing sheep and other animals. Perhaps predictably, his hand slipped and he cut a big gash through my hair. The only option was to clip all of it, leaving me with a bald head that I had to keep covered with an old cap. I wanted to stay home as much as possible, but Mama insisted that I fulfill a promise to visit my grandparents, who were then living in Columbus. Later, Grandma wrote saying that they had enjoyed my stay and that I was a nice boy, but that I had a peculiar fixation on wearing my cap in the house—even at night, when I went to bed.

. . .

Daddy always paid the field hands for their day labor and gave credit or cash loans to tenant farmers at our little store. This is where he kept his careful records of all advances (loans) and credit sales. Saturday was the only time when the store stayed open, but we would also unlock it whenever a customer showed up at our house, often at mealtime, just to buy merchandise worth a few cents. There would be a knock on the back door, and Daddy would take the key ring off his belt and toss it to one of us children. This was usually my job, but sometimes my sister Gloria helped as a clerk in the store, either on these daily visits or on Saturdays.

In addition to their clothing, Daddy expected our farm workers, whether day laborers or tenant farmers, to buy other necessities, such as plow points, rope, mule collars, hand tools, side meat, sugar-cane syrup, meal and flour, lard, sugar, salt, kerosene, and tobacco products, at our store. We also sold some patent medicines that our customers used to counteract the dietary and sanitary symptoms of hookworm, dysentery, pellagra, malaria, diarrhea, and typhoid, including calomel, quinine, castor oil, paregoric, Epsom salts, iodine, milk of magnesia, and the extremely bitter 666. I've never been able to forget those who would buy a ten-cent bottle of castor oil, go outside, and drink it all in a few gulps! We children, remembering its heavy slickness and terrible taste, would almost throw up while watching.

In addition to learning about working duties on the farm, I was also expected to know about the woods and swamps, and Daddy would teach and quiz me about basic survival techniques. He knew that my friends and I spent many days roaming the back side of our farms, sometimes several miles from the nearest field or road, and he wanted to be sure I was safe. In addition to swimming, the use of firearms, and the recognition of poisonous plants and reptiles, I had to know how to find my way even under difficult circumstances. I learned that there was never a problem in knowing directions if the topography was varied enough or if the distant sound of a highway or the sight of a heavenly body could indicate direction. He taught me how to look at the moon during either day or night and tell the direction of north, and would ask me at unexpected times to demonstrate this ability. The one difficulty was in the more remote, broad, and completely flat swamps, when clouds obscured the sky, when a compass was the only dependable guide. Daddy gave me one the size of a small pocket watch and told me always to carry it with me.

Once when I was fishing with Rembert on Choctahatchee Creek, we found an enormous alligator snapping turtle, the biggest we'd ever seen, pinned down by a tree that had fallen on it. It had begun drizzling rain, and it was time to take in our poles and leave the creek, so we took all our fishing lines, doubled them up, and suspended the monster from a limb to carry it between us and show it to our parents. It was almost sundown when we started walking out of the swamp. This time I had forgotten my compass, and as dark approached we realized we were lost. I began to get nervous, but a half-hour later we were delighted finally to see some human tracks—until we realized that they were our own. I remembered Daddy had told me that it was a natural human inclination to walk around in a circle unless we focused on specific landmarks.

About this time, the weather cleared well enough for us to see the sky, so we abandoned the turtle and began trotting westward, in a straight line toward Venus, which was then an evening star. We hurried forward, often forcing ourselves through clinging briars and holding up our arms to prevent the low tree limbs from striking us in our faces. After an hour or so, we reached a road, and I knew enough to follow it to the house of a black family—a long way from where I had expected to come out. I was both relieved and concerned to learn that Daddy had already been there, telling the family to be on the lookout for us. We were too exhausted to walk any farther, so the man hitched up his wagon and we began the journey of about eight miles to our home.

I feared confronting my father, knowing the anguish we had caused him and Mama, and how annoyed he would be because I had violated all the woodsman's rules he had taught me. We soon met his pickup and began the long drive back home. Daddy didn't speak to me until we drove up to our house and stood together in the yard. He looked at me for a few moments and then said, "I thought you knew better than to get lost in the woods."

I began to cry, and he reached out to me. Just being there enfolded in my father's arms was one of the most unforgettable moments of my life.

6

Boiled Peanuts in Plains

IT IS DIFFICULT for me to explain why the town of Plains is so attractive to Rosalynn and me. It is obvious that our family ties to Plains are strong. We still take our grandchildren and some guests to the family cemeteries, one north and the other south of the town, where our great-great-grandfathers, all born in the 1700s, settled, farmed the land, and were buried with their wives and progeny. Both of us grew up here, and at least one of us is related to many of the citizens, who are still our neighbors. Plains is where I've seen the members of my family laid to rest, and where we expect to be buried.

As a boy, I went to school and to church in this little town, sold boiled peanuts, hamburgers, and ice cream, and courted my sweethearts. It's where we raised our own children, built our first and only home forty years ago (the fifteenth house in which we lived after we were married), and struggled to make a living and deal with the end of racial segregation after we left navy life in 1953. Our Plains neighbors traveled all over Georgia to help me become governor, and to Iowa, New Hampshire, Florida, Wisconsin, Pennsylvania, and other states when I campaigned for president. The ties are many and deep.

There is a sense of permanence in Plains, of unchanging values and lasting human relationships, and the town has been a haven for us during times of political or financial crisis. Having visited almost 120 foreign countries and "seen the sights," we find the quiet attractions of Plains stronger with our increasing age, so that, no matter where we are in the world, we soon begin wishing we were back home. There is a sense of harmony here, of mutual respect between black and white citizens, a common willingness to join in ambitious projects to improve our town, and the strong influence of religious faith expressed in its eleven churches.

Modern conveniences like running water, telephones, and electricity haven't changed the appearance of the town since the earliest surviving photograph was taken in 1905. Main Street was and is primarily nine brick buildings, all with common walls except for one narrow alley halfway down the row. With the exception of my father's grocery store and the bank building, marked "1901," all are two stories high. When I was growing up, there were five small wood-frame structures on the west end of the street, which housed a café, a barbershop, the post office, a grocery store, and a filling station. Just across Hudson Street was the two-story drugstore with offices for doctors and nurses upstairs.

Plains is a circle with a half-mile radius centered on the depot and roughly bisected by the railroad and by U.S. Highway 280 going east and west, which until the mid-1950s was the only paved street. The town was laid out in the middle of a large pecan orchard, and almost every house has a few trees still in the yard. During my boyhood, when the nuts became mature, in November, people were eager to gather enough to pay the taxes, and didn't take a chance on passersby or squirrels sharing the harvest. "They don't hardly bounce twice before they're in a bucket" expressed how fast the annual harvest was on the way to market.

· · ·

With a few notable but seldom-mentioned exceptions, black and white people have always predominated in their own sections of town. In the country, of course, there was no way to separate houses by the color of their occupants. However, there were countless other distinctions that kept us socially and legally segregated.

The Plains I knew as a child hadn't changed much since its earliest days. I've read the old city-council minutes, which show that our town was established to be a law-abiding place. The use of houses for immoral purposes was forbidden, as was the sale or use of intoxicating drinks. It is obvious that this prohibition was interpreted very stringently. The "application of Floyd & Myers to sell Apple Phosphate was refused," state the minutes. Business licenses were designed both to raise revenue and to assist in shaping the moral climate of the town. In 1899, a flourishing livery stable, dealing in all the animals required for transportation and farm work, paid an annual fee of only $5, and the even more important cotton warehouse was charged $10, but owners paid twice this amount for each bagatelle game, and five times as much for a billiard table. Circuses were charged $50 per day to set up in Plains, and the daily fee for menageries was $5. License fees for theatrical, "legerdemain," or minstrel shows were discretionary with the mayor. In minutes from 1903 is this verbatim entry: "All persons selling bottled drinks as a beverage shall pay a licensed of 100 one hundred Dollars for privelige of selling same." However, this law was soon nullified by the advent of bottled Coca-Cola, Georgia's special contribution to the world, which was known to be heavily but legally laced with the extract of coca leaves and was always called "dope."

One ordinance that I violated as a boy stated that no weapons were to be used within the city limits, including slingshots, bows and arrows, or any kind of firearm. This prohibition was soon extended to include the cemetery, located about one and a half miles to the west. Safe and quiet streets were also important, as shown by a speed limit of ten miles per hour for trains and eight for automobiles. Understandably, no train whistles could be blown within the city limits. To correct original oversights, the city fathers soon outlawed bicycles on the sidewalks, games of chance, curing hides, tramps, Gypsies, loose horses, permitting any animals to run away with vehicles, and shoe shines on Sunday.

It is obvious that the fiscally conservative founding fathers of Plains believed in a balanced budget and kept a tight rein on expenditures. At first, all revenue came from licenses for business owners and professionals, and streets were maintained with seven days of mandatory labor by every citizen between the ages of sixteen and fifty (later restricted to males, and exempting schoolchildren). It was expected that the wealthier men would hire someone to take their place. But demands for improved services grew, and in 1901 an annual per-capita tax of $2.50 replaced the required work on the streets. With a total population of 346, this levy proved excessive, so no taxes were collected the following year, even though the city marshal's monthly salary was raised from $5 to $7.50. By September 1903, it had jumped to $10, but his pistol, purchased in 1905, had "to be repaid by same," which took at least a month's pay. Because of the large number of rabid dogs that appeared on the streets, this seemed to be a good investment.

The first record of strong public opposition to a council decision came in 1906, when, at the suggestion of a leading doctor, all hogs were ordered removed from within the city limits. There were no experienced farmers on the city council, as indicated by a February 4, 1907, entry: "Mule that was purchased for $30.00 found to be unable to work." Subsequently, the mayor was authorized to rent a replacement draft animal for fifty cents a day.

Judging from the frequency of journal entries on the subject, one of the most thriving trades in the early days was in fish or oysters, shipped in by rail or truck from the Gulf Coast. By 1907, new annual license fees had been established for some additional professions: $10 for a dealer in fresh meats, "except farmers selling beef by quarter or homemade sausage, souse or chitterlings"; $5 for blacksmiths; insurance agent, $10; banker, $10; photographer, $2.50; person shining shoes for pay, $1; and mercantile firms, from $2.50 to $10, depending on total capital ranging from $500 to more than $10,000. Hotels charging $1 a day paid an annual fee of $2.50, which was doubled for those charging $2 for a room. It is clear that Plains was expanding, and now had a population of almost four hundred. Each entry reveals that enticements of important professionals were also offered through tax breaks, with the license fee for a blacksmith being reduced to $2.50, and being completely repealed for the even more valuable physicians, dentists, and fertilizer dealers. Sometimes emergency expenditures were required. One December, for instance, there was an outbreak of smallpox, which was diagnosed and treated, with an eighteen-day quarantine supervised on every affected home, at a total cost for the medical team of $25.

In 1914, the holding of council meetings became erratic, and the members resolved, "Whereas the whole county is depressed owing to the very low price of Cotton, making Mony Scarce, and we See the necesity of Saving evry Cent posible, Resolved, That the Mayor and city council beleving that with rigid economy for the rest of year we can reduce our Tax Levy for the year, and hereby authorize the Clerk and Treas. to allow persons paying their Tax before the 1st day of December a discount of 50% on this years Tax."

These entries describe the Plains, Georgia, that existed almost unchanged when I knew it as a boy, except that now 715 people live within the city limits.

It's impossible to understand where I came from and how my life was shaped without knowing something about the other members of my family. Except for my father, his brother Alton (Buddy) was the most important white man in my early life, and was really the leader of the Carter family in Plains. As the oldest son, my Uncle Buddy took care of the family after my grandfather's death in 1903.

. . .

Buddy worked on a peach-and-grape farm for one season, supported his mother and four siblings on $25 a month earned as a clerk in the Oliver-McDonald Co., a general store, for four more years, and then started his own business, Plains Mercantile Company. He always relished an opportunity to answer my questions over the years, especially about his younger brother.

In many ways, the Carter brothers were quite different. My uncle was only six years older than my father, but I always thought of him as being in a different generation, much more settled in his ways. Both were deacons in our church, where Daddy taught a Sunday-school class and Uncle Buddy served as superintendent. Both of them were fascinated with baseball, but Daddy played it

Alton Carter (Uncle Buddy), 1960

well whereas Uncle Buddy was one of the executives who managed the Class D league. My father was an avid hunter and fisherman, but I never knew his brother to do either. Both men had inherited wine-making paraphernalia from my grandfather and made wine every year, but Uncle Buddy let everyone know that he gave his away. He had a reputation for having been quite a ladies' man before he was married, but he had never tasted whiskey, was the only man I knew who didn't drink Coca-Cola, and stayed at home on Saturday nights.

Daddy was a man of action. During working hours he didn't waste time in idle talk, but his brother was one of the greatest conversationalists I have known. Much later, when I would come home on leave for a few days from submarine duty, my father would always ask me a half-dozen standard questions, beginning with, "Are you pleased with your duty?" and "Do you need anything?" After that, I would have to volunteer information that I thought would be interesting to him. It was a completely different matter when I would go by Plains Mercantile Company. Uncle Buddy would ask me an unending stream of questions, about how a submarine was built and operated, how a toilet could flush underwater, the working of a dry dock, living conditions while submerged and on the surface, food preparation and service, how sailors were chosen, pay scales, recreation, armaments, the size of our beds, what we had to read, how often we bathed, what dangers we feared, our uniforms in winter and summer, race relations, and our experiences in different foreign ports.

During slack times in Plains Mercantile when I was growing up, I would urge Uncle Buddy to talk about our family, and he was eager to do so.

"When we first moved to Plains in 1904, Earl was just a boy around here going to school. He was not a bad young fellow, but we had some run-ins because he was not all that willing to treat me like

Earl Carter, 1917,
in officer candidate school

the head of the family. We finally decided that he should go off to Riverside Academy for a year, up near Gainesville, where he finished the tenth grade and got some military training. That was the most formal school any of us ever got—or any of our ancestors, as far as I know. After he came home he worked for a while as a clerk in the store, but as soon as he was seventeen years old he went off to Oklahoma and tried to sell some patented gas-operated flattening irons. After a year of barely earning living expenses, he decided to return to Plains.

"Earl was always restless when he was working under someone else around here, so, when the war came along, he enlisted in the army. He had real bad eyesight, but with his military training at Riverside and experience as a store clerk, they let him to go to training school, and he worked like the devil and became a first lieutenant in the supply corps."

I remarked that Daddy had told me that his outfit was scheduled to go to Europe when the war ended, but he was discharged and returned to Plains when he was twenty-four years old.

Uncle Buddy responded, "That's right. When he came back home Earl had a lot of ambition to be on his own, but he had to earn a living and took his old job back at Plains Mercantile Company. In addition, he opened up a little pressing club and hired a black man to operate it for one-fourth of the gross proceeds. He combined all this with taking care of our Webster County land, since I wasn't interested in farming. After a few years, Edgar Shipp put up fifteen hundred dollars and Earl started his own store down on the corner. Earl didn't talk to me about it ahead of time, but he did all right without hurting my business by going out and getting new people to come and shop in Plains.

"Your daddy was that kind of man. You know, some people work hard as they can all their lives and never have anything. Some others can lay their hand down, pick it up, and there's a silver dollar. That's the kind of man he was. Another thing about him was that, when it was necessary, no matter what kind of work it was—in the field or store or anywhere—he would just sail right in there and work like the dickens. That's how he got all this land around here. And he made you work, too."

I said, "Yes, sir, but I never fussed about it, because he was working a lot harder than me or anyone around him. Most times he would leave the house at four in the morning, while I was still sleeping, take all the hands to the field, and then come back to get me a couple of hours later."

Uncle Buddy said, somewhat defensively, "Well, I worked as hard as he did, but every time I made a dollar, Earl could make three."

.   .   .

Although Plains was less than three miles away, life there was quite different from the time I spent on our farm in Archery. My first acquaintance with the town's social life came through my grandmother Nina Carter, who lived alone in the same house our family had bought when they first moved here from South Georgia in 1904. She insisted on having company every night, so her various grandchildren were assigned this rotating duty. My day was Friday, and this weekly visit gave me a chance to become better acquainted with some of my town schoolmates and to play hide-and-seek, tin can, and marbles, and have rubber-gun wars with the neighborhood children. When I approached my teenage years, I began to go to prom parties sponsored by the town churches. After one of Mama Carter's neighbors, Eloise Ratliff, became my first sweetheart, I was eager to take my turn at visiting her.

To me, Mama Carter personified urban gentility, an affectation that she was committed to maintain. She was vain about her natural beauty, and concealed with ferocity any information about her age. Although there was always brandy in her cupboard, her favorite drink, at least in the presence of us grandchildren, was sassafras

Main Street of Plains, Georgia, 1925;
J. E. Carter & Company is on the corner.

tea. As a farm boy, I had the duty of keeping her supplied with the dried aromatic roots, which had the flavor of root beer and, she believed, great medicinal value. She did her own cooking and housekeeping, but we were expected to cut and bring in stove wood for the kitchen and coal for the living room fireplace, and to empty the two chamber pots every morning. Compared with those in our house, they were extraordinarily large and beautifully decorated, and she was especially proud of them. Unlike most other people, she didn't hide them under the bed during the daytime.

My grandmother had been born and raised near Greenwood, South Carolina, at a place on the railroad that was marked with her family name, Pratt. On a few occasions, my parents would take my grandmother and me and drop us off to visit with her family while they went on up north to see major-league baseball games. Even measured by Plains and Archery standards, this was an isolated, delicate, and ancient culture, since the Pratt women (all either widows or spinsters) seemed to have an aversion to changing anything around the family homestead. They were still carding wool and cotton, using a spinning wheel to make thread, weaving cloth, and churning butter in a small barrel mounted off-center on a turning shaft. They didn't have electricity, a radio, or even Aladdin lamps, depending entirely on candles and a few kerosene lamps in rooms that were always darkened by pulled shades to prevent fading of the furniture coverings; they went to bed every evening, even in winter, while there was still daylight outside.

I remember that their front yard was a maze of head-high ancient boxwoods, and many of the agricultural implements they used had long ago been replaced on our farm by more efficient ones. I explored the small plantation with some of the black boys whose families worked the land, but the Pratt women were so afraid that I would get hurt or in trouble that they restricted my movements severely. I knew when my folks were supposed to return, and they teased me afterward because I leaped from the bed, fully dressed and with my suitcase packed, when they opened the door to the room where I was supposed to be sleeping.

Over and over, I heard the story of how the children of the South Carolina family moved to Georgia through a series of marriages. My grandfather Billy's friend married a woman named Elizabeth Pratt, and her half-sister Lula came for a visit and married Billy's brother Dave. Then her sister Nina came down and married my grandfather. Their sister Mary came to visit and married our cousin Hall Calhoun, and their last sister, Carrie, came for a visit and married a doctor named Clebe Jowers. Later, their only brother, Jeff, came to see his sisters and married a girl from Damascus, Georgia.

My Uncle Jack Slappey and his wife, Ethel, my father's oldest sister, both played an important role in my early life. It was customary for us rural children to bring our own lunch to school in a paper sack or a lard can. It usually consisted of side meat or ham in a biscuit, peanut butter and jelly, or fried chicken, and sometimes a sweet potato or even a peach puff for dessert. I don't remember that we drank anything except water from the school spigot. Since Mama was usually out nursing and Daddy always left the house very early in the morning, he decided that Gloria and I should eat dinner with his sister Ethel. He paid her five cents a day for each of us, and during dinner hour we would go to eat at her house, just around the corner from the school.

We didn't like the idea very much. Although Aunt Ethel was a good cook and the food was hot and nutritious, she was not always punctual with the meals, and sometimes we would have to wait and miss most of the baseball or other games that were hotly contested every day on the school grounds.

The other problem was that there was very little money during these years for farmers to pay Uncle Jack for his veterinary services, and he was often compensated not just with chickens and eggs, but also with rabbits, squirrels, raccoons, and opossums that had been

The Carter family, 1943. *Left to right, top row:* Uncle Wade Lowery, Alton, Uncle Will Fleming, Donnel Carter, me, Willard Slappey, Daddy, Jack Slappey; *front row:* Mama, Aunt Jeannette, Aunt Lula, Ethel, Ruth (with Lynn), cousin Nina Pratt, Gloria, Hugh's wife, Ruth Godwin (with Sonny); *kneeling:* Billy.

trapped or treed by his clients. There was a long line of small cages behind the house to hold these wild animals, carefully tended by Uncle Jack's black helper, Gene May, and they were a regular feature of our diet. Aunt Ethel mastered the best ways to prepare these dishes, and we liked the pieces that were parboiled and then dipped in flour and fried—the same way squirrels and rabbits were cooked at our house.

Possums, though, had their own special character, and Mama wouldn't dream of cooking one at home. Knowing them to be scavengers, Uncle Jack insisted that Gene feed them clean foods for at least a week before they were brought to the kitchen. They were always baked whole, smothered in sweet potatoes, apples, or other fruits, vegetables, and spices that never adequately concealed their unique taste. I am sure that there are few living Georgians who, in their lifetimes, have eaten more possum meat than I have.

Not eating what was prepared was not an option, either at Uncle Jack's or at home. Barring a provable illness, we were expected to eat what was put on the table, and in generous portions. Mama and Daddy were quite proud of the special provisions they had made for us, and regularly inquired about the meal arrangements, both to us and to Aunt Ethel. No matter how much Gloria and I complained to each other about the possum or the tardy meals, we never shared these negative feelings with our parents.

One special advantage in our relationship was that Jack and Ethel liked to drive over to Americus on Saturdays, do a little shopping, and then just sit in their parked car, usually in front of the five-and-dime store, to watch the crowds move along the sidewalk. They were very flexible in their schedule, and were always good for a ride if we wanted to go to the Rylander Theater for a movie. Since our parents rarely went to the county seat except on business or for baseball games, this was a good source of transportation. Everyone in the community knew about this habit of Uncle Jack's, and it was a good way for farmers, while shopping in Americus, to make arrangements to have their pigs castrated or their dogs vaccinated, or to talk about a sick mule.

When Jack and Ethel's favorite parking place was not available, it was still easy to find their car. During waking hours, Uncle Jack was seldom without a cigar in his mouth, and he always smoked five-cent cigars, either Tampa Nuggets or Hav-a-Tampas. Over a period of years, the cigar smoke permeated everything around him, including the interior of his automobile. This was a distinctive aroma, not all that unpleasant, but in a veterinarian's car it was combined with the odor of all the medicines he carried and sometimes spilled in the trunk and back seat. Everyone walking by could tell that his car was there.

There was something especially attractive about the Slappeys' home, but it took me a long time to realize what it was. At last it became clear, by comparison with the other family homes I knew. Unlike the Carters, Uncle Jack was always easygoing, and generated a relaxed atmosphere in their house, with an emphasis on pleasure and creature comforts. In contrast, my Uncle Buddy's house was one of the most impressive in Plains, and it was kept impeccably clean by Aunt Annie Laurie, whom we called "Lala." Its hardwood floors always gleamed with wax, the dining room had a real chandelier, and everything had to be in its place. Their two boys, Hugh and Donnel, even had their own rooms upstairs. Both Uncle Buddy and my daddy were always ambitious and hardworking, and imposed strict discipline within their homes, both of which felt like temporary places of respite between more important periods of hard work. There was often a feeling of intensity or rigidity around the places.

The Slappeys had two sons of their own, but they were older than we and usually not at home. Their older son, Linton, had a mental problem; he would probably be diagnosed now as suffering from manic-depression (bipolar disorder). With modern medicine, he could have lived a normal and productive life, but in those days he was a problem for his parents. He was very intelligent, but had a tendency to become increasingly hyperactive, and made the other citizens of Plains nervous with his antics. As he walked up and down the streets, Linton made brutally frank comments, often at the top of his voice, and was a knowledgeable and unrestrained public commentator on the most sensitive and personal happenings in the community. If a man had been fired from the railroad, couldn't pay his grocery bill, or was secretly visiting a widow or another man's wife, Linton was likely to know and to promulgate the news, and not in diplomatic language. The shocked or embarrassed townspeople would finally convince Uncle Jack to let Linton go back to the state mental institution, until he calmed down and was permitted to return home. Some of us looked forward to those times when Plains was enlivened with his presence.

The Slappeys' other son, Willard, was a handsome young man who was a favorite of the county girls. He graduated from Auburn

University and became a successful veterinarian in North Carolina. He had been one of the first Plains boys to go off to work in Roosevelt's Civilian Conservation Corps, where he received room and board and a dollar a day for doing various kinds of conservation work.

My Uncle Buddy thought Jack was too easy on his boys. In later years, he once told me, "I raised my boys to mind in the first place—and I kept them busy. Your daddy did the same thing."

I agreed. "I never dared to cross Daddy. He never ordered me to do anything. He would just say, 'Hot, do you want to mop cotton tomorrow, turn sweet potato vines, prune watermelons, pull fodder,' or whatever? and I would just say, 'Yes, sir, Daddy.' "

Uncle Buddy continued, "I also tried to keep my boys out of trouble. I remember once when Joe Williams, Oscar's brother, had one of these pool outfits. He put it downtown, and all the boys wanted to play it, but I didn't want my boys to hang around a poolroom. I always thought a poolroom was a bad place for a man, much less a boy. So I bought an amateur pool table and put it upstairs. They and their friends played two or three months, and then it died down."

I didn't mention that I had been by the poolroom several times—with my daddy.

Since he had served as mayor for twenty-eight years, including all the time I was growing up, Uncle Buddy was my prime source of information about the town. One day I asked him if there had ever been any exciting events in Plains.

"Well, the biggest thing that ever happened here, and the most people I ever saw at the depot, involved the McTyier family. The oldest son in the family was Roscoe, and it was well known that he had moved south to join the Florida land boom in the 1920s. We all believed that he had struck it rich down there. One day his mother got the sad news by telephone from the Western Union operator in Americus that a casket would be arriving in Plains on the three-thirty train, containing Roscoe's body. The town was in a tizzy, not knowing exactly how to handle such a thing, with Roscoe already embalmed and no one knowing what church he might have joined in Florida, so we didn't even know which preacher would give the funeral sermon.

"I was mayor at the time, and the McTyier family came to talk to me and the undertaker, Ross Dean. We finally decided that there should be something of a short funeral service at the train station and then a procession to the cemetery, where all three white preachers could say a few words.

"Almost the entire town was assembled when it was time for the train to pull into the station, and the people watched Ross Dean's best pair of matched gray horses proudly pull the hearse around in a big circle and then park at the loading platform to pick up the casket. Everybody was lined up with the train's baggage compartment, and nobody noticed a nice-looking fellow who got off with his suitcase and began asking people on the edge of the crowd about all the hoopla.

" 'We're here for the funeral service of Roscoe McTyier.'

" 'But *I'm* Roscoe McTyier,' he said."

Uncle Buddy's throat tightened up and his voice rose an octave when he gave the punch line, and we both laughed a long time before he continued.

"His mother almost fainted, and began to tell people that God had answered her prayers with a miracle, but some people in the crowd seemed disappointed. Neither the McTyiers or me were ever able to find out how Roscoe's telegram got changed into a notice that he was dead."

Since few people lived in Plains, its major strength came from farm families who traveled for miles into the town, for trade and for pleasure. None of the field hands or tenants and very few of the small landowners that I knew during my boyhood days had an automobile or a pickup truck, and a buggy would have been an inappropriate affectation, used just by old and relatively prosperous people. So almost everyone traveled by foot or on wagons, which served multiple purposes both on and off the farm. My father, who drove a pickup truck to town and from one field to another, still used two-mule wagons to carry workers, plows, fertilizer, and seed to our fields, and small sleds within the fields to drag shocks of grain or peanut stacks to the threshing machines.

I had a balloon-tired bicycle as soon as I was big enough to ride it. Not only was this a pleasure for me, but with a basket on the front handlebars it made a good delivery vehicle when Mama needed something from town in a hurry. I also rigged up a haywire hitch on the back so I could pull a little wagon when needed. As a teenager, when I couldn't borrow Daddy's pickup, I rode my bike to and from the prom parties in Plains, often stopping by my girlfriend's house to give her a ride on the bar in front of my seat. After the parties, I'd ride home a lot faster, especially when passing the haunted house and the cemetery. I carried a flashlight so I could see the road on the darkest nights, and would just pull over into the ditch when a car was coming.

In addition to my work on the farm, for which I was paid nothing for doing chores and, until I could plow a mule, a child's wage of twenty-five cents for a full day's labor in the fields, Daddy always encouraged me to earn additional money. Even from my earliest days, he made sure that I understood the basic principles of commerce, and he urged me to seek employment that used my developing talents when I was not needed on the farm. I didn't realize until much later how exceptional this training was for a small boy.

I began selling boiled peanuts on the streets of Plains when I was five years old. This was my first acquaintance with the outside world. As soon as the nuts began to mature on the vines, I would take my little wagon into one of the fields nearest our house, pull a load of peanut vines out of the ground, carry them home, pick the peanuts off the vines, wash them, and soak them in salty water overnight. The next morning, as early as possible, I boiled the peanuts for a half-hour or so until they were cooked but still firm, filled about twenty half-pound paper sacks (forty on Saturdays), and carried them to town in a basket, either walking down the railroad tracks or riding on my bike.

I had some regular customers who would buy about half my peanuts every day, and seemed grateful for them. My best customer was the cobbler, Bud Walters, who was one of the community's most notable citizens. One of his feet had been badly injured when he was a teenager, and he had learned to walk around the house and yard on his hands, even going up and down the stairs. This built up his arms and chest greatly, and when his foot was healed enough for him to walk again (though always with a limp), he took up boxing as a sport. One Saturday night, Bud decided to fight one of the itinerant pro-fessional fighters who came to Americus, and we joined dozens of people who went from Plains to support him. He defeated the chal-lenger for a prize of $5 and became something of a hero to us boys. At our urging, and with an adequate audience, he would empty his pockets and walk around on his hands in front of his shop. For me, the best thing about Bud was that it took two bags of peanuts to sat-isfy his craving for a whole day.

The visitors to Plains were almost always polite to me, in either accepting or rejecting my offer of a sale, but some of the regular traveling salesmen had to make jokes at my expense.

My biggest problem was with the set of loafers who hung around the two filling stations and John Woodruff's livery stable. The stable was the focal point for the most intense and negative gossip, and the men would become bored with their own repetitive conversations. They sat in a semicircle just inside the entrance of the wide barn door, on either upended nail kegs or sagging stools and straight chairs.

Mr. Woodruff had a little office just beyond where the men sat, and he moved back and forth to join or escape the idle talk. Each man had his own place, except that they would rotate when each loser had to give up his chair at the checkers game during the day. Coca-Cola bottle caps served as the checkers, turned up or down to indicate the two sides. Even aside from the verbal comments, it was a fairly noisy game, as the contenders slapped the bottle caps down to emphasize a good move or one made in frustration or anger, and the serrated edges of the downturned pieces scraped deep grooves connecting the centers of the squares, which had to be deeply incised with a pocketknife to prevent their total obliteration.

I always expected to be the butt of the men's jokes, particularly as noon approached and they knew from my return appearance that I still hadn't sold out of peanuts and was more desperate for a sale. They would offer to buy a bag if I would feed the mules or sweep the area where they sat, and sometimes I would agree.

There were three or four veterans around town, my father's age, who were on disability pensions because of World War I injuries, two of them suffering from mustard-gas damage to their lungs. They were the only men in town not expected to work, since their government payments exceeded the income of a sharecropper or the wages of a day laborer. They provided the core of the permanent discussion groups. One of them was especially obnoxious to me, but I had to accept his teasing in order to maintain my customer base.

One day when I was about eight years old, he said he would buy some of my last peanuts if I could show my ability to follow instructions. He was to indicate by his finger movements how I should move, and I agreed. I watched his fingers closely, and moved back and forth and from side to side as he directed. Finally, all the men burst into laughter when my bare feet stepped on a still-burning cigarette, making me leap into the air in pain and surprise. Some days I dreaded the boiled-peanut routine, but if things went well I would have no peanuts left by noon and would ride my bike home with a dollar's worth of change in my pocket. This was an opportunity that lasted throughout the summertime.

Few people knew more about the Plains community than I did. I became something of a fixture on the streets and in the business establishments, and the adults tended to act as though I didn't exist. I'm sure my parents never fully realized that my potential customers used such foul language, told sexually explicit jokes, and commented frankly on the transgressions of their fellow citizens. Among other things, I learned which men went to the whorehouses in Albany, whether they favored black or white prostitutes, and how much these adventures cost.

I also knew about some of the serious crimes that were committed in our region. One tragic and horrible measure of poverty in those days was the lynchings that occurred, at least partially because of growing competition even for the least desirable jobs, which in the past had been saved for black workers. As the Depression deepened, an Atlanta organization adopted the slogan "No Jobs for Niggers Until Every White Man Has a Job." The number of lynchings in America quadrupled in 1933 over the previous year, and remained equally high during the hard times that followed.

I knew of only one such terrible murder in the vicinity of Plains, having heard of it first among the black workers on our farm and then, later, in guarded conversations at the filling station. It did not involve a black insult to a white woman, but the local newspaper said it was the result of "impudence bordering on assault" by a black worker toward a landowner south of Plains. Though I never knew for sure, I could have made an educated guess about which men were involved. There were a few who had no regular relations with black people, always spoke disparagingly about them, referred often and favorably to Ku Klux Klan activity, and impressed me as weak and cowardly. They were the scum of the community, and a source of embarrassment to law-abiding citizens.

It was not easy to conceal anything in Plains. People were vigilant about any passing car, especially one that might be parked in an unaccustomed spot. An unexplained absence from a home or place of business was sure to arouse a flurry of questions and comments from interested neighbors. Almost universal attendance at church and PTA meetings and the need for frequent shopping excursions at a time when few people owned refrigerators all permitted maximum exchanges of facts or gossip. Garden clubs, quilting bees, visits to the barbershop or beauty parlors, and the permanent circles of loungers downtown were social institutions with participants who were hungry for sustained conversations. For instance, everyone knew about one spinster who displayed her nude body in a front window while her suitor would drive his car slowly past her house.

A positive thing about this community omniscience was that we were as eager to relay information about someone who might need assistance as about some scandal. It was a common practice at the beginning of every church service for the pastor to enumerate such needs, and for people in the congregation to compete in giving more up-to-date information about the case or to add more concerns to the list.

We were bemused by some of the idiosyncrasies of our neighbors. One of the local farmers, Lester Sewell, was a compulsive talker, and eagerly sought any forum within which he might pontificate, even when he realized that no one was paying attention to what he was saying. He could be seen plowing in his own field, accompanied by a small boy he hired just to walk or ride with him, who was expected never to speak, just to listen.

Lester's Uncle Al, who had moved to Plains from Alabama, refused to change time zones and, like my father and others, deeply resented the government's imposition of Daylight Savings Time as contrary to God's law. Throughout the last decades of his life, Mr. Al lived by Central Standard Time, rising later than his neighbors, eating dinner at two o'clock in the afternoon, and retiring when it was dark in Alabama.

I was fascinated when a dramatic and closely watched change took place in the culture of our community that affected the mule-trading business. Although there was always a brisk trade in draft animals, Mr. Woodruff got in debt and went to Uncle Buddy for help. After some bargaining, they agreed that Uncle Buddy would furnish the money for the mules and horses, Woodruff would do the buying, selling, and trading, and they would split the profits.

After a few weeks, my uncle became concerned about some of the reported transactions and decided to accompany Mr. Woodruff, so he could learn more about the wholesale end of the business and be more involved in that part of the trading. They bought mules mostly in Atlanta but also in Montgomery and Troy, Alabama. "Then," Uncle Buddy often recounted, "we would come back home and sell them to the farmers like hotcakes."

However, about a year later, Uncle Buddy went to Athens to visit his son Donnel at the University of Georgia, and Woodruff took the mule truck to Atlanta. When Uncle Buddy arrived there a day later, he learned that his partner had been around to the mule merchants asking for a $5 kickback on each mule. Uncle Buddy didn't say anything to him until they returned to Plains. Then he went around to the stable and confronted Mr. Woodruff. They decided to split up, and agreed to divide the seven mules still in stock. These were almost equally good animals, so, at Woodruff's suggestion, my uncle had his choice of three mules, and Woodruff kept the four that were left.

Uncle Buddy soon developed one of the largest livery-stable businesses in Georgia, and twenty years later was selling from five to eight hundred draft animals each season (November to April), with mules trading ten to one over horses. Until the last three or four years of his mule trading, his primary sales were to farmers, but after everyone, even small landowners, shifted to tractors, draft animals were being sold by them, not bought. Almost all of these last horses and mules were sold by the pound, and many of them were slaughtered for dog food.

. . .

My main asset in the boiled-peanut business was the Coca-Cola deliveryman, since peanuts and Coca-Cola made such a good combination. The grown men in town drank "dopes" all day, usually throwing pennies to the cracks between floorboards to see who would pay. The man with his coin nearest the center of a crack was out, and then those remaining threw again until the final one would have to set up the crowd. They rolled high dice to make the same decisions in one of the filling stations, but this wasn't approved in the grocery stores, being too much like gambling. We boys rarely if ever drank a Coca-Cola, preferring to spend our money much more wisely on the big RC Colas, or sometimes on the even larger Double-Colas. Moon Pies were the best bargain at the fast-food counter, but my favorite order, at least as a salesman, was always boiled peanuts and a dope.

My first business as an investor and a property owner was launched in 1932, when I was eight years old. At planting time that year, cotton was at the all-time low price of five cents a pound, or $25 for a five-hundred-pound bale, and there was a tremendous surplus of almost two years' production in the warehouses. From the sale of boiled peanuts on the streets of Plains for three years, I had accumulated enough savings to go to the warehouse with Daddy and buy five bales, which we brought home and stored in a shed. Several years later, when the local undertaker died, I sold my cotton for eighteen cents a pound and bought five tenant houses from his estate, which I rented by the month: two for $2 each, one for $2.50, and two for $5. Every day, I knew that the houses were earning a total of fifty-five cents.

I couldn't afford to pay for much upkeep, but I would give the tenants a few boards or furnish a windowpane so they could do their own repairs. I rode my bike to make several visits each month until I finally collected all the rent, and continued this effort until I left home for college. Daddy took over the collections for me until I had been a midshipman at the naval academy for about a year. Then he got tired of listening to incessant demands for repairs and improvements and sold the houses for about three times what I had paid for them—a modest return for my eleven-year investment.

By the time I reached high school, my cousin Donnel Carter had gone off to college, and I became partners for about half the months of the year with his brother, Hugh, in special sales on Saturdays. The bank building was still vacant following its bankruptcy, and we used its front window for access to the large crowds that packed the only sidewalk for their weekly shopping. Our sales were limited to hamburgers and triple-dip ice-cream cones—five cents apiece. Hugh agreed that I could also sell my peanuts from the same stand, as long as I didn't push them ahead of our main products.

During the warm months, we met behind Uncle Buddy's house early on Saturday mornings and laboriously turned three enormous ice-cream freezers until the vanilla-, chocolate-, and fruit-flavored mixtures were frozen. Then we packed layers of crushed ice and rock salt around the containers, which kept the ice cream firm for the rest of the day. Hamburgers were an easier matter, and we could sell them even in cool weather. We mixed and squeezed together a half-pound of ground beef, a loaf of moistened lightbread, and a big onion, and fried the patties on a kerosene stove. We sold them in buns with catsup and mustard. Our only real competition came from a black man named Chick Tyson, who offered fried-mullet sandwiches for the same five-cent price. Hugh, who was my senior in the business, would make me walk up and down the street, shouting to the milling crowd, "Ice cream, you scream, we all scream for ice cream. Three dips for a nickel." I was always glad when the last freezer was empty.

Although anyone visiting sleepy little Plains today would find it almost unbelievable, I have never seen the streets of New York City more lively or closely packed than Main Street in our town on Saturdays during my childhood. Despite its small size, Plains was a major trade center for its own citizens and for all the farm families in the western half of Sumter County. Hundreds of customers would crowd into the stores, and many more would use this trading day to assemble on the only sidewalk, to meet with their friends or just to relish the electric atmosphere. It was almost impossible to walk down the sidewalk during the late afternoon and early evening, and much easier to move by going out into the street, where vehicles also had to creep along. The area behind the stores was almost equally crowded, with families loading their accumulated purchases into cars or wagons before heading home.

I also worked in my Uncle Buddy's store whenever he needed me, usually late on Saturday evenings. Plains Mercantile was open from daylight until dark on weekdays and stayed open until the last customers left on Saturday, sometime between ten o'clock and midnight. (On slow nights, I would still have time to take a date to the late picture show in Americus, where we would cuddle in the back row.)

In addition to Uncle Buddy's two sons, there were two men, Guy Dominick and Dennis Turner, who helped sell the enormous array of dry goods, groceries, and farm supplies. Mrs. Mary Lou McTyier Burnette ran the ladies' department upstairs, which was rarely visited by any males, even clerks. In addition to regular work, I helped with the annual inventory, just after we sold everything possible during the Christmas season. This was a position of honor, not only because of the mathematical computations required, but because it made me privy to the store's secret code marked on every item on the shelves to indicate its wholesale cost.

Despite the competition for sales, there was a sense of camaraderie among the clerks and the many traveling salesmen who served the store. A few of them were serious and all business, but good humor was the normal hallmark of a skilled salesman, and there were almost invariably a few new jokes told during a working day in the store. Some were clean enough to be told to Uncle Buddy and his boys, but others were fit only to share with the men who hung around the barbershop, filling station, and stable.

Dennis Turner was one of the funniest men I ever knew, and he was always searching for an original practical joke or funny remark that would add to his reputation. One that was repeated for years occurred when one of the local hunters came in to buy some shotgun shells. He asked Dennis what ours cost, and was told, "Two-fifty a box." The man replied, "I can get them for two and a quarter in Preston." Dennis asked, "Why didn't you buy them over there?" The man responded, "They're out of them right now." Dennis paused a moment, and then said, "Well, our shells are only two dollars when we're out."

Plains Mercantile Company carried a complete line of goods, and even competed with the filling stations for gasoline sales. In fact, one of our main attractions was the first gas pump where customers could watch the fuel flowing directly into their tanks. The buyer and people up and down the sidewalk would watch closely as we moved a big handle back and forth to pump gas from an underground reservoir up into a glass container that could be set to hold from one to five gallons. After the valve to the storage tank was closed, the gas was drained by gravity through a hose to the automobile. Pennies were precious, and gasoline was twenty cents a gallon. I've got some old tickets from the same time that show that oil was ten cents a quart, bread was five cents a loaf, twenty-four pounds of flour cost sixty-five cents, eggs were twelve cents a dozen, and shoes and overalls sold for as little as a dollar a pair.

Christmas was by far our most important holiday, for its religious meaning but also because of the frenetic business that absorbed the Plains community. This was an extra opportunity for me to help Uncle Buddy as a clerk. We cleared out the front of the store about two weeks before the big day, set up special tables, and began putting out the Christmas toys that had been hidden upstairs. We would bring down load after load on the hand-operated elevator. The store was always closed one entire weekday afternoon for this lengthy process, and immediately after school the front windows would be filled with little children's faces, their noses pressed to the glass while they examined what they hoped would appear under their trees on Christmas morning. We also had special items in the grocery department, including holiday candies, oranges, tangerines, Brazil nuts, English walnuts, and packages of seeded raisins. The fancy presents would be bought by landowners, railroad employees, and folks that worked in sawmills or at the hospital, but toys were out of the question for the children of most farm workers; after a normal crop year, Santa Claus was likely to bring only a couple of oranges and some raisins. With an average annual income of $70 a person, tenant farmers could only deal in symbols.

My usual request to Santa was for books, but I remember one dismal Christmas morning when I awoke with several cherished books under the tree—and a bad case of measles. Mama warned me to stay in my darkened room and not use my eyes, and later chastised me severely when she found me reading under the bed. Though we usually had toys and other gifts at our house, we also relished the rare fruits and nuts. Christmas was about the only time we ever had grapefruit, and one of our favorite events was sitting on the floor around Daddy's chair while he peeled the fruit, divided it into sections, applied some salt, and handed out pieces to us three children in turn. He said frequently that we reminded him of baby birds in a nest crying out to be fed worms.

We didn't like oranges as much, because we had them at other times and they had a vivid association with castor oil, that all-too-frequent remedy for many ailments, sometimes used just to prevent possible future problems. Mama or Daddy warmed the oil at the fireplace and let us eat a slice of orange to help counteract the terrible taste as we tried to swallow a large spoonful—quite a change from the baby birds in a nest.

There were always interesting things happening in Plains. All the brick buildings had flat, "built-up" roofs, and our local carpenters were reluctant to work with the hot melted asphalt and tarpaper, which were usually applied during the summertime, when the roof surface was extremely hot. Since many of the other nearby towns had used the same architectural design on store buildings, this created job opportunities for bands of Gypsies, who traveled from one place to another to do the undesirable work. Their annual visit was an exciting time for our town. There was always a lot of haggling back and forth between the storeowners and the roving repairmen concerning the quality of work done last year and charges for the current jobs. Excluded by ordinance from the city limits, the Gypsy families would set up their camp outside of town, and, justifiably or not, all the regular citizens were on alert to guard their property closely.

The Gypsy men always had some horses or other animals to sell or exchange. They knew horses well and were skilled at emphasizing good traits and concealing any defects; it was a real challenge for Uncle Buddy and Mr. Woodruff to come out even in any trades they made. My uncle seemed to like the Gypsies and kept in touch with their leaders throughout the year. He felt that they would keep their word, but that he had to be on guard to understand exactly what they were saying in a bargaining session. He reminded me that they had come from Europe to Georgia before the Carters, owned a lot of property in the state, and traveled around just because they preferred a nomadic life. Sometimes I would go out near the Gypsy camp with some other boys to watch and listen at a distance as they sang and danced. We were particularly intrigued by the beauty of some of the young Gypsy girls, but both sets of parents prevented any possible intermingling.

As a constant visitor to the streets to sell peanuts during the summer months, I was blessed with the opportunity to see other attractions. Medicine men brought their trucks into the main street to hawk their wares from the canopied bodies, and this would often create a traffic jam, with many people succumbing to the spiel about the magical curative powers of oils and liniments guaranteed to restore hair, strengthen manly vigor, purify the blood, and cure syphilis and consumption. Even the teetotalers in town felt that it was permissible to sip bitters for their health, although everyone knew that only recently had the law been changed to reduce the permissible pure-alcohol content from 40 percent down to 24 percent. Other concoctions were designed to calm the nerves and to control unruly children. When the foundation for our present home was being dug in Plains in 1961, I found a small bottle in the ground embossed "Elixir of Opium."

My favorite demonstrations were those by the salesmen for ax companies, who would arrange with a local sawmill to place a couple of twelve-inch-diameter logs in front of the stores near the railroad tracks. The salesman was almost invariably a little fellow, dressed as a city slicker, who would challenge any of the local men to demonstrate their prowess with a favorite blade. There were eight sawmills around our community in those days, each with a dozen workers, and many of them were very proud of their strength and skill. But they were never a match in these contests. After all our local heroes had been timed in cutting through the log, the small man would take off his coat, leave on his vest and derby hat, and cut through the log much quicker with a withering series of short and precise strokes using whatever single- or double-bladed ax he was promoting.

Another fascinating sight was the itinerant fishmonger who brought hundreds of pounds of catfish, packed in ice, to the street for public sale. Each buyer had an option: to purchase the fish as they were or to have them skinned and dressed on the spot. Money was scarce, and people were accustomed to doing their own work at home, even the difficult job of skinning catfish; but the charge for cleaning fish was only one or two cents a pound, and to watch the magical process was worth the extra cost. The vendor would hold the fish by the tail, make one swipe to embed its head on a sharp, protruding nail, and in two quick strokes with special pliers remove all the skin. This was an art that I practiced a lot, with little success, on the catfish we caught from Choctahatchee Creek.

The most highly organized event was a small circus that came to town every year, always preceded by a spirited negotiation between the owners and the city fathers concerning the license fees and the character of the exhibits. Some of the men around the filling stations said that in other towns the same circus featured a striptease where the girls took off "every stitch of clothes," and as an older teenager I witnessed such an exhibition in our county seat, but this much-discussed opportunity was never offered to the spectators in Plains. The main event, with animals and performers, took place in one ring, but all around were various other exhibits—deformed people and animals that were either alive or preserved in formaldehyde, tests of strength and accuracy, and various games of chance. We speculated on which of the young women workers might be the ones who performed in the more liberated communities. One of the most exciting times was immediately after the circus folded its tents and left, when we children would examine every square inch of the remaining grass to find coins that had been lost. Once I found a quarter and two nickels.

Plains may have been a small town in an out-of-the-way corner of the rural South, but to me it was an exciting, vibrant place, where it seemed to me that a boy could learn as much about life as he could in New York or Chicago. Yet the general character of Plains was one of peace and stability, with people going about their daily business, attending almost every possible service at the various churches, supporting the school, maintaining pride in our fine hospital, and suffering together when crops were short or a personal tragedy struck a family.

Except as employees on the job, patients of doctors, customers at the business establishments, or when arrested and tried for some crime by city officials, the black and white citizens in town were not even acquainted with each other. It was only on the farms that the races were mixed enough for us to really know each other—or think we did, though we whites could not realize how severe was the anguish of our neighbors who bore the extra burden of racial discrimination.

7

Breaking Ground, to Be a Man

My father, 1941

EVEN FOR US CHILDREN, personal problems and pleasures were always secondary to economic concerns. We realized that everyone on the farm was affected by the interrelationship of prices, crops, noxious weeds and grasses, moisture, and the condition of the soil in our fields. I felt that mine was a special role, because for the first thirteen years of my life, until Billy was born, I was the landowner's only son, and I was increasingly proud when my father discussed farm management decisions with me.

Daddy sometimes worked in the field with us when I was a little boy, but by the time I was big enough to plow a mule he was strictly a manager of the land he owned, except for a few special tasks: cutting ripe watermelons, weighing picked cotton at sundown, operating the syrup mill, and sometimes working around the peanut picker. I was eager to grow bigger and to learn as much as possible, to become like him, able to oversee the farm's complex and interconnected processes.

On rainy or other "off days," I would often wake up to Daddy's question, "Hot, do you want to ride with me today?" Even if I had something else planned, I always replied, "Yes, sir." I relished the times we could be alone together, and felt that a refusal would be disrespectful of my father. These were the times when Daddy drove from one field or farm to another, and examined carefully what was happening in each one or what needed to be done. I listened carefully to exchanges between him and the tenant farmers on the other farm we owned in Webster County, and as we drove to the next destination he would analyze what we had just observed.

One day when we were riding together, I asked Daddy how he got started in business. He seemed eager to respond.

"Well, your godfather, Mr. Edgar Shipp, had an interest in a packing plant, and was one of the first men in Sumter County to buy and sell meat and lard on a big scale—several railroad boxcars at a time. In the spring of 1914, he bought several carloads of salt-pork sowbellies at a low price, and happened to have them when the war broke out in Europe. The market skyrocketed, and he made a killing on the meat. He traded for a good bit of land with the money, but he was not a farmer and got tired of fooling around with tenants and sharecroppers, so he sold it and then owned a grocery store and a warehouse.

"One day, I think about the time you were born, he invited me over to his office in Americus and asked me if I wanted to run my own store in Plains. I was eager to do it, and rented an empty building down where Main Street runs into Bond. I proposed the name of 'Shipp & Carter,' but he insisted on 'J. E. Carter & Company,' saying that he would be the 'Company.' He helped me buy the stock of merchandise, and I got Will Kennedy to run the meat counter and Oliver Smith to help me with the other groceries and dry goods.

"We had a good enough business, but I had been getting more and more into working our family's farm in Webster County, and Buddy put it on me to take care of it. I began to learn about row cropping, some things about livestock, but more than most farmers I studied timber and what it was worth. If a farm was run-down and might be for sale, I looked it over real good, figured what the trees were worth and how I might get the fields in shape, and made an offer. Then I could get it fixed up and either keep it or get rid of it for a profit. Sometimes, after selling the timber, I wound up with the land for practically nothing. I soon saw that this was a lot better way to make money than in the store business, where there were two or three others in Plains with their own loyal customers.

"Mr. Shipp agreed with me, so I decided to close the store, pay off what I owed him, and become a full-time farmer. This was in 1928, when farm prices were pretty high and most folks felt good about the future. The Plexicos had the place out in Archery and were wanting to move to town, so we agreed on a price for the land and just swapped houses. I kept the store open for about two more years, figured out what we would need for a farm commissary, and sold the rest of my inventory in town.

"Now, you know the places we own, and they're doing pretty well, but we had a hard time for a few years when farm prices went way down, a lot of times below what it cost to make a crop. I just held on to the land, even when it wasn't worth anything."

This was the first time my daddy had ever talked to me like this, and it was obvious that he was proud of his financial success. I was certainly familiar with our farmland, none of it more than six miles from Plains, because I had worked with other hands in all the fields, and on off days my friends and I had explored every region of the woodlands. Also, I sometimes helped Daddy by keeping notes when he cruised the timber to determine the value of new land that he was bargaining to buy. We would walk back and forth through a woodland tract, using a compass to maintain straight courses as he examined each tree, measured its girth, estimated the length of the usable trunk, and called out the information for me to record.

As soon as I was able, I was eager to learn how to operate the implements on the farm. Each step was an indication of maturity. My first tools were, most naturally, a hoe and a hatchet for weeding crops and chopping stove wood. My big ambition was to plow a mule, but this task was usually reserved for full-grown men, since it required enough size and strength to hold the plow handles and at the same time to manage the mule with plowlines going to the bridle bit. For most farmers, that was about the limit of the current technology, except for plowing two mules at a time. Daddy was not interested in accommodating my ambition, so I naturally turned to Jack Clark, who would sometimes let me walk immediately in front of him behind the plow handles, imagining that I was the one managing the mule and plow.

After several years of begging, I finally had my first real lesson in solo plowing in our home garden, when it was time to turn under about half the patch so it could be replanted. I wanted to do everything by myself, so Jack Clark let me go into the barn lot and catch Emma, the most docile and well-tempered mule, hitch her to a simple turning plow, and direct her to the garden gate with shouts and tugs on the plowlines. It was very difficult for me to push down on the handles so the point of the plow wouldn't dig into the pathway. With Jack's fine adjustment of the clevis hitch, the plow's natural course was at an even depth, and after the first furrow was turned around the plot, I found that Emma simply walked steadily forward in the proper direction, stopping to be turned at each corner. I've rarely had a more satisfying experience.

After this, my desire to learn everything possible about farming was even more intense, but I had to be able to do a man's work. This equaled any other ambition I've ever had in my life. It involved learning how to plant and cultivate a crop. The theoretical teaching took place while I was with my father on his daily visits to the various fields, and the practical experience came, step by step, when I adjusted and used turning plows, harrows, fertilizer distributors, planters, and cultivating equipment.

I was permitted to do some land breaking and harrowing at a fairly early age, when errors or inaccuracy were not costly. I just needed the strength and intelligence to take care of the mules and not damage anything. When I could do this, Daddy increased my daily wages from a child's pay of a quarter to the fifty cents that competent teenagers earned. At first, either Daddy or Jack Clark would help me with the adjustment of the harness, plow stock, and plow points. It was instantly apparent if everything was not right, but not easy to discern how to correct a problem. In breaking land, the mules could refuse to cooperate, or the plow could dig in too deep, tend to surface, or pull to one side or the other, but the only adverse consequences were frustration and wasted time in stopping to make changes.

A turning point came when Daddy finally entrusted me with the cultivation of his precious crops, beginning with corn and, a year or so later, with cotton and peanuts. The long days in the field were tiring, but in addition to the exaltation of being treated as an adult, the skill required made it challenging, and gratifying when successful. Emma plodded unerringly alongside the growing plants and made a gentle turn to the right or left to "gee" and "haw" commands. She also knew how to turn around at the end of a row and enter the next without stepping on the crop, and never seemed to be startled or frightened by thunder or a flushed rabbit or quail. I didn't resent the feeling that Emma was the boss of our operation.

There would be three or four plowings during the growing season, each one more shallow and distant from the base of the plant to protect the roots just under the surface. Thanks to the precise instructions and advance warnings I received, and the numerous tales told among farm workers of crop damage done by others, I worried that any mistake of mine could be a disaster. The growing plants represented the culmination of hundreds of hours of work, and the hope and expectation of the future harvest. Some errors were immediately obvious to every observer and could not be corrected. There was no way to replant cotton, corn, or peanuts after they had been stepped on by a mule or plowed up by an errant blade. An even worse mistake could be made by plowing too deep or close to the row, because the damage would not become evident for a day or two, after a good portion of the field had been permanently injured and wilted in the sun.

But I soon learned that, with a properly adjusted plow and well-behaved mules, the plowing could go like a dream. I preferred to plow without wearing shoes, and I remember vividly the caress of the soft, damp, and cool freshly turned earth on my feet. The burning surface sand and the ubiquitous stinging nettles were brushed aside by the plow blade that I was following down the furrow. Although Daddy had some two-horse cultivators that could plow both sides of the crop row with one pass, most of the cultivating was done with single plow-stocks, one side of the row at a time. The apparently infinitesimal passes around or up and down a large field accumulated in a gratifying way, so that at dinnertime or sundown my personal accomplishment could be seen and assessed exactly. I felt that this was doing all I could possibly do, and that no one on the farm, no matter how strong or experienced, could do it better.

The skill with which crops were cultivated separated the successful farmers from those destined for failure. The habitual mistakes of some farmers were never corrected, and this is easy to comprehend when the complexity of the issues is realized. There were dozens of conflicting decisions just related to plowing: an understanding of land topography; absorption or rapid runoff of falling rain; the path of inevitable drainage; how to handle last year's crop residue of weeds on fallow land; which crop best fit the soil type in a field; optimum crop rotation; when to break land so it could be most easily worked in subsequent plowings; how to minimize clodding and maximize the friability of the earth; how to preserve scarce moisture during seedbed preparation; the best juxtaposition of fertilizer and the sensitive seed and hungry emerging plants; how to adjust the plow points and when to resharpen them so they cut smoothly through the furrow; how close and deep to plow so that rapidly growing weeds and grass could be destroyed while slower-evolving crop plants were nourished when both were intertwined in the same row; when to cease cultivation so that from then until harvest time the crop could prevail over the competing weeds; and, in the case of peanuts, when to plow up the constantly evolving kernels so that an optimum number would be mature.

In addition, of course, there were many decisions about crop varieties, the control of insects, the types and spacing of seed, and fertilizer formulas, quantities, and methods of application. All these decisions and many others had to be made daily, usually alone, by men who were often illiterate and under constant pressure to balance the needs in their fields with the severe limits on their time, ability, and equipment.

Along with everyone else on the farm, I also had to learn how to care for the mules, horses, and other livestock. A constant concern when plowing during the hottest months was that the draft animal would get too hot, which occasionally resulted in permanent injury. Mules were known to be much smarter than horses, but also craftier. Some of them learned to feign exhaustion to get a desired rest and had to be urged on, often with blows, to get their work done. However, most mules that stopped at the end of a row and refused to begin another were assumed to be approaching the limit of their endurance. If they didn't recover after a few minutes, they had to be returned to the barn lot for the rest of the day. We had a few horses, and they were much more inclined to work themselves past the point of recovery—sometimes to death.

There was also a delicate balancing act that confronted me and every other worker in the fields between getting the most work done and not becoming debilitated by heat exhaustion or sunstroke. We all understood the symptoms and dangers. The worst was sunstroke, which we called "the bear." "Don't let the bear get you" was a constant admonition for those of us who worked in the field during the most sweltering days. If someone quit sweating, his body temperature could almost immediately jump up five or six degrees, and death was a real threat. We knew to put such a man in the shade, pour our drinking water on his body, and rub his arms and legs. This was an event that warranted a visit to a doctor, and usually meant a week or more of no hard work in the field. It also shattered the macho image that all males wanted to maintain. "The bear got Ed Washington" was an expression of sympathy, but also a derogatory assessment of Ed's strength, vigor, and judgment.

Heat exhaustion was also a serious concern, but the symptoms of dizziness and nausea gave a few minutes' advance warning before someone reached a critical stage. Cramps were another affliction, which could be prevented by keeping up our salt intake. Any extended illness was a devastating blow to a family, and the economic loss was considered by the poorest to be worse than the personal suffering involved. Most of the sharecroppers lived in isolated places, had no transportation except a mule or perhaps a wagon, were chronically malnourished, and were barely scraping by financially with purchases of basic food and clothing. In times of sickness, their only recourse was to call on my mother for home treatment, since they considered expensive hospital care to be out of the question.

Although most of our draft animals were mules, we also kept about half a dozen mares for fieldwork, for riding, and to mate with our jackass to produce mule colts. We usually had at least one female jackass, or jenny, to bear a colt every now and then. When our young draft animals were old enough, we introduced them to harness by hitching them to a heavy sled in an open field. The next step was to let them pull a small one-horse turning plow; then they were hitched in tandem with an older mule, and eventually trusted to do cultivation of a crop.

Daddy owned about twenty-five or thirty mules and horses at any one time, a few of which were leased out to tenant families who didn't have their own. Although a casual observer might think they all looked the same, we knew every one by name, age, and idiosyncrasy. Some obeyed verbal commands, would work in harness with certain others, could handle a wagon going down a steep hill, seemed willing to perform a task, or permitted a rider on their backs. Most, however, lacked one or more of these good characteristics.

My father was quite familiar with animal husbandry, and I learned from him to treat problems like scours, mastitis, a calf reluctant to be born, and the dreaded screwworms. There was a magic "blue medicine" (copper sulfate) that every farmer kept on hand for animals, used like Mercurochrome or iodine on us boys. Daddy paid out money to a veterinarian only when absolutely necessary. For example, we usually castrated our own pigs, but when there were several dozen at one time and we were busy with fieldwork, he would sometimes call on my Uncle Jack Slappey and his assistant, Gene May, to do this difficult and sometimes dangerous work. I remember that, one day when Gene was catching the pigs, one of the mother sows attacked him, knocked him down in the sloppy pen, and began to bite and tear with her tusks into the screaming man. Daddy, Uncle Jack, and Jack Clark finally beat the sow off with boards and sticks, and rescued Gene and what was left of his ripped overalls.

We gave the finest possible care to our livestock from birth to maturity, because they were a major source of food and income. At the same time, there was no squeamishness about the killing of edible wild game or tame animals on our farm. We never heard of anything as strange as a vegetarian, and it would have seemed ridiculous for any of us to expect the meat on our table to be furnished by a slaughterhouse or some other distant and impersonal source. Daddy kept a small herd of beef cattle, mostly for sale on the hoof, and we produced a large number of hogs.

The processing of pork was an important event, etched vividly in my memory. Beginning with the first cold days of winter, but avoiding a new moon, we would slaughter hogs, usually twenty at a time. (Daddy usually didn't pay much attention to the moon's phase, but he respected the deep concern of the other workers on the place, who were careful about when to plant and harvest aboveground and root crops, to breed animals, to can fruits and vegetables, or even to dig post holes.)

Killing hogs was a challenging job, requiring the help of our entire family and all other available workers on the farm. Each person had a specific job and knew what to do. The hogs to be slaughtered were herded into a small pen, and either Daddy or Jack Clark would go among them with a .22-caliber rifle and shoot each one precisely, aiming so that death was instant and the bullet didn't go into the carcass in such a way that the prime meat cuts might be damaged. Then they cut each throat and let the blood drain into a large pan as soon as possible. I remember that when I was small Daddy was disappointed that I was repelled by this process. He turned to Jack and said, "The sight of blood is too much for the little boy." Later, to please him, I suggested that I might perform this first stage in the hog-killing ceremony, and was relieved when he declined my offer.

We built fires under dish-shaped cast-iron syrup kettles and some tilted steel barrels, and the slain hogs, each weighing about two hundred pounds, were immersed in almost boiling water for a precisely timed interval, long enough to loosen the hair but not long enough for it to be "set." Then we placed each carcass on a flat board frame about the size of a door and scraped off the hair with dull knives. If needed, more scalding water was poured on the tough hair to loosen it. When clean, each carcass was hung up by its heel tendons on sharpened sticks or singletrees and slit open with a sharp knife, and the internal organs, including the liver, heart, lights, and kidneys, were lowered into large washtubs and then separated for processing. This array of hot-water receptacles and other paraphernalia would cover the entire area in front of our barn.

While the rest of us scraped and gutted the hogs, Daddy and Jack Clark divided each carcass into hams, shoulders, spareribs, side meat, backbone, tenderloin, pork chops, heads, jowls, and feet. Alongside the commissary, the women would be boiling the fat into lard and cracklings in large black iron pots, cleaning the small intestines for sausage casings, and processing the inner organs and trimmings. Most of the lean-meat scraps and a lot of other parts were cut into small pieces and fed into a hand-cranked grinder to be made into sausage. None of the hog's body was wasted. We had very little storage room in our small icebox, cooled by fifty-pound blocks of ice, and other families on the farm had no way at all to refrigerate food, so everyone would have something of an orgy for the next few days, gorging on fresh brains (scrambled with eggs), pork chops, pig steaks or tenderloin, and the few other cuts that were not to be cured. It was nice to feel that we were fulfilling a duty by eating all the delicacies we wanted—so they wouldn't spoil. Later, about the time I finished high school, Daddy rented a large drawer in the Plains Freezer Locker, to supplement the vegetables and meat Mama preserved at the school canning plant.

Daddy used a standard formula of borax, salt, and other spices for the stuffed sausage, and a secret one of his own for curing the hams, shoulders, and some of the sides containing high-quality streak-of-lean bacon. After the cuts were trimmed to shape, we had to rub each tiny crevice thoroughly with Daddy's mixture, to give a proper flavor and to repel any probing insect. The fire in our backyard smokehouse would be lit and kept burning for days, using certain woods, mostly oak and hickory with a few pieces of persimmon or sassafras, to cure and preserve the meat. We suspended each piece and the long tubes of stuffed sausage from nails driven into the ceiling joists, and Daddy would inspect them and the fire several times a day. Once thoroughly cured with spices and smoking, the meats would be hung from rows of small steel pipe suspended by haywire from the ceiling of the commissary. Everyone in our family was proud of the quality of Daddy's cured meat. The uncured fatback, containing almost no lean meat, would be rubbed and then buried in coarse salt, until sold for a few cents a pound in the store.

For a few months each year, on every other Saturday morning in the spring and fall, I went with Daddy to the regular meetings of our beef club. There were eight members who took turns slaughtering a steer when the group assembled at his house. All of us pitched in to help with the work, and the carcass and innards were divided up, with a rotating system for allocating the different cuts of meat. The host usually kept the hide and blood. There was some grumbling on the way home if the beef was ill fed, but most of the farmers knew each other and tried to maintain a good reputation in the club. As during hog-killing time, we gorged on beef during these weeks.

Crops were best when planted on rested land, and every winter we cleared new ground with crosscut saws, axes, and a stick of dynamite under the stumps. After we removed all the trees and bushes from new ground in some of the flatter and better-drained woodlands, the first planting was always watermelons. This was my favorite crop, because I had a special role to play in its production, and harvest time was an exciting adventure. My friend Rembert Forrest lived about five miles north of us, and his father also grew watermelons, so he sometimes joined A.D. and me with the pruning. Periodically during the growing season, we had to walk through the fields with jackknives, spotting the damaged or deformed melons and removing them from the plant so they wouldn't sap the nutrients away from the good fruit. Although this was a difficult job for a fifty-acre crop, it required some degree of judgment and was much better than mopping cotton, hoeing, or toting drinking water to workers in the field.

A bonus was that Indian artifacts were more likely to be found during the first year after a field was stripped of its cover, cultivated, and exposed to the beating rain. Since most of the new ground tended to be in the lower fields, nearer the swampland, and this was where native villages had often been located, pruning watermelons could put me ahead of my daddy in our artifact-collecting competition.

The timing of the watermelon harvest was crucial to hitting the right market, and for a number of years our region was in a good competitive position. Daddy would hire a man from a nearby community who was expert in judging maturity and quality to join him, and they decided which melons were ready to be cut for sale. Each melon chosen was stood on end, so that we toters could see them and carry one or two at a time to the wagon. If we struck it exactly right at the beginning of the season, a good melon might be worth as much as a dollar, delivered to the railroad siding in Plains. Two weeks later, the market might be flooded and the price so low that the melons wouldn't pay the freight cost to Cleveland or Chicago.

During watermelon season, there would be a string of empty boxcars parked in Plains, each one to be loaded by my daddy or one of the other farmers. Swept clean and filled with a bed of wheat straw, a car would hold from five to nine hundred melons, depending on their average size. Government inspectors were responsible for the quality and approximate uniformity of size. It was exciting to go through the field, load the ripe melons on sleds or wagons, transfer them to trucks, ride with them to Plains, and unload them in our boxcar. We boys would discuss the crop like adults, watch the government inspector open the melons with his special long, thin knife, and worry if some defect was found in our load. It was embarrassing to haul unripe or diseased melons back home, so every effort was made to ensure high quality from the field.

There was also a limited market for melon in the nearby stores, and we would go in Daddy's pickup as far away as Atlanta if he heard that profitable sales could be made there. During the season, we always had a pile of lower-quality watermelons in front of our commissary to sell, usually for a dime, with a sign alongside the road to attract passersby. Melons that might not qualify for sale or, toward the end of the season, even those of high quality still unsold would be worth as little as a nickel each. Any lower price made them more valuable as hog feed. There were always plenty to eat; even a small boy could dispose of a half or sometimes a whole melon. When they were especially plentiful, we ate only the hearts, leaving the seeded parts for the animals and birds.

Another crop planted on recently cleared land was sugarcane, which often followed watermelons. Syrup was a major item in our retail sales in a broad area around Plains. Most landowners had a small cane mill, used to make syrup for the family. This was a much-superior product to molasses, which was sold in bulk or barrels by sugar manufacturers as a byproduct from their large mills. It was used as a cheap substitute for syrup and sugar by the poorest families and as a source of protein in animal-feed mixtures.

The first cane mill on our farm was a rudimentary outfit that consisted of a mechanical grinder and a large shallow cast-iron cooking pan about six feet in diameter. A slow-moving mule pulled a long pole around and around a set of intermeshed gears through which the sugarcane stalks were fed, and the squeezed juice dribbled out into a large bucket or tub. Daddy put up a sign and sold some of the juice for five cents a glass to travelers who stopped at the roadside, and the rest of it was carried in buckets and poured into the cooking pan, under which a hardwood fire was maintained. Water evaporated as the juice boiled, leaving thicker and thicker syrup, while impurities floated up and were continuously skimmed from the surface. These "cane skimmings" were poured into a barrel alongside the cooking vat. Quickly fermenting with the heat, they became a potent brew within a few days, which Daddy usually let the cane-mill workers imbibe—but not until after noon on Saturdays.

As the syrup thickened, Daddy would test it by letting a drop fall into a glass of cold water. Knowing that it would thicken considerably when it cooled after the fire was removed, he had to make a quick judgment about when it was ready. Syrup too thin was inferior on biscuits or hotcakes, and crystals of sugar would precipitate if it was too thick. As was his custom, Daddy produced more than our family could eat, and sold the excess in our commissary, packaged either in one-gallon tin cans or in quart bottles. He designed a label that he later used on all our packaged farm products, printed with the words "Plains Maid" above a picture of a beautiful young woman. He soon began to deliver syrup to some of the same stores that sold his milk drinks.

As the demand increased, we planted more and more sugarcane on our farm, until the batch process finally became too time-consuming; in 1937, Daddy installed a large syrup mill alongside a small stream on the back side of our farm and hired a neighbor to help him supervise the operation. Instead of a mule as the source of power, we had a large steam boiler that drove the grinder and also provided steam heat under a long flat pan that could be inclined at different angles. A constant supply of juice was fed through a pipe into the top of the pan and forced by tin baffles to run back and forth across the hot surface. Tilting the pan up and down and adjusting a few small gates determined how long it took the juice to reach the bottom of the pan, at which time it had become syrup of the right consistency. We even used a hydrometer instead of a syrup drop in a glass of water to determine its consistency. This was truly a scientific operation!

Ten or fifteen acres of cane made a lot of syrup, which created a challenging job for all of us. I did everything possible to avoid having to cut the cane and haul it to the mill. Although I was a proud and growing teenager, this was work almost beyond my capability. Rattlesnakes and water moccasins loved the sugarcane fields, and cutting cane stalks with a razor-sharp machete was an excruciating and dangerous task. We would plow around the field and then burn it to remove the lower leaves, but this was only partially successful.

The heat was almost unbearable, with the tall cane cutting off any breeze in the fields, and the edges of sugarcane leaves cut like serrated knives. I much preferred working in the mill. I learned how to fire the boiler, to keep the steam pressure at the proper level, and how to burn the squeezed stalks, or "cane pummlings," as supplementary fuel without smothering the fire. On occasion, Daddy had to sell some of the Plains Maid syrup through wholesale distributors, but he didn't like to lose a substantial part of his profit to any middleman.

Corn was not a cash crop, bringing only around thirty cents a bushel, but it was crucial for feeding both animals and humans, and provided the foundation for our Southern diet. We didn't let anything go to waste. After the ears were mature and before the stalks completely withered, we would go into the fields and strip off all the leaves, bind them into small bundles, and stick them on top of broken-off stalks to dry. This fodder was used throughout the year to feed livestock, along with the ears that were harvested later. Corn also fed the small and hidden stills that produced moonshine whiskey, or "white lightning," for personal use or for sale to neighbors. (Although Daddy made wine every year and experimented with home brew, we never owned or approved of any of the whiskey stills that were sometimes found in the remote swamps of our property.)

Second only to corn, we depended on sweet potatoes, which were high in carbohydrates and vitamins and grew well on our farm. At Mama's request, Daddy always planted a large patch near the home site, to be shared with everyone on the place. We began enjoying the crop in midsummer, to be cooked and eaten immediately, and completed the digging before first frost. We handled the tubers carefully and stored the final harvest outdoors in cone-shaped hills, separated from each other by layers of pine straw and covered with dirt for protection against rain or freezing. They were dug out one by one, or as needed, and could last until the following spring. There were almost unlimited recipes for them, and there was rarely a paper sack or tin lard-can at school or in the field that didn't carry a baked sweet potato in season.

Other common food crops were okra, peas, and greens, particularly collards, turnips, and cabbage. Some more ambitious tenant farmers grew watermelons and kept a few hogs, a small flock of chickens, and perhaps even a milk cow. With the open-range laws, however, they had to be careful that their animals did not enter any unfenced fields until after the crops were harvested. Hunting, fishing, and trapping were important sources of additional meat, used to supplement the cheap pork fatback that was used for grease, for seasoning, and as a source of protein.

We harvested wheat, rye, and oats in late May or early June, cutting it with hand scythes and binding the stalks into bundles, which we then stood upright in shocks until dry. These were later hauled to our stationary threshing machine, which Daddy always set up near the back of the barn. We stored the bagged grain in cribs, while an enormous pile of straw accumulated nearby. We children loved getting a running start in the barn loft and leaping as far as possible out of the door, to sink deep in the soft straw. Although it had no food value, the straw was baled and used to pack watermelons for shipment and as bedding, both for the animals and for some of the mattresses of the tenant farmers.

One of my greatest pleasures was taking our grain to Jim Price's mill. This was something Daddy also enjoyed, so we usually made the trip in his pickup instead of in one of the farm wagons. I was thoroughly familiar with the place, because Mr. Price was a Baptist and let Daddy and his church-school students spend the night at the mill on occasion. We boys fished and swam in the pond, explored the sluice-gate arrangements, and slept in the millhouse. After the customary boys' games, including corncob battles, we listened to Daddy read from Paul's letter to the Corinthians about us being "ambassadors for Christ," and finally lay down to sleep on crocus sacks or bags of grain. There was a wonderful odor of freshly ground wheat and corn, and all the sharp edges of the boards and tables seemed to be rounded off smoothly by the millions of grains that had moved over them during generations of use.

The place came alive in the daytime, and it was intriguing to realize that this grain from our own fields was being pulverized by the huge rotating millstones, and our own meal, grits, and flour were sifting down into troughs and being sacked up to be carried home. We ate the fresh meal by the handful as a special treat, although it was so hot it burned our fingers. While Mr. Price did his work, even busy farmers could relax with each other with no sense of guilt that this idle time violated the strict work ethic of people like my father. Fortunately, this was a fairly frequent excursion, because there was a limit on how long our supply of milled grain could be stored. Back home, the meal and flour had to be protected from mice, and were kept in metal bins or left in bags suspended by haywire from the ceiling. Weevils were inevitable, though, and a fine sifter was always used in the kitchen to remove them before any dough was made.

The single most important economic factor in our lives was the price of cotton, which, during my boyhood, varied from a low of five cents a pound to a high of almost thirty cents. Unlike all the other crops we grew, however, there was always a cash market at the prevailing price, which was set internationally and could not be unfairly manipulated in any local community. Also, lint cotton did not deteriorate when stored for years by owners, until the market might change to their benefit. However, this option was not enjoyed by most farmers, who had to sell at harvest time to pay their debts and prepare for the next year.

An important advantage for big landowners was the ability to control or monitor the sale of cotton after it was harvested. The handling of the cotton through the ginner and the warehouseman helped to ensure that the renter or tenant could not surreptitiously market any substantial portion of the product, as was possible with pigs, grain, and even peanuts. The fact is that both white and black sharecroppers and even landowners were, in effect, under the social and financial control of their wealthier neighbors, and of economic forces in faraway New York and Liverpool. There was no way for average Georgia farmers to understand, much less influence, the cotton market, and neither did they have any control over the price of things they had to buy.

These inherent disadvantages were exacerbated by the uncontrollable tendency of cotton farmers toward maximum production, either to benefit from last year's higher prices or to maintain a given level of family income when cotton was cheap. During most years, therefore, the total supply of cotton exceeded both American consumption and the relatively strong export market in Europe. Economists, journalists, politicians, and the farmers' own regional leaders realized that this suicidal overproduction had to be stopped, but no one knew how to convince individual farmers at planting time.

Louisiana's Governor Huey Long urged other governors to follow his lead in passing legislation prohibiting the planting of *any* cotton in 1932. They agreed in theory, but failed to act, and the Louisianans had to back down. Most small farmers knew nothing of these campaigns, and they were too independent and disorganized to take concerted action even if they had wanted to do so. I agreed with the tenant farmers on our farm that if other farmers reduced their planted acreage there would be higher prices for those who did not participate in the plan.

Everyone knew that cotton had shaped the relatively unchanged and largely unfavorable economic, racial, and societal relationships among our people for seven generations, since the invention of the cotton gin in 1793. But during my boyhood it seemed that farmers were doubly cursed. On top of the national agricultural crisis, our community was increasingly afflicted with attacks on the cotton crop by boll weevils and worms. In just a few years, crop yields fell by two-thirds. Even so, it was not feasible for a farmer to abandon a lifetime of experience and dependence on cotton. The only choice was to struggle against the insect invasion.

With cheap labor, we first attempted to pick the insects by hand, and a few farmers, including my father, used geese in an equally fruitless attempt to roam the fields and perform the same task. Our first effort at chemical control was the use of simple traps placed in the fields, made of dinner plates filled with vinegar and molasses. Later, we tried arsenic in various forms, the most effective being calcium arsenate, which was at least a partial remedy for the plague. We continued to use arsenic, a poison deadly to both humans and insects, until it was supplanted much later by DDT and other organic chemicals introduced during World War II.

Beginning as a small child just able to carry a gallon bucket, I had a continuing job during the growing season of mixing arsenic, molasses, and water in a large barrel and then helping to apply it by hand to the central buds of every cotton plant in Daddy's fields. We would begin this process with the stalk about a foot high, when the first squares appeared, each of which would later develop into a blossom and, if things went well, into a boll that would produce the mature fiber about four months later. I had to carry the poison solution up and down the rows in a lard bucket, and place it on each individual plant with a cloth mop on the end of a stick. This mopping process had to be repeated about every five days, and during some rainy seasons cotton had to be poisoned as many as twenty times.

Mopping cotton was a terrible job. The molasses attracted swarms of flies and honeybees, which seemed to be immune to its lethal effect, at least while I was watching them. They would cover the barrel and buckets, and follow us through the field. I usually wore just short pants and never underwear or a shirt during the warm months, but for this job I preferred to protect my legs with long trousers. They would quickly become saturated with the mixture, and would stick to my legs in a most uncomfortable manner. In fact, everything about me was sticky. With evaporation, the layers of the sweet goo would turn to hard sugar, so that at night my pants wouldn't fold, but would stand erect in a corner or against the furniture. Covered with poison, they had to be laundered separate from the other clothing, so we didn't change them every day. It was particularly disgusting to put them back on in the mornings.

There was a dramatic change in what we did in the cotton fields when the harvest began. This, too, was backbreaking labor during the hottest time of the year, but there was an element of cleanness and competition about it that added spice to each day's work. We moved slowly up and down the rows from when the heavy dew evaporated until sundown, bent over so we could reach the bottoms of the stalks, our fingers probing between the sharp burrs to pick each dangling lock of white seed cotton and cram it into long sacks that dragged behind us on the ground, suspended by straps that cut into our shoulders. Unlike when hoeing weeds or harvesting other crops, there was no element of common effort among the workers; all of us were on our own, totally independent, and competing with all the others in the field. We could look around and estimate how our work compared during the day, but we had to compensate for the fact that some of the workers picked two rows at a time. When our sacks were full or when we felt that we just had to stand erect for a few minutes, we would empty the picked cotton onto a burlap sheet about eight feet square, or sometimes pack it into large round white-oak baskets.

The excitement came at the end of the day, when Daddy, Jack Clark, or some other designated leader would weigh each person's harvest. A set of scales, known as "stilliards," was suspended from a strong beam, and the cotton was lifted from the ground by two men, the swinging weight balanced, and the amount called out and recorded for payment the following Saturday. Men avoided picking cotton when possible, partially because the women's more dexterous fingers gave them an advantage and they excelled in this task. During my years on the farm I increased from 50 to a maximum of 150 pounds a day, which was in the range of most adults. Rachel Clark, as small as she was, picked more cotton than anyone we ever heard of, reaching as much as 350 pounds when the yield was good and conditions were right.

Another great experience was to pack fourteen hundred pounds of seed cotton into high wooden bodies on our two-horse wagon and carry it to Cranford's gin in Plains, where a five-hundred-pound bale of lint was separated from the seed. The gin was on a one-acre lot completely surrounded by a high fence of corrugated tin to reduce the danger that sparks would blow into the gin from one of the ever-present trash fires in the town. We either took our ginned bale back to the farm or, more usually, stored it in one of the two local warehouses until Daddy decided on the best time to sell. We saved enough seed for the next year's planting, part went to pay Mr. Cranford for ginning, and we sold the rest, if any, for a small amount of cash or swapped it for cottonseed meal, which was used as a high-protein feed supplement for our animals.

In addition to our home place, we owned another farm in Webster County, about four miles north of our house going directly through the woods and swamp, but seven miles by the winding road. Our family had bought this land in 1904, the year they moved to Plains. Day laborers cultivated one of the large fields on the place, and black tenant families worked all the other land. To me, each of these tenant farmers is unforgettable.

They were superior farmers who had proven their competence and reliability while working by the day, had enough ambition and self-confidence to depend on their ability to support a family, and had managed their financial affairs well enough to purchase their own mules and equipment. There were eight families on the place, separated by woodlands; only two of the houses were within sight of each other. My daddy monitored all those who worked our land, visiting with them and inspecting their crops at regular intervals. Mobile in his pickup, he also provided some services for them, such as delivering supplies, sharpening plow points at the blacksmith shop at home, or summoning a veterinarian (my Uncle Jack Slappey) to care for their livestock.

Daddy treated the workers on our farm with meticulous fairness, and Mama's constant concern for them was well known. This gave us an advantage in attracting the best farmers, and I only remember one or two cases when a family voluntarily moved, to accommodate some personal need, to take a full-time job with a sawmill, or to move to a larger or better farm. In fact, when I returned after twelve years of college and service in the U.S. Navy at the time of my father's death in 1953, most of the same farmers were still working our land.

Unpleasant departures were rare. On one occasion, I remember, a man had been a good day laborer and wanted to work his own crop. My daddy agreed, and furnished him an adequate supply of equipment, two mules, a milk cow, and a few pigs, covering the cost with a mortgage on these things and the year's crop. The next spring, someone reported that the man had sold some of the mortgaged hogs. After the farmer admitted what was, in effect, a theft, he and Daddy worked out an arrangement for him to be paid in cash for the work he had done already, he was given credit for returned items, and he moved off the place. We then finished working and harvesting the crop with day labor.

The three families who worked the northern portion of the farm were quite independent of the others, and also related less to Daddy and me. Two were brothers, Richard and Virgil Johnson, who lived with their families in a copse of thick woods within a stone's throw of each other and worked different farms but shared a common barn. They and their nearest neighbor, John Ed Walker, cultivated our most productive pebbly land, but it was difficult to plow, and weeds and grass had a better chance to establish themselves during the extra day or so that it took for their heavier soil to dry out after a rain. They were competent and relatively successful, but they all preferred to give up farming in the late 1950s rather than shift from mules to small tractors.

Felton Shelton and his wife occupied the southernmost house on the farm. He was lighter-colored than most of the other share-croppers, was somewhat taciturn and competent, and had good judgment. He dressed properly, always wearing a shirt under his overalls with the collar buttoned. Felton was able to maintain an appropriate balance of bemusement toward the world in general and proper deference toward Daddy and other white adults. He had his own way of doing things and tended to ignore advice from my father unless it was presented strongly. Though he seemed to move at a slow pace, he always got things done.

Felton's relative independence probably came from his additional income as a basket weaver, a skill he had inherited from his father. He had permission from Daddy to cut down half-grown white-oak trees in certain areas of the farm, when they were about six to eight inches in diameter, and these provided the raw material for his craft.

I was intrigued with Felton's work, and Daddy let me spend enough time with him to help make a few baskets. After dragging the still-green logs back to his house with a mule, Felton would split them with an ax and a froe (a cleaving tool) down to long, wrist-thick pieces, and then use an old knife with a thick blade to separate them into ever-thinner strips for weaving the baskets. His standard product was about three feet in diameter and two and a half feet deep, and woven tightly enough to hold even wheat and oats. There were always a half-dozen in use around our barn and lots, and several in the cotton fields during picking time. For years, Felton's standard price was $3, but he went up to $4 when prevailing day wages were raised from $1 to $1.25. With some reluctance and on his own schedule, he would accept orders for special baskets, such as the square-cornered and oblong one that was used for our family's laundry, and smaller round baskets for gathering pecans, so that Mama and the women who helped her could carry them full of nuts. Even now, I use Felton's techniques in my home workshop to weave the bottoms of chairs that I make from green wood.

Next up the road was Wes Wright, a tall and lanky man, the oldest on the place. My impression, based on the frequency of Daddy's visits and the amount of detail in his advice, was that Wes was the least competent and ambitious of the tenants. He had disputes with some of his kinfolks and nearest neighbors. With little fanfare, Daddy let Wes's young nephew Lenard Wright move into Wes's apparently better place; the older man and his wife moved to the most remote land, near the creek, where he said he preferred to live anyway. Later, Lenard would become one of my best friends and my partner, shouldering much of my farming responsibility when I went off to serve as governor and president. He and his wife, Mary, were committed to providing a good education for their children, who today are college graduates and successful in their professions.

Arthur Bridges and his family lived just east of the land my father worked. He was a cousin of the Wrights, so they shared farming responsibilities and, as far as I ever knew, lived in harmony with each other after Wes changed places.

Willis Wright lived in the center of the southern group of farmers, his land touching that of Arthur, Lenard, Wes, and Felton. Willis was a patriarchal figure on the Webster County farm. Daddy's relationship with him was more consultative than instructive. It was usually at this stop that we would have a drink of water from the well, or sit for a few minutes on the porch. Willis was interested, and enough at ease, to question Daddy about market conditions, the relative value or quality of fertilizers or farm equipment, and even political matters. Willis didn't work on shares, but paid an agreed quantity of cotton and peanuts as rent for the use of our land. He had unlimited checking accounts at our commissary and at Plains Mercantile Company, and was able to pay cash for bargains he found at other stores. He had no sons of his own, but with help from some of his wife's relatives and even hired hands during seasons of heavy field work, on occasion, his farming operation was considerably larger than that of any other tenant. It was my impression that basic decisions about his crops were his own, with almost routine ac-

Willis Wright, 1976

quiescence from my father. When Daddy had duties elsewhere and left me on the Webster County farm, I spent as much time with Willis as possible. Along with Rachel Clark, he was instrumental in teaching me and helping to shape my values and opinions.

Willis was my mother's special friend, perhaps because he suffered from a serious kidney ailment. Willis would never come to our commissary or visit families on the home place without coming by for a conversation with Mama. Eventually, he had to have major surgery at Wise Sanitarium to remove one of his kidneys; Mama served as the nurse in charge of the operating room. During Willis's long recuperation at home, Daddy would take her to Webster County to see him during his routine trips, and Mama would stay with Willis while Daddy was visiting nearby sharecroppers.

Black families had remarkable success in becoming owners of their own farms during the Reconstruction era. By 1910, when a survey of the South was completed by the U.S. Department of Agriculture, about 25 percent of farm owners in the South were black citizens, owning sixteen million acres of land. However, their families' net production of crops (and that of equally small white landholders) was no more than the amount a slave had formerly produced on a large plantation three generations earlier. A few years later, in 1916, the editor of the widely circulated *Progressive Farmer* magazine began a strong but ultimately unsuccessful crusade for legislation that would have permitted white citizens to prohibit the purchase of farmland by blacks. Since that time, however, the goal of dominant white ownership has been reached by subtler means. The size of farms has grown tremendously, and racial prejudice in both private and federal lending agencies has channeled the limited capital available for heavy equipment and expansion to white farmers. Black land-ownership has decreased rapidly, in proportion to the increase in average size of farms.

I remember how surprised and disconcerted we were when, around lay-by time one year, Willis Wright proposed that he buy the farm. It was a reasonable request, but a startling one, impossible to grant. Although Daddy had bought and sold a number of tracts of farmland around the general community, this place was special. Its 215 acres lay in the heart of our original family property, none of which was considered eligible to be traded. In fact, some of Daddy's siblings still owned an interest in the land. Since Daddy and Willis were very close friends, the obvious solution was for Daddy to help Willis locate another small farm that was on the market.

One day during the next Christmas holidays, Daddy asked Mama and me to go with him to Webster County, and we drove directly to the house where Willis lived. When we arrived, we sat on the porch for a while, talking about his good crop that year, the state of his health, and plans for the next planting season. At a pause in the conversation, I could see that my father was struggling with his emotions. Finally, he blurted out, "Willis, I've decided to sell you the farm." This was a surprise to all of us, and an amazing event. Mama burst into tears of joy and put her arms around my father.

After the general commotion died down, Daddy told Willis to come to the store the following Saturday, to work out the terms of the sale. Before another year went by, there was a new concrete-block home on the site, painted green; with Daddy's help, the Rural Electrification Administration made it the first house in the area to be wired for electricity, early in the 1940s.

By the time I was sixteen, I knew about all the chores that had to be performed on the farm, was familiar with the animals and machinery, and was fairly proficient in carpentry and in the skills of a blacksmith. Both in school and from my father, I had learned at least the rudiments of agricultural economics, and was becoming qualified, if necessary, to succeed my father in his chosen career. Although this was my most likely future, I had developed a different goal.

It was my mother's brother, Tom Watson Gordy, who helped shape my childhood ambition and my future life. Daddy was as well educated as necessary for the times, having completed the tenth grade at Riverside Academy and served as a military officer, but he was determined that I would realize what seemed, in those Depression years, to be a distant dream: to graduate from college. No one of our Carter ancestors had ever finished high school, and it seemed then that any college opportunities were limited to the two free military institutions, West Point and Annapolis. Although Daddy had served in the U.S. Army, he hadn't appreciated the experience enough to insist that I follow in his footsteps.

Uncle Tom had joined the navy when he was quite young, and made a lifetime career of it. He was my distant hero, and through all the years of my boyhood he and I wrote letters back and forth, mine giving news about the family and his coming from the far reaches of the Pacific Ocean and filled with information about the exotic places his ships were visiting. I heard from him more than did anyone else in the family, and a letter or photograph from Uncle Tom was a memorable event in my young life that I was eager to share with my mother and the other Gordys. We all followed his career closely, and were excited when he changed ships or made the slow advancement from boot camp to seaman and finally to radioman second class. The United States Navy had two rigid dirigibles, the *Macon* and the *Akron,* and he was part of the rescue team when the *Macon* went down in the waters near San Francisco. He sent Grandma a small piece of the aluminum hull, which she cherished the rest of her life.

Uncle Tom was the champion lightweight boxer in the Pacific fleet, and a photograph of him holding a trophy and standing in front of the men he had defeated occupied the central location on his parents' mantelpiece. He had a flat nose and curly hair, and walked with something of a strut, like James Cagney. He married a San Francisco girl named Dorothy, and they had three children during the 1930s, the oldest son named for me. It was his service in the navy that captured my imagination, and my parents didn't object when this was my choice for a future career.

So, from the time I was five years old, I would always say that someday I would be going to Annapolis, and would become a naval officer. Although I might stand in our yard and admire the railroad engineers as they went by and tooted their steam whistles in answer to my waving hand, it was not their admirable job but the vague image of someday being on a ship that became my dream.

It's not easy for me to understand now why Daddy supported this unswerving commitment to such a distant dream. But perhaps the reasons were the obvious ones: the unattractive nature of farming in those years; his ambition for me to enjoy a superb education at a respected institution; or just a stubborn determination to reach a long-standing goal. In any case, with my parents' full backing, years before I graduated from high school, we sent off for some pamphlets to learn about the Naval Academy, and I adopted this as my exclusive goal in life.

8

Learning More About Life

THERE IS NO WAY to exaggerate the importance of sickness and medical care in our community for people of both races, or how much my mother's involvement in nursing affected my early years. Illness was a constant source of conversation and concern, and even those who were not directly related to our special local hospital, Wise Sanitarium, stayed up-to-date on the latest news about everyone's physical ailments. At the barbershop, filling stations, stable, grocery stores, school, and church, this was the foremost subject of conversation. With so many local nurses in the operating room, in the wards, and keeping medical records, there was no way to have any secrets about what was happening in and around the hospital. We knew who was sick, who was treating them, and often the details of the treatment.

Any serious illness involved the entire community. There were no miracle drugs in those days, and for our own protection we had to be familiar with such things as the dangers of tetanus, which we called lockjaw, and how best to deal with an epidemic of flu, mumps, measles, chicken pox, whooping cough, typhoid and typhus fever, and the still more dreaded polio. When one child came down with a case of polio, our school would close for a few days, and all of us began to imagine the symptoms: fatigue, headaches, fever, and a stiff neck. No matter how serious the disease, the patients would almost invariably stay at home, and not in the hospital. (Even much later, we never considered any alternative to my father's spending his final days, with untreatable cancer, in his own bed.)

We absorbed a lot of information, or superstitious beliefs, about the most prevalent illnesses. Everyone knew that for pneumonia, for example, the crisis would come on an odd-numbered day after the onset of the disease, sometimes as early as the fifth day but most likely on the seventh or ninth. At this crucial time either the patient would die or the five or six degrees of elevated temperature would break. In the white community (and I presume also among our black neighbors), special prayer services would be held in the patient's church, and during Sunday-morning worship and regular weekday prayer meetings all the congregations would pray for recovery or (in hopeless cases) for fortitude. I remember the gathering of wagons, buggies, and automobiles in the streets or roads around the home of a desperately ill person. Friends and relatives would bring flowers, firewood, fruit, and their best-prepared dishes, and take over all responsibilities for household chores during the final days. The number of people would increase in and around the house when it was expected that the attending physician would make an announcement of either continuing life or imminent death. Our prayers were answered when we heard the words: "She has survived the crisis!"

When the news was bad and the patient died, the whole town was drawn into active condolences, showing great respect and concern for the bereaved family. A group of women would be in the house around the clock, preparing food, welcoming grieving guests, cleaning up, and sparing the family as much burden as possible. Almost everyone attended the funeral service, the procession to the graveyard was always slow and stately, and for prominent citizens the mayor would direct that all the stores be closed. All other vehicles, whether local or passing through, had to stop and pull off the road as the procession passed; any people along the way who were not participating would stand facing the road, and men would remove their hats. The cemetery services were directed both by the local pastor and, depending on the secular membership of the deceased, by American Legionnaires, Masons, or Woodmen of the World. Before the casket was lowered into the grave, everyone was expected to come under the protective shade tent to embrace, or to shake hands and commiserate with the family. After these duties were performed, folks could then enjoy a kind of homecoming in the cemetery, with warm welcomes to all the out-of-town people who had come to honor the deceased.

Like everything else, the Lebanon Cemetery was segregated, with whites buried on the west side and black graves located to the east. All the funerals were impressive affairs, budgets straining to give maximum honor to the deceased loved ones. The largest ceremony was when Bishop Johnson died, and was buried in the cemetery at Archery. The procession of automobiles, mostly large and black, extended for more than a mile.

The epitome of social and financial distinction around Plains was to be a medical doctor, particularly one who practiced in the Wise Sanitarium. The doctors enjoyed extraordinary respect, almost as superhumans. In a time when now forgotten diseases were frequently fatal, it seemed that our very lives were constantly in their hands, and we appreciated their skills and the horrendous burden of their work. They were always on call, either within the hospital or, more often, to attend patients in their homes.

Even if my mother hadn't been a nurse, the hospital would still have been a center of interest for our family. When the three sons of Plains's first mayor, Doctors Thad, Sam, and Boman Wise, decided to build a medical center, they sold stock in the venture to people in the community. Although any profits seemed to be automatically reinvested in the building, equipment, or supplies, almost every family with any means had a direct financial interest in the hospital. Both stockholders and other citizens were walking advertisements for the hospital's quality of medical care—not in how healthy we happened to be, but in our repetition of folktales about the institution. We were firmly convinced that our hospital was the best, even compared with the famous ones in Atlanta and farther north.

One story, still repeated today after more than seventy years, was about a wealthy man from Americus who was in need of an unusual surgical procedure and traveled up to Johns Hopkins Hospital in Baltimore, Maryland, for treatment. When he arrived there, at great expense, the finest surgeons in America told him that his was a rare and difficult case. They advised him to go to Wise Sanitarium in Plains, Georgia, where a surgeon named Thad Wise was best qualified in the advanced techniques.

The people in our community knew that "we" could offer the best not only in surgery, but in anesthesiology and in radium treatment of cancer and other tumors. Our doctors were also famous for minimizing the use of medicines and for advising diet, exercise, and certain home remedies as the best cures and prevention of disease.

There was a great competition among the dozen or so doctors who served the people of our Plains community in those days. They were divided rigidly according to whether or not they were affiliated with Wise Sanitarium, and our family was convinced that the "other" doctors were inadequately educated, charged more for their services, were reluctant to make house calls, did not stay abreast of advances in medical science, and prescribed excessive quantities of expensive prescription medicines. The few known dope addicts in town were believed to frequent these physicians to receive repetitive doses of potions containing opium, morphine, or other narcotics.

The Wise brothers also had an excellent program for young doctors serving their internships, and the older citizens of Plains can still name those who went on to greater things, including an anes-thesiologist who earned a national reputation with innovative tech-niques, a famous ophthalmologist in Columbus, and the chief surgeon at Emory University Hospital in Atlanta. Just as fine, in our opinion, was the training program for registered nurses. At any time, there were about twenty young white women struggling through this rigorous course. Although they were extremely disci-plined and reduced to virtual peonage within the hospital environ-ment, they were the objects of admiration and some jealousy among the citizens of our town. We knew of no higher calling for a woman than to become a nurse, especially if she trained at Wise Sanitarium.

There is no doubt that these opinions of Plains citizens were in-fluenced by the nurse graduates who stayed to practice their skills among us and became the wives of fortunate young men and the mothers of a number of my schoolmates and me. Most of the nurses served in the hospital, working regular hours either on the staff or on private duty. Others, burdened with their own family responsi-bilities or reluctant to be on a rigid schedule, "went on call" when it was convenient for them, usually nursing in a patient's home. After my sister Ruth came, in 1929, mother often chose this latter option.

During her earliest years after graduation and before going on private duty, my mother served as the nurse in charge of the operat-ing room. On my bookshelf I have a copy of the 1921 *Lippincott's Nursing Manual*, which Mama used to prepare for her state board examination, and which served in later years as a handy reference guide. Her pride in it was indicated by her signature, "Miss Lillian Gordy," inscribed in nine places, often followed by "Wise Sanitar-ium, Plains, Ga." On the preface page are listed the "1922 girls in training," with "Miss" preceding the last names of twenty-three young women. I still remember most of them: "Miss Webb," "Miss Arrington," "Miss Pennington," and "Miss Abrams." For the rest of their lives, they called each other either by their first names or by "Webb," "Arrington," and "Gordy," reflecting their strong and per-manent sense of sorority.

Most of the manual describes the regular duties of a nurse, with special attention to the use of Latin words and abbreviations and the translation of doctors' prescriptions. There was a fairly thorough presentation of symptoms and standard treatments for the common ailments of the time, most of them now of concern only to people in Africa and a few other places in the Third World, and some then-fatal infections like strep throat, which killed my Uncle Buddy's wife. For some reason, the entry on syphilis is heavily underlined.

I particularly enjoyed reading the section on "Nursing Ethics." With one exception, the nurse is expected to treat the attending physician with the utmost respect, almost reverence. There is no advice on how to respond to improper personal advances by a doctor, presumably because such a perfect person would never create an uncomfortable situation. The exception was if called on a case by a doctor who was known to have performed an abortion. The advice is to refuse, "for you could not afford to associate in private nursing with a criminal or a malefactor of this type."

I notice that the corners of some pages are still turned down. One of them is a description of how a nurse could "ethically" give a discount for her services to a poor family without embarrassing them. There was a sample bill included. The standard charge was $28 a week, in this case $80 for twenty days, but with a discount, called an "allowance," to pay for the pleasure of living in the patient's home. If there were small children there, "the nurse should take the place of the mother, provided she does not have to neglect the patient."

Since a good portion of physicians' time was devoted to making house calls, the doctors treated a few of the nurses as physician's assistants, and entrusted them with fairly advanced duties in the delivery of medical care when the doctors were nearby. Since we lived several miles from town among neighbors who were very poor and whose best transportation, if any, was a mule and wagon, my mother cared for many of them almost as a doctor, often providing both diagnosis and treatment. There may have been other nurses who did this, but I never heard of it. Mama was a special person, who refused to acknowledge most racial distinctions and spent many hours with our black neighbors. She never charged them anything for her help, but they would usually bring her what they could afford—a shoat, some chickens, a few dozen eggs, or perhaps blackberries or chestnuts. One prize payment was a wagonload of extremely flammable "turpentine chips" that we used for years to start fires. She kept the Wise doctors informed about her cases, and they supplemented her medical care when necessary.

There was a surprising frankness of discussion within the families of the medical professionals—at least in our home. Even in the presence of us children, my mother and father would talk about administrative problems within the hospital, the relative competence of staff members, the rare cases of drug addiction, and love affairs between the doctors and nurses. There was always an attractive unmarried nurse, either in training or already practicing as a professional, to pair up with an available doctor. Physicians were immune to disparaging gossip, although it was generally known, at least in our family, which doctors and nurses were "living in sin." For some reason, it seemed to me that this phrase did not have such a negative connotation when applied to the doctors. Most people seemed to feel that dedicated physicians had a right to enjoy the few hours when they were off duty, and the community did not condemn their sexual peccadilloes.

The community, apparently including her husband, accepted the fact that Miss Abrams, my godmother, lived with Dr. Thad Wise, who was a widower. I became at least indirectly involved in this love affair when Miss Abrams became pregnant and bore a son, who was named for me. The baby died after only a few weeks, however, and was buried in the family cemetery of her husband, with whom she had not lived for several years.

After Mama nursed her patients, she tried to keep up with their subsequent condition. Some of the more destitute ones had to be moved to what everyone called the "po' folks' home" of Sumter County, and sometimes I would go with her to visit them. I don't remember exactly where they were, but I recall a large and somewhat run-down former plantation home with a broad front porch and a large vegetable garden on the side for white folks, and two old houses nearby for blacks. Regardless of age or sex, all able-bodied residents were expected to work in the adjacent gardens; those who were too feeble sat in a somnolent state, seeming to observe little of what occurred around them. Mama worried about these old folks and felt strongly that more should be done to care for them. I remember how pleased my mother was, and the excitement in the "po' folks' home" when the government dole went up to $10 a month for white people and $6 for blacks.

While Mama focused on her profession, Daddy was exploring every opportunity for diversifying his farming operation and for marketing what he produced. Although cotton remained his main cash crop, Daddy was one of the first to shift to greater dependence on peanuts. Primarily on our home place, he used almost every source of additional income compatible with the land and markets in our local area. He didn't believe in having anything around that could not contribute its part to the overall farm economy. Sheep, geese, hogs, milk cows, chickens, horses, and jackasses were carefully tended, and they or the products derived from them were handled so as to yield the maximum income.

Furthermore, whenever possible he carried his products all the way to the retail level. When we sheared sheep, Daddy arranged for our wool to be traded to a manufacturer of blankets, which were later sold in our commissary and in Uncle Buddy's store. It seemed to me that the sheep were more trouble than they were worth. I don't know why, but we never ate any mutton at our house, even after lightning killed thirty out of our fifty when it struck a large oak tree under which the flock was huddled during a thunderstorm. They were foolish and helpless, and eventually Daddy sold them. One of our best bird dogs had begun to acquire the terrible and apparently uncontrollable habit of attacking and killing the lambs. Obviously, it was the sheep that had to go.

Throughout the South, a century of concentration on cotton production had depleted soil nutrients, and much of the topsoil was lost to wind and rain, often leaving bare subsoil in fields scarred by ever-deepening gullies. Most landowners had little if any money for improvements or adequate fertilizer, and many were just looking for a way out. It was a shame how run-down some of the farms became, but when Daddy bought such a farm, he would transform it. I helped him terrace all the fields by carrying the target while he used his spirit level to lay out gently sloping contours. Then we would plow along this line over and over with our largest turning plows to create a bank of earth to control erosion. He was a director of the Lower Chattahoochee Soil and Water Conservation District, and followed strict procedures on using vetch, clover, and other cover crops and a long-range plan of crop rotation to rebuild soil fertility. We would all join in making repairs on the house, barn, and fences, and then Daddy would choose a reliable tenant farmer or else work the place with day laborers for a year or two, before it was ready to be resold for a good profit.

To me, my father seemed all-powerful, yet we knew that he shared with other farmers a sense of almost total impotence in the face of unpredictable weather conditions and the remote and mysterious economic system that set prices for hogs, timber, cotton, and peanuts. Our part of Georgia receives about fifty inches of rain during an average year, mostly during the spring and early summer, with a relatively dry period in the fall and winter. This is usually a favorable pattern for both planting and growing, with maximum moisture to make seeds sprout and young plants grow and then a drier season for harvesting. However, depending entirely on draft animals and hand labor, small variations in the rain pattern could be devastating. There was no thought of irrigating crops in those days, and, compared with present times, expected crop yields were quite modest because of the inevitable periods of drought, sparse plantings, little fertilizer, and rudimentary equipment. The first week or two without rain was not particularly deplored, and was not even mentioned in Sunday-morning prayers in church. The dry ground permitted the mule-drawn cultivating plows and hoes to restrain the ever-encroaching weeds and grass.

However, when no plowing was possible because of several successive days of rain, the noxious plants were uncontrollable. Something like the terrible creeping and oozing things in horror movies, Bermuda grass, coffeeweed, cocklebur, Johnsongrass, beggar-lice, and nut grass would emerge from what had been a cleanly cultivated field, and in a few days our entire crop of young peanuts and cotton could be submerged in a sea of weeds. Often, despite the most heroic efforts by the best farmers, parts of the crop would have to be abandoned. Although partially salvaged, the remaining young plants were heavily damaged by the aggressive plowing and hoeing. During these rainy times, Daddy would pace at night, scan the western skies for a break in the clouds, and scour the community, often far from our own farm, to recruit any person willing to hoe or pull up weeds for day wages.

It was not natural for my father to admit a mistake, and as a child I was inclined to consider him omniscient and infallible. Daddy was bold and innovative in his farming operations, and it was inevitable that some of his projects would prove to be ill advised.

One year, Daddy decided that there was a lot of money in tomatoes, and planted ten acres of them instead of our usual one row in the garden. We had a bountiful harvest, but so did everyone else in Georgia, and our best efforts to sell our truckloads of the carefully packed baskets were fruitless. Not to be thwarted, Daddy decided to convert the entire crop into catsup, and obtained a home recipe from the county agent. He studied the formula, and multiplied it by more than a hundred in order to fill all the bottles he had bought and labeled. We built a fire under the big cast-iron basin normally used for making syrup, cooked the first large batch of tomatoes, combined the juice with the proper condiments, and started boiling the mixture. After an hour or two, Daddy realized that the brew was all boiling away and that he had mistakenly kept the juice and fed the tomato pulp to the hogs.

We started all over again, this time using the pulp to make a suitably thick final product, which we bottled and capped like soft drinks. It tasted good, and we were all proud of the result. We filled a good portion of the commissary floor with bottles of catsup, which Daddy began to deliver to the same merchants who were already selling our milk drinks and sugarcane syrup.

A few days later, when I went to the commissary to sell some snuff or tobacco to a noonday customer, I noticed several shattered bottles and spilled catsup everywhere. From then on we were afraid to go in the store: the catsup was fermenting and exploding with great force. Daddy hastily visited all the stores and picked up the surviving merchandise. Our hogs enjoyed more than two hundred gallons of spoiled catsup. We no longer discussed tomatoes in our house.

One important source of income was high-quality honey, which we sold either in the comb or centrifuged to extract the pure nectar. At that time, when few pesticides were in use, wild honeybees were prevalent, and all of us were on the lookout for swarms of them somewhere in the trees on our farm. We would rush to the swarm, sometimes the size of a basketball, and shake the limb or use a long stick to dump the big wad of bees into one of our empty hives. Daddy maintained about two dozen hives, and we processed the honey, consumed what we needed for our family, and sold the rest.

In addition to what we called "tame" bees in our hives, we were always on the lookout for wild bees that had made a hive inside a hollow tree. Sometimes it would take several hours to cut down a big tree, split it open, and gain access to the stored honey, while wearing head nets and subduing the angry insects by puffing smoke on them from a small pot containing pieces of smoldering burlap bags.

The nearest my father ever came to death on the farm was when he was routinely taking honey from our hives and was unexpectedly attacked by a horde of bees. He had been stung many times in the past, but this time he had a violent reaction to the multiple stings, and his body swelled to an amazing size after he rushed to the house and lay on the bed, with the stingers protruding from his skin. (Bees are the only insects that leave their implanted stingers behind.) Luckily, my mother was at home, and I remember her stripping off his clothes, scraping the bee stingers from his skin with a knife blade, and applying a paste of baking soda before we took him to the hospital in Plains. Daddy sold all the hives; after that we used store-bought honey.

There was only one time that I remember feeling embarrassed for my father, and it was not based on a momentous event. To match Miss Mary Lou Burnette's women's-clothing department at Plains Mercantile Company, my Uncle Buddy traded with a men's-clothing manufacturer to send a representative to the store every few months to offer custom-fitted coats and suits. Daddy had never had anything but ready-made clothing, and all of us were excited when he was measured for a three-piece "tailor-made" suit.

We waited impatiently until the package finally arrived in the mail, and gathered around while Daddy opened the box. No one disturbed the suit, but we looked at it and were permitted to finger the beautiful fabric. We looked forward to the following Sunday, when Daddy would be putting on his new finery for church. It was an important day for our family, but it turned into a disaster. When the big moment came and Daddy put on the trousers, they were at least four inches too long, and the waist would have fit the fattest man in town. Our incipient laughter died immediately when we saw the stricken expression on my father's face. He returned the merchandise to Uncle Buddy and refused to consider having the suit altered or being measured for clothes again—at least until fifteen years later, when he went off to Atlanta to serve in the state legislature.

Daddy wore thick eyeglasses, and I never saw him outdoors without a hat—a gray felt fedora during the cold months and a straw Panama hat of the same basic design when the weather was warm. Unfortunately, another constant feature of his appearance was a cigarette in his mouth or hand. With the approval of the government, tobacco companies had distributed free smokes to him and other soldiers during World War I, and he became addicted to the strongest brands, usually smoking at least two packages of Home Runs every day. To save money during the worst Depression years, he bought gallon cans of tightly packed shredded tobacco, cigarette paper in

Earl Carter, 1950, as candidate
for the legislature

large packages, and a small machine that my sister Gloria and I used to keep him supplied with home-rolled cigarettes. There were no health warnings in those days, so we didn't know about the almost inevitable cancer that would cause his premature death.

My father's independent nature rebelled against an addiction that controlled him, though, and this brought about one of my most memorable conversations with him. One day, about the time I became a teenager, I was shocked when Daddy told me to come into the bathroom and shut the door. After desperately trying to remember all my recent activities that might have displeased him, I finally decided that he was going to tell me about the sexual habits of birds and bees.

Instead, he said, using a rare and solemn form of address, "Jimmy, I need to talk to you about something important."

"Yes, sir, Daddy."

"There is something I want you to promise me."

"Yes, sir, Daddy."

I was relieved when he said, "I don't want you to smoke a cigarette until you are twenty-one years old."

"No, sir, Daddy, I won't."

He then made an unnecessary commitment. "When the time comes, I'll give you a gold watch."

I kept my promise, and so did he. I was a midshipman at the Naval Academy when I reached legal maturity, and I went to the store in Bancroft Hall and bought a package of cigarettes. I took one puff, didn't like it, and never smoked another. Unfortunately, my mother and my three siblings took up Daddy's habit, and all died of cancer.

We always kept turkeys on the farm, to supplement our diet on special occasions like Easter, Thanksgiving, and Christmas. One of the mysteries of my young life was why Daddy decided to buy one. During the week before Thanksgiving, we were visiting our Webster

County farm and, apparently on the spur of the moment, Daddy said, "I've heard that Mrs. Free has some white turkeys. Maybe we ought to go by her house and get one." I had met her once or twice, and remembered that she was an attractive young widow with long black hair who was respected for continuing the work of her former husband on their family farm. Daddy said he had read an article about these newly bred white turkeys with a lot more breast meat than the ones we had, and I was eager to see the new creatures. We drove the five or six miles to Mrs. Free's farm, and finally stopped in her front yard.

Daddy said, "We'll go in the back." The widow opened the door a few minutes after Daddy knocked on it.

They exchanged greetings, Daddy introduced me, and then he said, "We've come for one of your white turkeys."

She smiled and replied, "Well, Earl, I've sure got plenty of them left that I need to sell between now and Christmas."

Daddy turned to me and said, "Hot, go out behind the barn and be picking out a good one."

It was easy to find the big flock, and I was intrigued with their color and how much bigger and fatter they were than those in our yard. I was a little disconcerted, though, because they all looked about the same. A black worker soon came out of the barn, and I told him why we had come and described my assigned duty. He and I finally settled on the biggest one, and before long we had the turkey in an old crocus sack, tied tightly but with its head sticking out of a hole.

I waited for Daddy at the pen for a long time, but he didn't come, so I lugged the turkey back up to the house. After shuffling around in the back yard for quite a while, I got up nerve enough to blow the pickup horn, and shortly thereafter my father and the widow came out to join me. They seemed especially eager to be helpful.

"I've been paying for the turkey, and we can pick any one we want," Daddy remarked.

"Joseph will help you catch it," said Mrs. Free.

"It's already caught and in the pickup," I said, somewhat brusquely.

I never said anything to Daddy, but I've never passed Mrs. Free's place since then without wondering how Daddy knew to go to the back door and where the turkeys were . . . and why it took him so long to settle up.

9

Learning About Sin

A S A FARM BOY I spoke two languages. One was heavily in-
fluenced by my playmates' African heritage, with special
pronunciation and inflections. All of us white children habitually said "ain't," but with my friends on the farm a ghost was a
"haint," "eaten" was "et," "going" was "gwine," "rode" was "rid,"
"himself" was "hisself," "saw" was "seen," "am" was "be," "yesterday"
was "yestiddy" with the accent on the middle syllable, "rinse" was
"rench," "help" was "holp," and we didn't bother with final "r"s, "g"s,
or "d"s on other common words. A sufficiency was a "bait," as in
"We et a bait of plums." Absolutely correct was "mighty right," and
the opposite was, "You better say Joe ('cause you sho' don't know)."

Sometimes even Mama couldn't understand what our black
neighbors were saying, and I was proud to interpret. I made my
share of mistakes when trying to shift between the two dialects.
Mama teased me for years for rushing into the house when we first
moved to the farm and reporting to my parents, "I rid in the wagon
and driv the mules!" With my life confined to a small area around
our farm, I also had limits to my understanding. Once, Daddy took

the family thirty miles to the east to see the flooding Flint River. Never having seen a large stream, I asked, "Wheh de ribber, Daddy? Is it down in dat creek?"

In our house and at school and church, we were drilled in the proper use of white folks' language, but even the best efforts were not always enough. I remember being chastised by my English teacher once when for "food" I used the Archery word "t'eat," which I presumed was a contraction of "to eat." Sulking, I found the word in the classroom dictionary, and raised my hand to inform the teacher of her mistake. She smiled, and asked me to read the definition. I glanced at it and tried to back out of the confrontation, but she insisted that I read aloud: "The mammary protuberance on a female's anatomy, through which milk is discharged to a baby or young animal." I had always thought this was a "tit."

As my linguistic mishaps suggest, going to school added a completely different dimension to my life. From age six until I entered high school, I was two different people: a self-confident young man on the farm with my family and close friends, and a timid and somewhat defensive boy in school with my classmates. In school I had to confront white boys in a competitive environment. I knew a few of them from Sunday School at the Baptist church, but these were brief encounters with parents always present. I was very small for my age, no taller than my younger sister Gloria, and I soon learned to concentrate during the recess periods on sports that didn't depend on size or strength.

I usually came out second best in the personal contests I couldn't avoid, but I was accustomed to wrestling and fighting with A.D. and Edmund, and the bigger boys on the school grounds learned that I was willing to inflict and take punishment if it was necessary. I could read and write when I entered the first grade, never had any trouble with the lessons, and usually had good enough grades to match the smartest girls. The only thing in which I really excelled throughout my school years was in reading more books than any of my classmates. When not at work, I usually had a book with me, and read on rainy days, Sunday afternoons, in bed at night, at the table during meals, in my tree house, on the toilet, and between and even during classes at school.

The Plains High School building was an imposing brick structure, its entrance framed by four white columns and enormous white-cedar trees. On the main floor were an auditorium, which we called "chapel," the superintendent's office, a library, and ten classrooms to house the eleven grades (with the second and third grades in the same room). A smaller second story was used for typing, shorthand, home economics, and, in my final school years, the lunchroom. The classrooms were not wired for electricity, but each had an entire wall of large windows that gave enough light for reading except on dark, cloudy days.

School attendance was required until the age of sixteen, but the law was not enforced strictly, even for white students, if parents could prove to the school principal that they really needed their school-aged children to help make a crop. I was expected to attend all 180 days of the school year, and I envied the poorer boys who moved more freely between the field and classroom. I never imagined that they might consider my full-time schooling a blessing. With Daddy running his farm business and Mama nursing, my sister Gloria and I were pretty much on our own in the daytime during our elementary school years. There was no school bus then for those of us in Archery, and we usually rode into Plains with the older Watson children, whose father was the Seaboard Airline Railroad section boss. They had an automobile, and Daddy provided the gas and oil.

A bus did not begin coming by our house until I was in high school. A makeshift affair, with a small yellow body mounted at an angle on a wrecked and partially straightened chassis, it was called the "cracker box"; it always appeared to be moving down the road sideways, like a crab. I was honored during my senior year to be designated a schoolboy patrolman, and wore a white woven belt over my shoulder and around my waist as the symbol of my authority. I helped the driver maintain order on the bus, and had to open the door, step on the ground, and look both ways before the vehicle could cross a railroad track.

These niceties were only for white children, of course, since buses weren't provided for colored students. So far as I knew, there were never any discussions in those days, either at school or at home, about changing the racially segregated system. In fact, I envied A.D. and the other black boys because they could walk just a half-mile to their classes in the St. Mark Church building, and weren't expected to attend school every day. Fifteen years later, when efforts were being made to avoid integration by belatedly honoring the "equal" part of the Supreme Court's "separate but equal" mandate, a few buses were run to the largest schools for black children, their fenders painted black to maintain a clear, though symbolic, racial distinction between the students even on the way to their classrooms.

Despite its small size, with fewer than three hundred students in eleven grades, our Plains High School was superb. This was primarily because of Miss Julia Coleman, the school superintendent and the best teacher I have ever had. She walked with a limp, had failing eyesight, and never raised her voice to scold or in anger; her only marriage was to our school. She was totally dedicated to her profession, evidently seeing something special in us rural children. I thought at the time that I was one of her pets because she knew I had a burning desire to go to the U.S. Naval Academy, but I later discovered that many others in my class had the same impression about themselves. Miss Julia was just as interested in preparing most of her graduates for their predictable lives as housewives, railroad and sawmill workers, or sharecroppers.

Even in the earliest grades, Miss Julia encouraged the teachers to promote reading, which led to my first school victory and an introduction to "foreign food." Miss Tot Hudson was the teacher of the second and third grades, and I won a contest by reading the

Julia Coleman

most books. The prize was to eat dinner with Miss Tot at the home of our undertaker, Mr. Ross Dean. Mama made me wear my Sunday clothes that day, and I was overwhelmed by the prospect of dining in such a fancy city home. For some reason, they served sauerkraut, a dish I found both strange and vile. Having been taught by my father to clean my plate, I struggled with the unsavory mess, convinced that Mrs. Dean had made some kind of terrible mistake in the kitchen. My misery was somewhat assuaged when Miss Tot awarded me a framed print of Thomas Gainsborough's *Blue Boy*, which hung in a prominent place in my room until I went off to college.

Miss Julia wanted us to be widely acquainted with the literary world. She maintained long, challenging lists of great books and made sure that all of them were in our school library. She got extra books for me from the county library and even mentioned in chapel my reading *War and Peace* when I was in the fifth grade. She played great music for us on a small gramophone and drilled us in recognizing classical masterpieces and their composers. She did the same thing with paintings, holding up prints and challenging us to write down on our tablets the names and artists. We had to declaim in front of the class, reciting poems and Bible passages; we stood in line for spelling bees; and we had constant "ready writing" contests. Our teachers would put three subjects on the blackboard and we had to choose one of them and write about it within a time of fifteen or thirty minutes. We also held monthly debates in the classroom, after doing a lot of research on the assigned subject. Everything was competitive, but Miss Julia had a way of limiting the arrogance of the fast students and easing the embarrassment of the slow ones. Plains High School was always a formidable competitor in the district and state meets in one-act plays, debating, spelling, and ready writing.

Mr. Y. T. Sheffield worked directly under Miss Julia as our principal, math teacher, and athletic coach. He was also the ultimate disciplinarian, and worked closely with our parents to ensure that our performance on the school grounds met the high standards set by him and Miss Julia. The last thing we students wanted was to be sent to see Mr. Sheffield, because his judgments were quick and sure and his punishment was severe. Our classroom teachers would usually give us one warning about improper conduct; the next step was, "Take this note and report to Mr. Sheffield." The girls might have to stay after school or get a few licks on their open palms with a ruler, but we boys had to remove everything from our hip pockets, bend over with our hands against the wall and breeches tight across our butts, and take from three to seven licks with a heavy and narrow board. This punishment was rare enough so that everyone in school—and at home—knew when it happened. My father's standard practice was to supplement the punishment we received at school, usually with restrictions for days or weeks from the radio, travel, or other cherished pastimes.

If two of us got into a fight, Mr. Sheffield's presumption was that guilt was equal—unless it was obvious that a bully was abusing a relatively defenseless adversary. One of my most brutal fights was with one of my best friends, Bobby Logan, who lived in Plains. We were in the boys' restroom when we had an argument about Dr. Boman Wise's daughter, whom we were both dating. There wasn't much room to move around, and no one was there to break us apart, so we

Julia Coleman and Y. T. Sheffield

both took a lot of punishment. When we were finally exhausted and stopped pummeling each other, the first thing we agreed was that we would clean up and do everything possible so that Mr. Sheffield wouldn't know about the incident.

All of us boys played sports before school started in the morning, at recess and dinnertime, and at least a few minutes after school hours until our bus loaded. We were lucky because the cracker box made two trips, and the one to Archery was last. All of us loved to play baseball, including farm boys like me who couldn't go out for the school team because springtime farm work interfered with regular practice. One leader would throw a bat to another, and we would alternate fists up to the top of the handle. The last one able to grasp the bat well enough to throw it over his shoulder got first choice of the boys assembled to play, and sides were then chosen alternately. The second level of baseball was scrub, when kids yelled "batter, catcher, pitcher, first, second," and so forth until a maximum number of about fifteen were chosen. After the arguments were over, we'd have three batters, a catcher, backstop, pitcher, and then the rest of the team, sometimes with several infielders and outfielders. Whenever one of the batters made an out, he would go into the last field position, and everyone moved up a notch. A ball game could go on for an entire week, always resuming where the school bell or a departing bus had interrupted. The biggest boys were the arbiters of disputes, with Mr. Sheffield as the final judge.

Some of the students, boys and girls, preferred basketball, which we also played on campus throughout the school year. I went out for basketball and made the varsity team during my last two years. This was really the most important sport as far as interscholastic competition was concerned, because games were played at night and parents with day jobs could attend. Half our contests during the season were at other schools, to which our teams traveled on a school bus. There was always a girls' game before ours, and the long trips in the dark gave us a chance to pair off on the back seats and do some enthusiastic petting.

I was by far the smallest one on the team and acquired the name "Peewee," from a comic-strip character. But I was also the quickest, and we depended a lot on fast breaks whenever our team got the ball on the opponents' end of the court. (I grew three inches, to five feet nine inches, during my first year in college, and was proud to make the intramural all-star team.) During the winter season, I usually walked home from school in late afternoon after basketball practice. I liked baseball more, but Daddy didn't want to spare me from work during the spring planting and plowing.

Our other sports on the school grounds were horseshoes, handball, spinning wooden tops, dodgeball, and marbles. Mr. Sheffield also used our out-of-class times for the track team's practice in running, jumping, vaulting, discus throwing, and the shot put. A few of us were obsessed with tennis, and we played whenever possible at our homes or on one of the three courts in town.

In many ways, school was a cruel place, with cliques and pecking orders established among the children. One hierarchy was based on physical strength, in which the older boys usually dominated. Almost by definition, these were the poorer students who had failed several times to be promoted and so were older than their classmates. I was not large enough to be competitive in combat, and didn't suffer much from these potential confrontations. Another established pyramid was based on academic standing, on which the accumulated grades placed each student precisely. The very slow learners eventually dropped out of school, and the talents of others were channeled away from mathematics and literature and into home economics or agriculture, so they wouldn't "waste their time" in advanced mathematics and literature. There were no social promotions then just because a student was a year older, except on rare occasions when students were totally unable to meet the minimum standards and parents insisted on their going up after being kept back for at least a year. There were not many of these, perhaps one or two in an average class of twenty-five. Instead of a diploma at graduation time, they received an equally ornate certificate stating that they had attended school for at least eleven years.

I'm still embarrassed to recall our social order based to a great degree on the economic status of our parents. Within a fairly broad range, all the students were accepted as approximate equals, but there were always a few who were different. Their dresses and shirts were made of washed guano-sacks, and their odor, hair, teeth, and complexion showed that their families were not accustomed to washcloths, soap, or toothbrushes. I don't recall abusing them myself, but neither do I remember being their champion when others refused to sit near them or made disparaging remarks about bad odors, lice, or itch. These relative outcasts could either shed quiet tears and endure, or quietly drop out of school.

There was certainly no assurance that I would ever go to the Naval Academy, so I prepared for other future possibilities. The most natural would be as a farmer, so, along with more than half the other boys in high school, I concentrated on the Future Farmers of America (FFA) program. We took classes in the care and management of draft animals, beef and dairy cattle, hogs, crops and pastures, forestry, poultry, farm equipment, and other related subjects, such as pest control and food processing. In the workshop, we practiced carpentry, blacksmithing, welding, and furniture making. Our agriculture teacher worked closely with each of our fathers to ensure that our work at school was compatible with what was being done on the farm.

The FFA was a tight-knit organization at the school, state, and national levels. We had competitions all the way up in public speaking, record keeping, the raising, showing, and judging of prime animals, and other crafts important to a successful leader in agriculture. (The only skill in which I excelled was cutting a rafter to fit a complicated roof design.) We derived a lot of unexpected advantages from this combination of academic and practical instruction. I was one of the FFA officers at school, have been to national conventions, and am an honorary lifetime member. The agricultural studies have been of great benefit to me, especially during my time in politics. I also studied typing and shorthand, which I used throughout college and in my writing career.

There were twenty-six members in my high-school graduating class in 1941, but none of the others went on to get a college degree. No senior college served the one million people who lived in Southwest Georgia, and we would have had to go to Auburn University in Alabama, or almost two hundred miles away, to the University of Georgia in Athens, and pay both tuition and boarding expenses. Several of the girls had some further education at the local vocational school or at junior college, where they learned to be secretaries or bookkeepers, but most of the boys went back to the lives of their parents, which often included hard manual labor, heavy smoking, and irregular health care. (They led good and productive lives, but I noticed that at our fiftieth class reunion the death rate among my classmates at the U.S. Naval Academy was only half what it was among those from high school.)

The only time I directly disobeyed the principal was on April 1 of our senior year. The boys in my class all decided to slip away from school and spend the day in Americus as an April Fools' joke, and stuck to the plan even after Mr. Sheffield got wind of it and forbade our leaving. We attended a movie and visited the newspaper office, where we inserted a news article about our "delightful outing." When we returned to Plains, the principal, Daddy, and some other fathers were waiting for us. Mr. Sheffield informed us that we were all being given a zero in every class for a week and would have to take a maximum whipping of at least seven licks before being readmitted to classes.

I was petrified as I rode home with my father in our pickup. He didn't speak for a while, just clutched the steering wheel and clenched his teeth.

Then he said, "Are you ready to quit school for good?"

"No, sir, Daddy."

Gloria, 1943

Class of 1941.
I'm at lower right.

"Have you given up on going to Annapolis?"

"No, sir."

"Why did you disobey Mr. Sheffield?"

"I don't know, Daddy."

"Are you prepared to take your punishment at school?"

"Yes, sir."

"You won't get the same thing at home this time, but, except for going to school, you'll not leave our yard and fields for a month."

"Yes, sir, Daddy."

I took the whipping at school, which was the last one I ever had; my reduced grades saved me from having to make a valedictory speech.

The churches joined the schoolhouse at the center of our spiritual, educational, and social lives. Every day of my eleven years at Plains High School began with a chapel service in the auditorium. After routine announcements by the school principal or superintendent, and perhaps some entertainment by a student, we pledged allegiance to the flag, usually sang "He Leadeth Me" or "Onward Christian Soldiers" and then "America the Beautiful," or "Dixie," and recited some Bible verses. Sometimes we had a visiting speaker, most often one of the three (white) preachers in town. Only then, after about a half-hour, did we go to our individual classrooms for daily lessons.

The two dominant white churches in Plains were the Methodist and the Baptist, although our town was different from most others in also having a small Lutheran congregation. My family were Baptists. None of the churches had full-time pastors, and it was customary for the two major congregations to visit back and forth on alternate weeks, with no preaching on the fifth Sunday. By far the largest and most important service, at least for me, was our weekly Sunday-school class. Daddy taught the junior boys, aged nine through twelve, and also worked with the Royal Ambassadors, the equivalent of Boy Scouts in other communities. Even before I was old enough to be in his class, he would take me along on overnight camping trips and on afternoon swimming or other outdoor excursions. There was also a training union for young people, where the emphasis was on our global missionary program. But the main attraction was the frequent parties sponsored by the church and held at different members' homes on Friday nights. These were the most important social events of our young lives, where parents expected their children to pair off with future spouses.

In our worship services, the Methodists and Baptists had few detectable differences, except that we Baptists chose our own preachers, whereas the bishop and district superintendent decided who would serve the Methodist church. The people of Plains seemed to prefer more moderate preaching, so we were not afflicted with the kind of harsh fire-and-brimstone sermons that we sometimes heard in other churches. Unfortunately, this meant that, except during revivals, our church services induced more somnolence than excitement. My sister Gloria and I often amused ourselves in church by commenting on the appearance of the other worshipers, and especially enjoyed estimating how long a couple had been married by how similar their facial features had become.

Rosalynn's grandfather, a Baptist, would not permit their family to play cards, fish, or go to movies on Sundays, and both congregations strongly condemned alcoholic beverages. (Many devout Christians, including my parents, assumed that Saint Paul's advice to Timothy that he "use a little wine for thy stomach's sake and thine often infirmities" took precedence over the local church's prohibitions.) But the Methodists must have been stricter in the early years, because the patriarchs of two of the most influential families in our church had been expelled by the Methodists for dancing in their younger days.

Our black and white Baptists had worshiped together in Lebanon Baptist Church until after the War Between the States, when emancipation led to separate services. Later, when the town of Plains was established, the white congregation took the more pre-eminent-sounding "Plains Baptist Church" as their name, and the black congregation retained the former name for theirs.

The largest church in town is still Lebanon Baptist Church. There are a number of other National Baptist and African Methodist Episcopal churches within the city limits, and also in almost every rural settlement. Lacking transportation except for wagons, the black worshipers had to have their churches near their own homes. Although there has been some consolidation in the past fifty years, most of these churches are still active, and we sometimes visit them, although the more remote churches have relatively small congregations of older people. There are now eleven church congregations in and around Plains, and St. Mark AME Church in Archery is still a dynamic force in the lives of its members.

The high points of our church year were revival weeks, or "protractive meetings." They were always held after crops were laid by and before harvests began, and carefully scheduled so that both Methodists and Baptists could attend the services of the other. In preparation for the revival, the pastor and deacons would visit every family in the community that had not accepted Jesus Christ as Lord and Saviour, and the deacons and others would hold nightly prayer meetings to seek God's guidance for the coming services. Our churches invited outside evangelists to preach, some of them quite famous in their own home churches or because of the high administrative offices they held, and they would move into our community for a week of fervent and intense worship. We entertained the visiting pastors almost like royalty, with each host family attempting to outdo the others in presenting delicacies at the dinner and supper tables.

We had two services daily—one in the morning, heavily attended by housewives, and the other at night, for a more general audience. This was usually the time when children, typically at least eight years old, would accept Christ as Saviour and subsequently be baptized into full church membership. (Daddy was more conservative than some parents, so my sisters and I waited until we were about eleven.) By then we had been carefully instructed in Sunday school and in training union, and understood the meaning of these decisions, which were considered without question to be the most important of our lives.

Newcomers to the community were expected to join one of the churches if they hoped to be successful in business or to play a full role as Plains citizens. The few "lost souls" knew they would be visited each year, and some had become experts in certain passages of scripture, seemingly eager to mount an argument on theology or to use the visits to point out the hypocrisy of some church members. On rare occasions, the members of all churches would celebrate the salvation of one of these well-known sinners. "Old man Jackson was saved last night!" was a happy message that would sweep through the community.

By the time I went away to college, no one in Plains had ever been divorced. As far as we were concerned, divorce was a sin against God committed only in Hollywood and among some of the more irresponsible New Yorkers. The oath given during the marriage ceremony was considered to be inviolable, based on the words of Christ himself, who, when questioned about marriage, referred to the first binding of Adam and Eve: "For this cause, a man shall leave his father and mother, and shall cleave to his wife; and the two shall become one flesh. Consequently they are no longer two, but one flesh. What therefore God has joined together, let no man put asunder."

For some reason, this Biblical command was considered to have priority over the one against adultery. Even as a child, I knew of several incompatible couples who had actually separated but were still maintaining the façade of marriage. In some cases, the wife or husband was cohabiting with another person, but no legal acknowledgment of the marriage's dissolution was ever sought. Early suspicions about the indecent arrangement were usually confirmed when both the adulterers would quietly cease attending church services.

One of the most notable cases involved two white families who lived in a fairly remote area near Archery. In what was obviously a totally harmonious arrangement, the two husbands simply swapped wives and a total of nine children. Perhaps to minimize false rumors, one of the husbands came over to our house and described their decision to my father. Other children were born to the new couples, and the resulting common-law marriages remained intact thereafter, but the parents stopped going to church.

Although I didn't know much about them at the time, there were a number of active organizations and a few semisecret fraternal orders in the community. Upstairs, above the general stores, was a meeting place for the Woodmen of the World and the Odd Fellows, and there was a Masonic lodge in Preston, nine miles west, which had earlier been located in Plains. One or two of the wealthier Plains men became members of Kiwanis or Rotary clubs in Americus, our county seat. There were Women's Missionary Unions, garden clubs, and other organizations that gave women a chance to meet for their own pleasure and for the benefit of the community. My mother always found an adequate excuse not to join them or, at most, to attend meetings only rarely. She was a member of the "Stitch and Chat" club, but she worked most of the time, never did any sewing, and had little interest in gossip. Much later, after she had retired from nursing, she played poker every Thursday afternoon with a small group of women, always for dimes. Even her grandchildren learned to stay away from her when she came home with a smaller bagful than she had taken to the game.

The Parent-Teacher Association was a dynamic group that played a strong hand in public-school life. On monthly PTA days during the school year, there was an intense competition among the students to have both parents and grandparents present, and the school auditorium would be full of citizens who discussed and debated the school curriculum, building repairs, classroom supplies, plans for public events, and the identity and qualifications of teachers. All members of the local school board attended, and had to answer questions and respond to the demands of the gathering if there was a consensus. One policy, for instance, was to provide for widows or single women by giving them top priority as classroom teachers, and firing any of them who married to make room for one in greater need of a job.

When I was thirteen, Daddy built a cabin and a small pond a few miles from our home, and it became a favorite place for fishing, swimming, and entertaining friends. It had a pool table, a second-hand jukebox, and a large open room for dancing. Every now and then, one of the hands and I had to take a pair of mules over to the cabin the morning after one of my parents' parties to pull a guest's automobile out of the pond. The simple explanation was always, "The brakes didn't hold." These guests were the gentry of Plains and Sumter County, who met to eat steak or fried chicken and to round-dance or Charleston to Victrola music. The men and women drank beer, wine, and bonded whiskey together (bought from the local bootlegger, since ours was a dry county), and we children were always excluded from these events.

It was completely different when Mama and Daddy consorted with other farm families. They would usually take us children along, and the main dish was fried chicken or barbecued pork and Brunswick stew. A few musicians played fiddles while one of them called big-circle square dances. Everybody drank sweet iced tea or lemonade with the meal, and afterward the men passed around homemade moonshine in fruit jars between square-dance sets, usually with Coca-Cola chasers. Honoring the clearly understood proprieties, men would always imbibe out in the yard, unashamedly but separately from the women, a few of whom slipped a drink in the kitchen. There were always comments about the clarity and taste of the 'shine, just as a chef's main-course or special dessert dishes would be evaluated in a fancy restaurant. Obviously, we children looked forward to the farmers' dances, where the smaller boys and girls were treated as though we were invisible, young teenagers were invited to join the adult dancers, and the oldest boys made something of a passage to adulthood when finally permitted to have a toddy with the adults.

Everyone knew that my daddy liked to have a good time, and he and Mama almost always went out somewhere on Saturday nights. The first parties I remember were their evenings with the nurses and doctors from Wise Sanitarium. It was a group of about five or six couples, whose leader was Dr. Sam Wise, the second of the three brothers. The other two were married, but Dr. Sam, a bachelor, was always dating the prettiest of the unmarried nurses. I guess they rotated parties among the various homes, and I always dreaded it when my parents were hosts. They would push back the dining-room table and chairs, use our small breakfast room as a bar, put us in bed early, and let their hair down. They must have thought that pulsating gramophone music, raucous laughter, and loud talking didn't penetrate our thin walls and doors. Dr. Sam had lost a leg during a childhood disease, and we could hear his special rhythm as he made our floors resound with the loud taps of his wooden prosthesis. Sometimes the parties would last until it was almost time for Mama to fix breakfast and get the family off to church, where Daddy had to teach his regular Sunday-school class.

One of the more unforgettable events of my life took place on one of these Saturday nights. I had gotten old enough—about twelve—to think that we children deserved more consideration when we were trying to sleep. About three o'clock in the morning, with the party in full swing, I decided I'd had enough. I got out of bed, put on my pants, and left the house, slamming the door behind me. With all their noisemaking, there was no way the partygoers could hear me. I went out, climbed about ten feet up in a large chinaberry tree in our back yard, and went to sleep in my tree house, a small framed enclosure sided with crocus sacks. A few hours later I heard the automobiles leave, and shortly afterward my father walked out in the back yard and called, "Jimmy! Jimmy!" I could tell that he was angry, but I was not yet through pouting, and decided not to answer. I heard him go back into the house, and all was quiet.

I waited a while and then climbed down and slipped back into my bed, beginning to dread what was going to happen next. It wasn't long before Daddy came in and called me. I sat up in bed, rubbed my eyes, and pretended that I had just awakened.

He said, "Where were you last night?"

"Out in my tree house, Daddy."

"Didn't you hear me call you?"

This was the difficult time. I had never confronted my daddy with direct disobedience, but I knew that lying was the ultimate crime in our house.

I hesitated a moment, and then said, "Yes, sir."

"Go out to the garage and wait for me."

I had gotten a number of whippings in my life, but this was the one that hurt most. Later, Mama described to me how worried both of them had been, and how Daddy had not been able to go to sleep. Unlike past times, she didn't express any regrets for the punishment I had received. But it was the last whipping I ever got from Daddy.

We children had our own parties, usually sponsored by the church. Since it was taken for granted that we would attend Sunday school and preaching services, these events were not scheduled to recruit new members or to promote loyalty; they were just the normal expression of a human desire to get together for a good time. As little kids we pinned tails on donkeys, played drop-the-handkerchief, musical chairs, and hide-and-seek, and enjoyed homemade ice cream, cookies, and cake. Beginning at high-school age, we enjoyed frequent "pound parties," still church-sponsored but at private homes, to which each of us would take a pound of refreshments. Over a period of time, we learned what kind of food to furnish, so that everyone didn't bring the same Kool-Aid, peanut-butter-and-jelly sandwiches, ham and biscuits, potato chips, or pound cake. I realize these events were carefully orchestrated by our parents to let boys and girls learn the social graces and take the first steps toward courting. Each party consisted of a series of about a dozen proms, in which we strolled or danced together, each lasting ten or fifteen minutes. Most host mothers imposed a strict rule against having two successive proms with the same girl, and insisted that we check into the "staging area" between proms. The prom cards were monitored by the chaperones so that wallflowers didn't have too many gaps in their lists.

Drivers' licenses were not required in Georgia until 1940, and many of us young farm boys were competent truck drivers, because our fathers needed us to deliver fertilizer and seed to the fields and to run other errands. I still rode my bicycle to most parties, but my father began to let me use his pickup on special occasions when I was twelve years old, as long as I went directly to the prom party and then straight back home. Since everyone in the community knew all the operating vehicles by sight, and often just by sound, it was highly unlikely that I could violate his instructions and go undiscovered. Later, at the ripe old age of fifteen or so, I would just get his comment, "Drive safe."

By then, we also had a lot more chances for private dates, but we still depended on the prom parties, where strolls down the town streets or country roads led naturally to snuggling in back seats or dancing at Magnolia Springs. All of us learned the basic one-step and two-step, with a waltz thrown in every now and then, to the slow and romantic songs. However, during most of my high-school and college years, jitterbugging was the standard dance step, and we strove to be imaginative and unrestrained in twirling our partners right, left, forward, and back. The older boys we tried to emulate could perform the most intricate and innovative steps while appearing totally bored, despite the calisthenics they were orchestrating.

Even as preteens, most of us boys had our own steady sweethearts (at least for a few months at a time), and we wanted to spend most of the party with them. This was not difficult with more understanding hostesses and chaperones, or when we used flexible prom cards or swapped with other couples after we were out of sight of the hosts. At any time there was a particular girl who was the center of my attention. After I lost Eloise to a newcomer in town, who was older than the rest of us and had his own car, I dated girls named Ann, Betty, Roxie Jo, and Marguerite, and would sometimes meet Americus girls to sit in the back row in the movie theater. These were all "nice girls," and our courtships were relatively innocent by modern standards, sometimes including heavy petting but within prescribed limits. I had taken a private oath never to say "I love you" to anyone other than the girl I intended to marry, and I kept this promise until I fell in love with Rosalynn. A few girls were known by all the boys to "go all the way," and they were available at the price of a movie, perhaps a hamburger, and the public knowledge of the illicit relationship.

My farm work became more serious and burdensome when I was a teenager, but I also found opportunities during slack seasons of the crop year and on rainy days for more advanced adventures. My friend Rembert Forrest and I bought a wrecked pickup, stripped everything from the chassis except the seat, and used it on the back roads to visit each other and to go to the woods and swamp areas for fishing and hunting. Mr. Forrest was in the sawmill business and kept an underground gasoline tank on his farm. We would buy a few gallons from him on occasion, but I remember one Saturday afternoon when he was away from home, the tank was locked, and we needed some gas. We devised a clever solution. We found the ground-level filling pipe for the main tank, opened it, and repeatedly lowered strips from a white cloth guano-sack on a strand of haywire down the pipe, let them soak, and then squeezed the gas into a bucket until we had enough for our afternoon ride. I don't remember that we ever paid for it.

One of the most personally embarrassing of my escapades with

Rembert was when he and I went to my grandmother's house and she gave us some divinity candy she had just cooked—two pieces for each of us and two each for the other members of my family. The delicate white mounds of sugar, egg whites, and particles of pecans were too much for us to resist. Overcome with temptation and certain that our crime would be undetected, we ate it all except one piece each for my parents and two sisters. As fate would have it, Grandmama dropped by to see us on a Sunday afternoon a couple of weeks later. I still felt safe until she asked, "Lilly, did y'all enjoy the candy?" Mama replied, "Well, it was really good, but one piece wasn't enough to really get a good taste." I couldn't sneak out of the room quick enough to avoid the inevitable, "But I sent at least two pieces for everybody."

Until my last two years of high school, the black boys at Archery were my closest friends; I had a more intimate relationship with them than with any of my white classmates in town. This makes it more difficult for me to justify or explain my own attitudes and actions during the segregation era. A turning point in my relationship with A.D. and my other friends occurred when we were about fourteen years old. Until then, there had never been any distinction among us, despite the great difference between our economic circumstances. I lived in the "big house" and they lived in tenant shacks; I had a bicycle, my parents owned an automobile, and we went to separate churches and schools. I was destined to go to college, and few of them would finish their high school work. But there were no acknowledged differences of rank or status when we were together in the fields, on the creek banks, or playing in our yard or theirs, and we never thought about being of different color.

Around age fourteen, I began to develop closer ties with the white community. I was striving for a place on the varsity basketball team and developed a stronger relationship with my classmates, including a growing interest in dating girls. One day about this time,

A.D., Edmund, and I approached the gate leading from our barn to the pasture. To my surprise, they opened it and stepped back to let me go through first. I was immediately suspicious that they were playing some trick on me, but I passed through without stumbling over a tripwire or having them slam the gate in my face.

It was a small act, but a deeply symbolic one. After that, they often treated me with some deference. I guess that their parents had done or said something that caused this change in my black friends' attitude. The constant struggle for leadership among our small group was resolved, but a precious sense of equality had gone out of our personal relationship, and things were never again the same between them and me.

It seems strange now that I never discussed this transition in our lives with either my black friends or my own parents. We still competed equally while on the baseball field, fishing, or working in the field, but I was not reluctant to take advantage of my new stature by assuming, on occasion, the authority of my father. Also, we were more inclined to go our separate ways if we had an argument, since I was increasingly involved with my white friends in Plains. I guess all of us just assumed that this was one more step toward maturity and that we were settling into our adult roles in an unquestioned segregated society.

10

The Carters of Georgia

WHEN I CAME HOME from the navy, both my Uncle Buddy and I wanted to learn more about our family history. Compared with those in most other Southern states, Georgia's historical records are especially well preserved. When General William Tecumseh Sherman and his Union army approached Atlanta to destroy it in 1864, our secretary of state hastily piled the state's official documents into a two-horse covered wagon, hired a teamster, and told him to haul the load northward until he found a place away from military action. More than ten years later, the governor of Georgia received a letter from a man in Maryland stating that he had recently bought a farm and found a wagonload of papers, apparently relating to Georgia, under the shed of a barn. The records were returned to Atlanta, remarkably intact.

Uncle Buddy and I learned from minutes of the Colonial Council, dated February 1764, about "a petition of James Carter setting forth that he had been in the Province four years, that he had had no land granted him and was desirous to obtain land for cultivation, having a wife and children, therefore praying for 350 acres at a place called Mackintosh's swamp, near Briar Creek." Three years later, James was back, "praying for a purchase of 150 acres on N. side of creek called Rocky Comfort, and about six miles below the Indian trading path, for a cow pen." James must have had five children, because new land acquisitions were based on a "headright" system, with every head of family allowed one hundred acres, plus fifty additional acres for each other member of the household. The new landowner had to pay only the surveying costs and recording deeds.

This particular frontier area was just west of Augusta, Georgia, and was more fully settled a few years later by a group of Quakers who came from Orange County, North Carolina, and established a community named Wrightsboro. Although not a Quaker, a man of Scotch-Irish descent named Thomas Ansley came with them and acquired a land grant near the homestead of James Carter. Most of the settlers were relatively young, had large families and little money, were not familiar with slavery, and were accustomed to doing their own work.

When they heard about the Declaration of Independence, James was thirty-six years old and Thomas was thirty-nine. Life in their part of Georgia was both exciting and extremely difficult for the two men, who were not pacifists like their Quaker neighbors and joined the Georgia militia in the struggle for independence. When British troops occupied their area, they moved their women and children into hiding in what is now eastern Tennessee, and fought the Redcoats in Georgia and the Carolinas until the war was over. Afterward, the families lived together in a close-knit community.

Thomas's granddaughter Ann Ansley and James's grandnephew Wiley Carter were married in 1821 and had eleven children, all of whom survived. Wiley was a strong-willed man who believed in defending his rights as a citizen. Courthouse records show that in 1843, when he was forty-five years old and the father of ten children, he had a heated argument with a man named Usry whom he accused of stealing some of his property. Wiley swore out a warrant and joined a posse under Sheriff Augustus Beall. Arriving at Usry's place after dark, they found the accused man inside his house with a loaded gun, shouting threats to kill Wiley. The confrontation lasted for eight hours, during which time one witness said, "The sheriff offered to break down the door but Carter advised against it, hoping Usry would become sober and give up." There was a one-day trial about six months later, and the sheriff's testimony described what happened: "Usry was evidently preparing to shoot Carter. Carter insisted in a friendly way that Usry submit to the warrant. Usry cocked his gun and abused Carter in a most offensive character. The two men were cursing each other and both raised their guns about the same time and fired. Usry was killed."

The jury declared Wiley Carter not guilty of any crime, but I've always suspected that there may have been some painful memories of the event, and perhaps remaining animosity between families in the community. In any case, after Ann delivered her last child and then died two years later, Wiley and his second wife, the widow Sarah Chestnut Wilson, finally decided to move farther west with the younger children; they established a home just a few miles north of what was then known as Plains of Dura.

Wiley was my great-great-grandfather, and his new land had been won in a lottery. This was an interesting process. As the Indians were pushed steadily westward, it usually took five years for their vacated land to be surveyed and divided up into lots of about two hundred acres each. Plats of each lot were traced on small cards, about the size of those now used in Monopoly games, which were deposited in wire cages, along with a number of blank cards. At highly publicized events, the cards were drawn one by one, in full view of the assembled crowds. Every white adult male was entitled to one free draw, married men or widows with children had two draws, and extra chances went to Revolutionary War veterans, those who had served honorably in certain public offices, or had some other distinction.

Beginning in 1805, members of my family won the right to own twenty-three lots of land in ten different counties, swapped some of the titles to gain contiguous acreage, and permitted five of these to revert back to the state. I don't understand why my kinfolks declined some of the land, since its price was just $4 for each hundred acres, to cover the cost of the surveying and deeds. It may have been because some of them were not ready to move westward and just chose to hold on to old titles rather than to establish new homesteads and clear fields.

Wiley and his second wife, Sarah, had one son, named Sterling Gardner, who was born in 1851 and moved to Roberts County, Texas, a few years after his father died in 1864. It was only in recent years that we learned what happened to him. He worked as a cowboy, served as sheriff and county judge, and wooed by mail and married a Georgia girl named Mary Howard Cheves, who had three children before she died in 1898. Sterling then traveled back to Georgia to court and marry his wife's younger sister, Loua Eugenia, who preceded him in death by a year. He directed in his 1921 will that he be buried between his two wives, but "tilted a little toward Loua."

When the War Between the States started, three of Wiley's sons, Littleberry Walker (age twenty-one), Wiley, Jr. (twenty), and Jesse Taliaferro (fifteen), volunteered for the Sumter Flying Artillery, and their unit served under General Jeb Stuart. They fought through Virginia, Maryland, and Pennsylvania, and all three men survived, although Wiley was wounded at Hanover Junction. According to regimental records and letters from the battlefront, they laid down part of the artillery barrage to cover Pickett's fatal charge at Gettysburg. A letter from one of the young soldiers read, "We get about a half enough to eat. That is green beef and flour and but very little salt. When we left Savannah, we had a hundred and twenty-five men. Now we have thirty-six able for duty. You can guess how we go." In a wonderful understatement, he added, "I am well but not satisfied."

Ulysses S. Grant accepted the surrender of Robert E. Lee on April 9, 1865, Abraham Lincoln was assassinated on April 14, and the three Carter brothers surrendered after six more weeks. Along with many other Confederate prisoners in the South, they were paroled eight days later, and walked back to their Georgia home.

Their father had died the previous year, and his children inherited small plots of farmland. Luckily, they knew how to work and make the most of what they had. Owning farmland in Georgia has not always been a measure of great wealth. Real estate varied widely in value, as indicated by our old deed records covering more than two centuries of headrights, lotteries, wills, and purchases. One two-hundred-acre tract of the family's land was bought in the 1700s for just five shillings; a five-hundred-acre farm brought £50 sterling. In the more populated areas, where passable roads evolved after the Revolution, prices for cultivatable land seemed to average about $2 per acre. Two generations later, in 1854, my ancestors recorded deeds showing that 653 acres of the same land was sold for $1,000 and a nearby tract of two hundred acres was bought for $500. Just before the Depression, my father paid as little as $3 an acre for some land we still own.

Uncle Buddy was able to tell me about my great-grandfather:

"After the war, Littleberry Walker lived and farmed the land where Souther Field is now, just east of Americus. It's the airport where Lindbergh soloed and bought his first airplane. My granddaddy died in 1883. Some later claimed it was diphtheria, but a news report in the *Weekly Sumter Republican* said he was knifed to death by his business partner, D. P. McCann, in a fight over the proceeds of a 'flying jenny' [merry-go-round]. The same newspaper reported the next week that his wife, Mary Ann, died 'due to grief at the shock of his death.' McCann escaped a warrant by running off to South America, and was never caught.

"Most families had their own cemeteries at that time, and the couple were buried out on the old Carter Place. Later, a man from Montezuma bought the farm and made a two-acre hog pen around the graves, so, when my Great-Aunts Annie and Nanny heard about this, they had the bodies moved to the Americus cemetery. The bodies were in expensive bronze caskets, so they must have been well off. Not wanting to admit the fighting story, they told everybody, 'By no means, don't open those caskets, because some diphtheria germs may still be in there.' "

We knew about Littleberry Walker, but no one seemed to know exactly where his father, Wiley, had lived or was buried, except that it was in an old settlement called Quebec. At Uncle Buddy's urging, I spent several weekends looking in known cemeteries in that general vicinity for Carter graves and wandering alone through various woodlands to investigate rumors about abandoned burial sites. One Sunday afternoon I noticed in some dense woods a cluster of large white-cedar trees, not indigenous to the area, and as I approached them I could see that the ground and bushes in the site were almost completely covered with knee-deep thick vines. Wading in through the underbrush, I saw an erect tombstone, but was disappointed to find that the name on it was "Hart," not "Carter." However, when I pushed more of the foliage aside and separated some of the vines, I found two or three stone slabs, a few inches above ground level. I knelt and scraped dirt off some of the incised letters, and finally saw the name "Wiley Carter" plus a few more letters and numbers.

Thrilled and excited, I began to uncover more of the inscription, but then every nerve in my body tingled and seemed to freeze from a sound that I had known and dreaded all my life. It was a rattlesnake, obviously very close behind me. I turned my head, and there it was, coiled about two feet from the grave on which I was kneeling, with its vertically slit eyes focused on me and its tail quivering. I stood erect very slowly, and remained still while looking carefully around for other serpents. The rattlesnake uncoiled, crawled toward me, and disappeared into a hole under the slab where I was standing.

I took several tremendous leaps through the vines and brush, got in my pickup truck, and went back home. The following week, after getting permission from the landowner, who turned out to be one of my distant cousins, I went back to the place with my brother,

Billy, and a small front-end loader, and we carefully cleared brush and vines from the entire graveyard. Later, my Uncle Buddy and I cleaned the inscriptions, put a coping and a chain-link fence around the graves, and erected a simple marker with a list of Wiley's family who had been born and lived on the farm. I learned, for the first time, that the Harts were close relatives.

It was also from Uncle Buddy that I learned about my grandfather William Archibald Carter, who was called Billy. Born in 1858, he was the second son of Littleberry Walker Carter. Billy didn't have much education, but he taught school for a while before going into the sawmill business. He worked for the rich Hand family in Pelham, Georgia, near the Florida line, married Nina Pratt, and then moved to a little crossroads settlement in South Georgia called Rowena when he was thirty years old.

Billy was strong, ambitious, and hardworking, and thrived in one of the most challenging frontier regions of Georgia. He acquired four hundred acres of land, a cotton gin, three sawmills, and a roadside store. His main income was from cutting virgin pine timber, sawing it into crossties, then hauling them five miles to the railroad station in Arlington. He also planted a ten-acre vineyard and made about three thousand gallons of wine each year, which, said Uncle Buddy, "sold like hotcakes for thirty cents a quart." Billy built a small schoolhouse on his land and induced one of his cousins to teach, but she became "frightened of the riffraff" in the community and moved back home. Except for his oldest son, Alton—my Uncle Buddy— who stayed there to help his father, all the family then moved to Cuthbert, twenty-six miles away, so the children could go to school.

Uncle Buddy told me, "My daddy worked like the dickens all the time, and he was tough. Let me tell you what I saw him do one day. He was at the sawmill, and he had a drawknife making some ox yokes. It slipped and cut his knee, pretty bad. There was blood shooting out everywhere, and he had to wrap his shirt around the thigh so he wouldn't bleed to death. He put a sawmill hand on a mule and sent him to our house, two miles away, to get a needle and a spool of white thread from Mama. Then he sat there and sewed that thing up himself—and went right back to work. He was just that sort of a fellow.

"Another time, he had a well digger come over to dig an open well—we didn't have any bored wells in those times. He dug down about thirty feet, then came and told Daddy he had got water all right. Daddy had agreed to pay him twenty-five cents a foot to dig it, and he went over there to measure it to see how much he owed him. You know, sometimes the digging is kind of crank-sided, and hard to get the bucket up and down. Daddy looked in and said, 'Jim, it looks kinda crooked, don't you think?' Jim eased up to the hole, looked in, and said, 'Yes, sir, Mr. Billy, this well sho' is crooked now, but when I left here it was just as straight as a dowel.' Daddy said, 'Well, how did it get so crooked?' Jim said, 'Well, I don't know, sir, unless the sun warped it.' "

I knew that my uncle had witnessed my grandfather's death, and I asked him to tell me how it happened.

"A fellow by the name of Will Taliaferro [he pronounced it "Toliver"] had rented one building from my daddy, but it got burned up, so he rented another for a kind of a store. In his place, Taliaferro had a pair of scales, a flat-topped J&P thread case, a can cutter, and a few other things that my daddy let him use. Taliaferro headed a crowd that was rough as pig iron, and I understand the folks are still the same way down there. They'd meet every Sunday to drink liquor, play poker, and just have a helluva hooraw. This hell raising was in my daddy's building, so he went down and told them they'd have to stop their carrying on—he was clean with it—but they didn't pay any attention to him at all. He went back again and told them if they didn't stop he was going to report them to the grand jury. Finally, he did report it, and the whole outfit got mad with him. However, they kept on doing the same thing, sometimes as many as twenty or thirty men there at a time.

"Finally, Daddy told Taliaferro to move off his property, which he did. He left the scales and other things in our building, but that little flat-topped thread case, he took it with him. Taliaferro then went up the road a piece and built a little store on his sister's land. When we got ready to gin cotton in September, we needed that thread case to use for a desk, and Papa told me to go up to Taliaferro's and get it, so I went up there and said, 'Will, Daddy told me to come up and get his desk.' He said, 'It ain't his no more. I bought that desk from him and paid him for it.' But he said he'd lend it to me. That was in the morning. I put it in the gin and worked on it that day, but that night I told Daddy what Will had said. He said, 'Will ain't paid me for no desk—I'll go over there and see him about it.'

"His store was not far from ours, about a hundred yards or so. He walked down the road to Will's door, and I got off our front porch and followed him a ways. I was close enough to hear every word they said. My daddy put one hand on each side of the door and said, 'Will, Alton said you claim you bought that desk. I don't remember anything about it.' Will said, 'You're a goddamn liar. I bought it and paid you for it.' When he said that, they went together. There was a barrel of bottles sitting there, and my daddy fell on the barrel, and bottles busted all around them. They fought there just a little while. I moved closer when they began fighting, but they broke apart, and my daddy started walking back toward our place. The fellow pulled a pistol out of his pocket and shot three times.

"One bullet hit Daddy in the back of his head. We got the doctor, and put Daddy on a train—we didn't have any automobiles then— and carried him to Cuthbert, where Mama was living. And he died there, after being unconscious for a day or so. That's the reason we buried him in Cuthbert."

I asked Uncle Buddy what they did with Taliaferro, and he replied, "Well, they arrested him, but he finally got off scot free. Now where my daddy did wrong was going over there to his store, and he was carrying a twenty-five-cent Barlow pocketknife, which he never opened. Everyone knew what kind of carrying on there had been—my daddy was just trying to make it a decent place to live. Taliaferro had a lot of kinfolks in the county, and some of his drinking buddies were always on the jury. They had three trials—two mistrials, and the third time they gave up, probably because by then the Carters had all moved away and the Taliaferro family were still there."

I knew we had some kinfolks named Taliaferro, but Uncle Buddy didn't think my grandfather's murderer was related to us.

It took Uncle Buddy and his uncle about a year to sell the land, gin, and sawmills, and then the family moved up to Plains to be near their kinfolks. They bought a house next to the Methodist church, and spent the rest of their money on eight hundred acres of farmland in nearby Webster County.

Our family made this move to Plains when Alton was sixteen, my father ten, and the town eight years old, with a population of about three hundred. Five years later, Alton joined with Ross Dean, the undertaker, to form a partnership called Plains Mercantile Company. The two trading centers were competitors until 1934, when Oliver-McDonald lost its dominant position and Plains Mercantile took over the two main brick buildings on the street, with the funeral business in the west end. Alton would go to Atlanta about once a month and to New York twice a year to buy dry goods and furniture. He was proud to tell me that on one occasion he joined in with other local merchants and bought fifteen carloads of furniture from High Point, North Carolina.

My Uncle Buddy also provided the town with banking service from 1920, when the Plains Bank went broke, until 1965, when private banks were banned by the Georgia legislature. He didn't lend money, but just ran a deposit-and-checking business for the town, often handling $40,000 to $50,000 per day during the harvest season. He said he never made a dime in banking, but it brought a lot of people into his store and gave him a chance for a sale. I think it also gave him a chance to keep up with what was happening in the community, because the depositors all expected a fairly extensive conversation when they showed up at the counter. In 1918, my Uncle Buddy was elected to the city council, and was mayor from 1920 until 1954, except for six years out of office when he served as a county commissioner. He was as tight with public money as he was with his own, and during all those years as mayor his monthly salary rose only from $1.50 to $2.

I never had many opportunities to discuss the history of our family with my father—he was already gone before I developed any real interest in my kinfolks. I knew more about my distant ancestors than about my current relatives. My daddy's folks were never tempted to have a family reunion or even an informal relationship, and I don't remember any visit to or from any of them, even though he had a number of first and second cousins who lived within ten miles of us. So far as I know, there was never any animosity, just a lack of interest in each other.

Unfortunately (I think), we had a somewhat different situation with my mother's clan of Gordys. They had emigrated from Scotland to Maryland and Delaware, then moved to the Carolinas; eventually, my great-great-grandfather Wilson Gordy came to live near Columbus when the Indians left, before 1840. He brought all his belongings in a large hogshead with an axle through its center, pulled down the narrow Indian trail by his one draft horse. It was an accepted fact that even Mama's immediate family members couldn't get along with each other long enough to enjoy a full meal together. Among her parents and siblings there was an intense interest in controversial subjects, some highly personal in nature, that almost guaranteed that some constantly threatening personal explosion would occur. Sometimes on the way to Sunday dinner in Richland after church, Daddy and Mama would try to guess what would precipitate the main argument of the day. After each of these encounters, it took a long time for wounded sensitivities to heal.

I wanted to know about Mama's family, and she was glad to respond to my questions:

"Well, first of all, let me tell you about Mama. She seemed to be real quiet, but she never let Papa push her around. For instance, Papa was quite a dandy when he was young. He was engaged to another woman, in Cusseta, before he even met my mother, and the wedding was all planned. I never did know if it was a forced wedding or not, but when the time came he got on the train and left town instead of going to the church. He stayed away about three months, then came back and started courting Mama. When they were engaged, he was twenty-five and she was just seventeen, but Mama was really feisty. She told him she wasn't going to even dress for the ceremony until she knew he was standing by and ready. She sat in a chair in the pastorium, with her wedding dress on the bed, until Papa arrived at the church and the preacher came over and certified that he was there. Only then did she get up, put on her wedding dress, and join him for the ceremony.

"Papa's first job was in Brooklyn [Georgia], just a crossroad with about a dozen families, where they moved immediately after the wedding. Mama always told us about the first meal she cooked. Papa brought home some oysters, and she said the more she boiled them the tougher they got.

"Mama took good care of the house and all of us children, with not much help from Papa. She had Susie, Annie Lee, and Albert, one right after another. Then Uncle Crockett either was shot or killed himself, and Mama took his boys, Thad and Rex, my double first cousins. They were Catholics, and we made fun of them when they knelt down to pray or said their catechism. So Mama had five babies at once, none old enough to go to bed without help. Then she skipped three years and I came along, followed by Lem, Jack, Tom, Elizabeth, and Sissy—all of us two or three years apart."

When I was a child, I would visit my grandmother Mary Ida Nicholson Gordy, who was calm and sedentary and seemed to be perfectly satisfied with her way of life. She would spend all day in the house and garden. She concentrated on preparing breakfast for a big family; when breakfast was over, she'd get the children off to school, clean the kitchen, and make up the beds. Then she would put on her sunbonnet and work in the large garden, bringing a wicker basket full of seasonal vegetables back into the house.

She always cooked a big dinner at noon, along with pies, cakes, or fruit puffs for a constant supply of dessert. After the dishes were washed, she would clean the rest of the house, wash and iron the family's clothes, and take care of the kids coming home from school, being sure that they did their chores and completed their home-work assignments. Then she had to prepare supper, which was often leftovers plus a few fresh-cooked items. By the time it was dark, we'd all go to bed. The next morning, she'd get up at four-thirty and make a fire in the woodstove while Grandpa, if he was home and it was winter, would make a fire in the fireplace.

Ida Nicholson Gordy, 1915

On Sundays, everyone went to Sunday school and church, so Grandma had to prepare most of the large dinner in advance, perhaps cooking just the biscuits and fried chicken after the services were over. For one afternoon a week, she joined some of the other ladies of the community in a quilting bee, all of them sewing while they discussed affairs of their families and the community. I can see now that hers was a complete life, not much different from that of most Southern women of the time. She was proud and grateful to serve the other members of her family, who more or less took her for granted.

My grandfather "Jim Jack" Gordy was as wide-roving and flamboyant as my grandmother was sedate and home-loving. He was born in 1863 near Columbus, Georgia, and moved with his bride to the small settlement of Brooklyn, where he established a one-room schoolhouse and taught for several years before moving ten more miles to the larger town of Richland. He was named for James Jackson, one of Georgia's Revolutionary War heroes, who accepted the final British surrender of Savannah and later served several terms as governor and U.S. senator.

In many ways, Jim Jack was a man's man. He was tall, slender, handsome, and always well groomed and neatly dressed. Even on workdays, he preferred to wear a bowtie —and never a pre-tied one. Jim Jack was intensely interested in politics and was known to be the most knowledgeable man in the two counties nearest his home. Our family was always proud of Grandpa's ability to predict local election results. He would write down the expected returns on election eve, put them in a sealed envelope, and give them to the county clerk to retain. When opened after the results were known, they always turned out to be remarkably accurate.

Grandpa also demonstrated a remarkable understanding of national elections. During years that long preceded a civil-service system in the U.S. government, he was nimble enough on his political feet to guess right in successive presidential elections, shifting party allegiance to retain his appointment as postmaster in Richland,

My grandfather Jim Jack Gordy, 1915

Georgia. When Harding was elected, he went to make arrangements for the position in the small Georgia town of Rhyne, the only Republican stronghold outside of Atlanta, where choice federal appointments were dispensed because of political support or cash payoffs. They had already sold the postmaster's position, but Jim Jack was able to become the chief revenue agent for our region. I heard my daddy say that this was one job for which Grandpa and his sons were especially qualified, having done business with most of the moonshiners in the area. Grandpa would take a "sociable" drink on frequent occasions, but I never knew him to be tipsy enough to lose his composure or bring ridicule on himself. He had two sons, though, who had serious problems with whiskey.

As a former schoolteacher, Jim Jack kept meticulous records of his work and expenses as a revenue agent. I have his memorandum book for October and November 1922, and it is fascinating to see how he traveled, gathered information, found and destroyed stills, poured out mash and whiskey, arrested moonshiners, and later helped to prosecute them in court. During this two-month period he destroyed thirty-six stills. Whenever possible, he traveled by rail, and then incurred his largest expense items by hiring an automobile to take him to the suspected site, at a cost of about fifteen cents a mile, including the driver, whom he usually swore in as his deputy. He ate most of his meals at country stores, at an average cost of about eighty-five cents, and never exceeded a dollar for a night's lodging at hotels in his district's various towns. The farthest he ever traveled was across the state almost two hundred miles to Savannah, where he joined his supervisor, Mr. Dismuke, to prosecute some cases in the federal court. The round-trip rail fare was $6.78.

Jim Jack's only unswerving political allegiance was to Tom Watson, a nationally known populist in his day, who served as a Democratic congressman in North Georgia but was disavowed by his party when he advocated equal economic treatment for black and white workers and small farmers. Cheated out of re-election, Watson joined the Populist Party and in 1896 was nominated as vice-president on William Jennings Bryan's Populist Party ticket. Later, he was twice the presidential nominee of the Populists, and became embittered by repeated defeats at the hands of the oligarchs against whom he raged. He was elected to the U.S. Senate after he changed his political philosophy almost completely and ran on a racist platform.

My grandfather considered his own greatest achievement to be recommending the concept of rural delivery of mail to Tom Watson, who was successful in getting the idea passed into law. The only mementos I inherited from Grandpa were letters exchanged with Tom Watson on this subject and a history book entitled *Life and Times of Thomas Jefferson.*

Watson had an effusive dedication of his book to the newspaper magnate William Randolph Hearst, who, he said, "has shown an earnest, fearless, and consistent interest in the cause of the weak and oppressed, as did Mr. Jefferson a hundred years ago."

Grandpa Gordy was a restless man, always seeming to want to be somewhere else when with his own family or with boring companions, but loquacious when he had a good audience or when he was especially interested in a subject being discussed. He fathered nine children and adopted the two boys who were orphans of his brother, but he never seemed to care much for their company. The only exception was my mother, whom he invited to serve as his assistant in the post office until she moved to Plains for nurses' training.

A couple of times each year, my mother would get word that "Papa has gone again." Grandpa would pack a small suitcase, get a supply of flour, meal, sugar, coffee, side meat, some liquid refreshments—and a good supply of books—and tell his wife, "Ida, I'm going out to the farm for a while." She had long ago learned that protests were fruitless, so she would tell him goodbye and expect to see him again in two or three weeks. They owned a small, remote place near Kinchafoonee Creek in Webster County with a tenant shack on it, mostly woodland with not enough open land to farm, a haven that Grandpa found preferable to the hurly-burly of home life. When he finally tired of the solitude or felt that his official duties couldn't spare him longer, he would return home as though he had just been down at the drugstore, with no thought of apologies or explanations for his absence.

My mother was proud of her relationship with Grandpa. "There was no doubt that I was Papa's favorite. Everyone in the family knew it. I guess one reason was that I didn't always accept what he said as the gospel truth, and would argue with some of his opinions. Looking back, I was always careful not to go too far with it, and to back off if it looked like he was getting too aggravated. In a lot of cases, though, particularly when he and I were alone at the post office, I think he liked for me to speak up so we could have something of a debate.

"I read more than anyone else in the family—except him, of

course—and I tried to learn about things that interested him. Sometimes he would give me a book he had just read, and we both looked forward to a fierce discussion about the subject. One thing I liked about working at the post office was that both of us could find time to read on the job. Another thing was that we probably knew more than anybody else what was going on around Richland. Papa had a way of absorbing the news, but always cautioned me about not repeating gossip we heard if it would hurt anyone. I loved Mama and Papa, but I have to admit that I was ready to leave home and go in nurses' training, and when I got to Plains I didn't go back very often."

I remember that, after I graduated from the U.S. Naval Academy in 1946, I borrowed Daddy's automobile and drove the eighteen miles from Plains to Richland. I stopped by my grandparents' home and enjoyed some sweet milk and blackberry pie while telling Grandma about my new career. She then told me that Jim Jack was downtown in Richland, "probably at the drugstore." I walked down there and, sure enough, found my grandfather with some other loafers assembled around one of the glass-topped tables, drinking dopes and engaged in a heated discussion of some local issue. I stood behind him for a few minutes, until one of the men noticed my uniform and indicated my presence to Grandpa. When he turned around, I could tell that he didn't recognize me, and I blurted out, "Grandpa, I'm Jimmy, Lillian's son." He shook my hand and said, "Boy, I'm real glad to see you again." Then he turned around and continued his previous conversation. After standing there a few minutes, I went back home and off to my first ship. That was the last time I saw him.

When long past retirement age, in his late seventies, Jim Jack took a doorkeeper's job in the state capital, just to be close to political life in Georgia. He died in 1948, the year I became a submariner, and I was not able to go home for the funeral.

The varying temperaments of the younger Gordys mirrored the stark differences in the character of their parents. The girls all married well and raised fairly stable families, in some ways like their mother, but the boys were more like Grandpa.

My uncle Walter Lemuel Gordy moved from one job to another, at one time working with his father when he was a revenuer but mostly as a traveling salesman. Lem was handsome and eloquent, dressed neatly, and got along well with the customers on his route. He always seemed to be selling some new item of transient appeal to rural families. I remember that one of them was a little aluminum gadget shaped like a doughnut, with a cord that plugged into an

The Gordy family, 1930, with my mother in the center, Tom behind her, and Lem on top.

electrical outlet and could heat a basin of water. No one had central water-heaters when rural electrification first brought power to farmers' homes, and this was a good way to get hot water without firing up the woodstove or fireplace to heat a kettleful. However, there was a problem with insulation or with the basic design, and Lem was soon faced with irate customers on his route who had been knocked across the bathroom when they were heating water while standing nude on a wet floor. Luckily, no one was electrocuted, but he had to change products. Another of his wares was a lightbulb that cost three or four times as much as regular ones but was guaranteed to last for ten years. Eager buyers snapped them up, but Lem had really been saddled (probably without his knowledge) with fancy packages containing regular bulbs. Even when he replaced the burned-out bulbs twice, the company still made a good profit, but he soon ran out of trusting customers. His income fluctuated wildly, and he was inclined to go on a bender when his luck was bad. But his wife, Lorraine, had a good and steady job in a large department store in Columbus, and the couple lived fairly well.

James Jackson, Jr., three years younger than Lem, became a hopeless alcoholic. When reasonably sober, Uncle Jack was a good housepainter, but whenever he received payment for a job the house owner and the Gordy family all knew that the money would go for beer and whiskey. He was a docile man who never hurt anyone while drunk, and would always go home when he needed some food and a place to sleep. Later in his life, after his parents were gone and I had come home from the navy, the sheriffs in our area knew to call me when Uncle Jack had turned himself in after a drunken spree to sleep it off in a jail cell. We finally got him to agree to enter the Anchorage, a treatment center for alcoholics in Albany, and he spent the last years of his life in and out of the place. I would pick him up at the jail and carry him there; he would sober up, go through therapy and counseling, and easily get a job painting. Inevitably, he fell off the wagon, and we would repeat the cycle.

The bright light in the Gordy family was my Aunt Emily, whom everyone called Sissy. Only twelve years older than I, she was a frequent and welcome guest in our home, and my parents and I followed closely her education and early career as a teacher. The biggest social event that ever occurred at our house was Sissy's wedding party. We set up tables under shade trees in the front yard, and borrowed folding chairs from the local funeral parlor. After some discussion with Daddy, Mama decided that the main dish would be chicken salad, which could be prepared in advance from the large flock of hens and fryers in our yard. The guests could also have a choice of sandwiches or a fuller meal served on dinner plates. My mother brought in several of the women on the place to help her

Emily Gordy Dolvin

prepare food for more than a hundred people, many of whom came all the way from Atlanta, the home of the groom.

The party got off to a fine start. Everyone was having a good time, and I was helping to replenish the supply of food on the front-yard tables. On one of my trips into the kitchen, I noticed a chicken flat on the ground near the back steps, spasmodically kicking its legs. It died as I watched. I went to find Daddy, and we began seeing other chickens perishing around the back yard. We realized that the folks eating chicken salad would be even more distressed than we were when they saw the kinfolk of their food dying around their feet. Daddy said, "Hot, you and A.D. run all the chickens out of the front yard while I keep them in back with some corn." With every-one in our farm family helping, we concealed the dead chickens from Sissy's friends until Mama was able to expedite their depar-ture.

Then we began worrying about what would happen to the guests a few hours later. Because of scarce refrigeration, all the rural families were quite familiar with the threat of food poisoning, and we began preparing for the worst. We finished picking up all the feathered cadavers, and had some hope restored when we found an open bag of nitrate of soda, which was used to fertilize the nearby cotton field, with a few chickens scratching and pecking around it. Daddy called Uncle Jack Slappey, the veterinarian, to come out, and he confirmed our diagnosis that sodium-nitrate poisoning was the problem. Our chicken salad did not threaten the lives of the wed-ding guests.

When the Japanese bombed Pearl Harbor, my Uncle Tom Gordy and about thirty other sailors were stationed on Guam, part of the radio communication system that served the Pacific fleet. With our military force incapacitated, it was inevitable that the island would be taken, and the men there were ordered not to resist. They were not trained for combat, at least in jungles, and it was likely that many

Guamanians would suffer if the Japanese had to fight their way through the island. Tom and the others were captured about a month after the war began, and taken to Japan as prisoners. Tom's wife, Dorothy, and their three children left San Francisco and came to Georgia to stay with my grandparents, who were then living near us in Archery. Dorothy was a beautiful and quiet woman, but this life on a South Georgia farm was totally different from what she and the children had always known in San Francisco, and her city ways were considered strange by Tom's kinfolks.

In the summer of 1943, the International Red Cross notified Dorothy officially that Tom was dead, and she began receiving a widow's pension. Everyone was heartbroken, and she and the kids moved back to San Francisco to live with her parents. After a year or so, she married a friend of the family who had a stable job and promised to care for her and the children.

Two years later, when the war ended and American troops entered Japan, they found Tom Gordy still alive! He had been working for four years as a fireman on a small, isolated railroad that hauled coal from some mountain mines down to the main transportation lines. Beaten and partially starved during the four years, he weighed less than a hundred pounds, and was suffering from severe phlebitis. He was transferred back to a military hospital in Georgia for treatment, immediately promoted to lieutenant senior grade, and given all the back pay he would have earned.

I was in the navy at the time. Tom wrote me about his situation and said that he still loved his wife and children and wanted to be with them. Dorothy quickly decided to have her second marriage annulled, but Tom was very weak, and unable to resist his mother and sisters, who convinced him that Dorothy had betrayed him and committed adultery while he was a prisoner of war. He got a divorce and was transferred to Florida, where he was put in charge of security at a large navy base near Jacksonville.

Tom was soon happily married to another woman, was promoted to full commander, and when he retired, bought and operated a prosperous tavern. He visited us in Plains every now and then, and was proud when I was elected governor. He always reminded me that he had been two grades my senior in navy rank; he died in 1975, not living to see me become commander-in-chief.

These were my kinfolks, and I presume that I inherited some of the characteristics of them all. The special background of my life in Archery, with a relatively protected and disciplined boyhood, helped prepare me for what was to come.

11

The Navy Versus Plains

A S I APPROACHED graduation from high school, the Naval Academy became almost an obsession in our family. If I slacked off at all from my schoolwork, one of my parents was sure to say, "You'll never go to Annapolis this way!" In fact, there was only one way to obtain admission to a military academy: to receive an appointment either from one of our U.S. senators or from our local congressman. Since senators had to share their five incumbent midshipmen with the entire state, we concentrated on our Congressman, Steven Pace.

Daddy deliberately increased his circle of friends throughout our region, determined to use his political influence to wangle my Annapolis appointment from our congressman. He supported Mr. Steve Pace strongly in every election, and contributed what he could afford to his campaign fund. At least once a year while I was in high school, Daddy would take me and my report cards over to the Pace home during a congressional recess, to brag a little about me and to repeat his request for an appointment. Having served for several terms, the congressman knew how to assuage supplicants without making a firm commitment, and I finished high school without a positive response. All our family were bitterly disappointed, but Congressman Pace suggested that I enroll at the junior college in Americus and wait for another year, when a possible appointment might be forthcoming.

In September 1941, I left home and moved into the dormitory at Georgia Southwestern College in Americus, where I concentrated on subjects that were recommended in the Annapolis guidebook for prospective midshipmen. But after a year we were disappointed again, and this time our visit with Mr. Pace was somewhat confrontational. Daddy was determined to get a definite answer, and I remember our staying on the front porch after it was obvious that our welcome was over. Finally, I heard the congressman say, "I'll give Jimmy an appointment next year, and he won't have to take the full entrance examination if he can make good grades in college." I had my doubts, but Daddy trusted Mr. Steve's firm promise, and we decided on the way home that I could benefit more as a student at Georgia Tech than at the local junior college.

After a year of engineering studies in Atlanta, where I was a member of the Navy Reserve Officers Training Corps, I got my Annapolis appointment, and served for seven more years in the U.S. Navy. As a result, I didn't move back to Plains until twelve years after leaving home; by that time my father had died and the Depression was a distant memory. Except for very brief vacations, I had not lived in Plains for almost twelve years, and except for infrequent letters and telephone calls, I had lost personal contact with the other members of my family and with my old boyhood friends.

While I was away, A. D. Davis got married; he eventually had twelve children, served four years in prison on a conviction of forgery, and then lived the rest of his life peacefully in Plains. His oldest son, A.D., Jr., is head of the family now, and is the spitting image of his father.

Rembert Forrest became a successful funeral director in New York, and is now retired with his family in Florida.

College freshman, 1941

Jack Clark died while I was still in the navy, and his wife, Rachel, moved into Plains to live in the new government housing project. As much as anyone I've ever known, she helped to shape my early life.

Alton Carter, my Uncle Buddy, married a retired schoolteacher, Betty Jennings, after his first wife died, and the couple continued the tradition of annual trips with my parents to major-league baseball games. After my father died, Uncle Buddy became a surrogate father to me, and helped to guide me through my embryonic years as a businessman and a politician. He lived until 1978, long enough to visit me in the White House.

.   .   .

I thought about my father often after I left home. It was not easy for me to put into words, even to my wife, Rosalynn, how my early years with Daddy had affected my life. I had strongly mixed feelings about him: of love, admiration, and pride, but also at least a retrospective concern about his aloofness from me. I never remembered him saying, "Good job, Hot," or thanking me when I had done my best to fulfill one of his quiet suggestions that had the impact of orders. The individual punishments he administered remained vivid in my memory. I used to hunger for one of his all-too-rare demonstrations of affection. Also, even though he was obviously proud of how well I did in the navy, I had a lingering question about why he never encouraged me to stay in Plains with him, even during the thirteen years before he had another son. Sometimes I thought about how he carried me along as the only child on an adult hunting or fishing adventure, but I remembered that it was usually Rachel and Jack Clark who taught me the intricacies of fishing and hunting with a dog.

With passing time, while I built a navy career and had a family, it was natural that Plains and my parents became hazier memories. Still, I thought I knew my father well, but it was not until I received permission from the navy to visit Daddy for a week during his terminal illness that I really understood how diverse and interesting and valuable a man's life could be. Now we all knew that Daddy's advanced pancreatic cancer would not go into remission, and I spent my few precious home days mostly at his bedside.

His accomplishments and the breadth of his interests were astonishing to me. In almost all facets of community life he was a respected leader, including education, health, agriculture, social affairs, and in his newly elected position as a member of the state legislature.

Our long conversations were interrupted frequently by a stream of visitors, black and white, who came to the door to bring a small gift or a special food delicacy, or to inquire about his condition. A surprising number wanted to recount how my father's personal influence, community service, and many secret acts of generosity had affected their lives.

I was at the pinnacle of success for a young officer of my rank and had never had any serious thoughts of anything other than a full naval career, feeling confident that I could attain the navy's highest rank. But now I felt besieged by an unwelcome comparison of the ultimate value of my life with his. On the long drive back to Schenectady, New York, where I was helping to prepare one of the two prototype nuclear-propulsion plants for submarines, I could not escape a startling and disturbing question: whether I wanted to resign my commission and try to follow in his footsteps in this tiny rural community. Rosalynn was shocked and furious a few days later when I told her that I had decided to do just that.

When I came back home from the navy in 1953, Willis Wright was still making a good living on his own farm, but he realized he was in failing health. He came to let me know that, if anything happened to him, and if his second and younger wife ever wanted to sell the farm, he wanted me to have "first refusal" to buy it back. This commitment was to be fulfilled almost exactly forty years later. Now the Willis Wright home is the only one still standing on our entire farm in Webster County, since the better fields are worked with large equipment and I've planted the less productive land in pine trees.

His black neighbors in the community looked to Willis for leadership, and they knew that the white people in our area also respected him. Quite early in the civil rights movement, there was a meeting of a few people in Willis's church, just north of our farm, where it was decided that he should be the first one who would attempt to register to vote in Webster County. He bought all his seed, fertilizer, and pesticides from me at Carter's Warehouse, and we purchased his peanuts and other cash crops during harvest season, so it was natural for him to come and tell me about it.

Willis still abided by the old proprieties in addressing me as a white adult: "Mr. Jimmy, I need your advice on something that's important to me and some of the other folks in Webster County. We had a meeting in our church, and there was a man there from the Justice Department. He told us that the law now guarantees that black people can vote and that some have registered in other counties in Georgia."

I assured him that this was correct.

"Well, I was chosen to be the first one, so early this morning I went over to the courthouse to the registrar's office and found that it was closed. I waited until almost dinnertime, and he finally unlocked his office and I followed him in. He asked me what I wanted, and I said I wanted to register to vote. He told me to wait a few moments and walked down the hall. When he came back, he brought out some papers and said I would have to answer some questions about citizenship."

I interrupted to say, "I'm familiar with those questions, and I couldn't answer them myself. There are thirty of them, and they're used only to keep Negroes from voting. They ask folks to give the legal definition of a felony, to quote portions of the U.S. Constitution, to explain when it is appropriate to depend on *habeas corpus,* and to name all the Supreme Court justices."

"Yes, sir," Willis agreed. "We discussed this at the church, and the man from Washington said that we no longer have to answer them in order to vote. I told the registrar this, and then he pulled a pistol out of a drawer and laid it on the counter. He was nervous, but he said, 'Nigger, you better think this over for a few more days, then let me know what you decide.' "

I asked, "Willis, what did you do then?"

He smiled and said, "That's when I decided to come over here and talk to you. We know you've had a boycott against your own business, and might be familiar with the problem." (Twice during those years, racist groups in Sumter County had organized boycotts against Carter's Warehouse because of my "liberal" racial views.)

I offered to go with him to the registrar's office, but he responded, "No, sir. It wouldn't mean nothing if you was there with me."

I advised Willis to tell the registrar that he had discussed the matter with me, and that I told him to go back and register. He did so, and the next time I saw him he said he hadn't had any problem.

Times were changing in Georgia, but slowly.

I've tried to understand how my upbringing and inherited traits have influenced my character and my attitudes toward life. There seem to be some connections, but the diversity among my siblings shows how tenuous these kinship ties can be.

Although Gloria was just two years younger than I and Ruth was born only three years after her, the difference in their ages and also in temperaments created an enormous difference in the way they related to me. My parents mentioned often that I almost died from colitis when I was three years old, and they surmised that this setback stunted my growth. In any case, I was very small through grammar and high school, whereas Gloria grew rapidly in her early years. For a while she equaled me in physical strength and was far superior in the tactics of surviving and prevailing in our childhood rivalry. She was always strong-willed and aggressive, so there was intense competition between her and me until we were both old enough to begin ignoring each other. Gloria and my father also had frequent confrontations, because she resisted his rigid standard of discipline. She was unflinching when Daddy punished her, either by restricting her to her room for a weekend or with a few licks on her legs with a limber switch. As a teenager, she even insisted on setting her own schedule for coming home from dates, and Mama spent a lot of her time covering up for Gloria and serving as her defense advocate with Daddy.

I was in the navy when she began dating a former soda jerk from Americus who had just finished flight training in the Air Corps. Over the strong opposition of my parents—perhaps because of it—they were married and moved off for service in a military base. Shortly after a baby came, she returned home with severe bruises on her face and body from her husband's beatings. With Daddy's help, Gloria was able to have the marriage annulled.

Later, she married a fine man, Walter Guy Spann, who was a farmer from Webster County and just the opposite of her first husband. Walter worked hard, took care of his land and equipment, minded his own business, and made a good living. He had a great interest in motorcycling, and over the years he and Gloria accumulated seven Harley-Davidsons, on which they would take long trips, including to Alaska and down through Mexico. They made many friends among the bikers, and Gloria gradually became kind of a "den mother" to them. She planted a large garden each year, canned the vegetables to serve their often unexpected biker guests, and arranged their farmhouse so the floor could be cleared for multiple cots or sleeping bags. Walter constructed a four-hole outhouse in the back yard, and they were able to accommodate several dozen bikers who were on the way to Daytona races or just cruising through the South. Everyone knew when Gloria and Walter had company, because there was a fleet of the big motorcycles moving down the highways and country roads around Plains. If the bikers were sick, she nursed them; if their motorcycles needed repairs, Walter helped them in his machine shop; and if their leather jackets or stitched insignia were torn, Gloria repaired them on her heavy-duty sewing machine.

One of my sister's proudest possessions was a big trophy she kept on the living-room mantelpiece. The state's Honda dealers had held a contest in Macon for the most beautifully decorated motorcycle, and Walter and Gloria went over to see the activities. Without their knowing it, a large group of Harley aficionados had attended and voted en bloc for Gloria's muddy bike, so she brought home the trophy.

After I returned to Plains from the navy, Gloria and I got along

The Carters, 1976:
Billy, Ruth, Gloria, me, and Mama.

well, but she never relinquished her independent spirit and unique character. When she was on her deathbed—with pancreatic cancer, like my father—her biker friends descended on Plains. For almost two weeks, two of them were always outside her hospital-room door. At her request, the funeral cortege consisted of the hearse led by a long double line of Harley-Davidson motorcycles. On her marble gravestone is carved, "She rides in Harley heaven."

By contrast, Ruth was my intimate friend and her daddy's little angel. One reason for this was that she was seriously ill when she was a baby in arms, and the entire family was assembled with the doctor for her impending death. Although I was only five years old, I remember vividly that Mama was disturbed when Daddy lifted Ruth's inert little body from the crib. She cried out, "Earl, what in the world are you doing?"

He replied, "I'm going to let her see the sunshine one more time," and held her up to the window so she could look out into the yard. When he put her back on the pillow, we all knelt down and prayed for her. Ruth survived and thrived. From then on, although Ruth had her normal ups and downs with boyfriends and school affairs, there was something special about her.

She married Dr. Robert Stapleton, a successful veterinarian, moved to North Carolina, and raised four children. Then she went back to college and studied theology; when I began to run for president, she was already famous as Ruth Carter Stapleton, a successful international evangelist and author of five popular books. Although she often spoke to huge crowds, Ruth was especially effective in small groups and as a personal counselor.

She knew how to help me at one of the lowest points in my life. When I ran for governor in 1966, no candidate got a majority of the vote, and the legislature ultimately chose the racist Lester Maddox. His symbol was a pick handle that he used to drive potential black customers from the door of his restaurant in Atlanta. I was deeply disillusioned. I could not believe that God, or the Georgia voters, would let this person beat me and become the governor of our state. Ruth drove down to see me, quoted a scripture from the book of James, and urged me to react to failure and disappointment with joy, then patience and wisdom, and finally by striving for a transcendent religious experience. At the time, I rejected her advice, but later I came to accept it and carved out a new political life for myself.

She also died at an early age from pancreatic cancer. But I still meet people who say, "Your sister Ruth changed my life."

To many people, the most interesting member of our family was my brother, Billy. He was thirteen years younger than I, and just a small child when I left home. I saw him only on my brief visits on leave from the navy, and during those few days in Plains I was more interested in being with my parents, our other relatives, or my old friends than with little Billy. Even then, he had a mind of his own. One hot summer day when I was in the kitchen and talking to my parents, Billy walked through the room and said he was going to take a shower and go out for a while. Daddy said, "Billy, this is the third shower today, and you don't need it." That would have changed my plans, but we soon heard the water running upstairs. Later, Billy walked through again, put a nickel on the table, and said, "This is to pay for the water." Despite this gentle rudeness, I could see that Billy was much closer to Daddy than I had ever been. They looked alike and had many of the same mannerisms.

No one had ever expected me to come back to Plains to live, and only long afterward did I realize how adversely my decision to do so had affected Billy's plans to succeed Daddy. My brother was fifteen years old at the time, and he stayed close to Mama and his girlfriend Sybil, who was only thirteen, while I was working hard to learn about fertilizer, farming, business management, and the personal characteristics and interests of farmers around Plains whom I was seeking as customers. A few times, Mama and I suggested that Billy work with me as he had with Daddy, but he usually made some excuse. The day he finished high school, he joined the U.S. Marines, and he and Sybil were married soon afterward. They left Plains and didn't return after his enlistment expired.

Late in 1963, I was serving in the state Senate. Our business was continuing to expand, so I asked Billy again to come back home to help me with the warehouse, and he agreed. I knew he was drinking a good bit, but he seemed to have it under control, and I never knew it to affect the good job he did as my partner. He had an easy rapport with farmers—much better than I with most of them—and he and I got along fairly well. I was boss when I was at home, and he was in charge when I was away campaigning or serving as governor. There were times when we had disagreements, and he would stomp out, slam the door, get in the pickup, and scratch off. He never failed to come back, though sometimes not until the following morning.

Mama always said that Billy was the smartest of her children, and none of us argued with her. He read at every possible moment—books, magazines, newspapers. Every morning by about six-thirty, when I arrived at the warehouse, he had already absorbed all four newspapers that came to Plains. Billy was a walking encyclopedia on subjects that he found interesting, including international affairs, American politics, and especially baseball. He earned a lot of money betting with unsuspecting people who questioned his seemingly foolish comments, which always turned out to be factual.

When the international news media moved into our town during the 1976 presidential campaign, Billy became a center of attention. He drank more, talked more, and saw his deliberately outrageous statements quoted as serious comments (and later used to ridicule him when his reporter "friends" turned on him). He was always good for a delightful quote. When one of the reporters remarked that Billy was a little strange, he replied, "Look: my Mama was a seventy-year-old Peace Corps volunteer in India, one of my sisters goes all over the world as a holy-roller preacher, my oldest sister spends half her time on a Harley-Davidson motorcycle, and my brother thinks he's going to be president of the United States. Which one of our family do *you* think is normal?"

After I was inaugurated and we walked down Pennsylvania Avenue, our family left the reviewing stand and moved toward the White House for our first visit. Not surprisingly, we were surrounded by news reporters, and my press secretary, Jody Powell, said, "Now, don't anybody stop to answer their questions." Mama replied, "Jody, you can go to hell. You might tell Jimmy what to do, but not the rest of us." The TV cameras quickly focused on Mama, and the first question was, "Miss Lillian, aren't you proud of your son?" I waited for her congratulatory words, but Mama answered tartly, "Which one?"

It was not much later that Billy realized that alcohol had gotten the best of him, and he volunteered to go into therapy. He was sober for the next ten years, and became a key spokesman for Alcoholics Anonymous. He was just fifty-one years old when, once again, pancreatic cancer brought death to one of the people I loved.

Until her death in 1993, my mother was the matriarch and real leader of our family. Although she lived a relatively restricted and disciplined life when we children were at home, she blossomed forth after my father's death, and during her last forty years she seemed to be searching constantly for whatever was interesting, challenging, and gratifying.

Her first job was KA fraternity housemother at Auburn University, where she mothered about a hundred rambunctious boys. Back home in the Plains community, she paid no attention to the restrictions of racial segregation. In 1964, when Lyndon Johnson decided not to campaign in the Deep South and received just a handful of white votes in our county, Mama volunteered to manage his campaign office. Almost every day, when she returned to her car she found it covered with graffiti, the windows soaped over, or the radio antenna tied in a knot. Her only compensation was to be a delegate to the national Democratic convention.

After opening a nursing home for some friends in Plains and operating it for a year, she volunteered for the Peace Corps, just asking that she be sent "where people have dark skins and need a nurse's service." She completed her tour near Bombay, India, at the age of seventy, then came back home and made almost five hundred speeches, telling her audiences not to let age or public opinion restrict the scope of their adventures.

Mama established her new home in a little isolated cabin in the woods, bought one of the first satellite antennas, and monitored Auburn's football team, professional basketball, and the major-league achievements of her beloved Dodgers. She was a favorite guest on Johnny Carson and other talk shows, because her discussions were just as lively and irrepressible as her public speeches.

. . .

Now I'm the only one left from my Archery family, and I'm ever more thankful that Rosalynn and I are living in the village where we were born, just a few minutes away from the sources of our most pleasant and enduring memories.

I never knew how unusual the members of my family were until I came to know Rosalynn's relatives after we returned from the navy to live in Plains. A Sunday dinner at her mother's home always included a long, pleasant, rambling discussion of what appeared to me to be minutiae. The casual conversation of a grandchild with a playmate or the illness of a distant relative would be thoroughly analyzed, always in a congenial manner. Collectively, they knew almost everything that had happened in our town, the churches, or the school. Even when some potentially controversial subject arose, such as a local election, there didn't seem to be any rough edges to the discussion. The contrary opinions of everyone around the table were politely respected. After we finally finished the meal and cleared off the table, those who weren't washing dishes would sit on the front porch and continue a detailed discussion of the weather, the status of the crops, or interesting tidbits of news about the families of people who happened to be passing by on the road in front of the house.

There were and still are annual family reunions of the Smiths and Murrays, always after church services on a Sunday in summer or fall. All of us wear name tags with a distinctive color representing the now deceased person from whom our part of the family happens to be descended. Prizes, usually a dollar, are given to the oldest, the youngest, and the one who has traveled farthest to attend—often several hundred miles or across the continent. After a thanksgiving prayer and an indescribably bountiful and delicious covered-dish banquet, folks admire all the babies, marvel over how much the children have grown since last year, visit with each other for a while, and then return home. It is surprising how enjoyable it is—and inconceivable to me that the members of my family on either side would do such a thing, year after year.

In most ways, the Plains I live in today is almost the same as it was when I was a boy. But in one way, change has been dramatic and positive—in the area of racial attitudes.

This was an issue that troubled my mother during my political years, when the news media began to probe our family's history. One day she said, "Jimmy, one thing bothers me. Reporters have criticized your daddy lately about not being for racial integration. What they don't recognize is that he died in 1953, when there was no such thing as integration and nobody had ever heard of Martin Luther King or any civil-rights movement. Your daddy always rejected all the racist organizations that degraded or persecuted black people, and both races always knew him to be fair and helpful. I was real controversial in the community sometimes, but he supported everything I did to help black people and to treat them well." She was right, of course.

I have focused this book almost exclusively on the distant past, beginning seventy years ago, to understand and explain myself better, to recount interesting experiences, and perhaps to bring some perspective to our rapidly changing present circumstances as we enter a new millennium. These sometimes random recollections are my most vivid ones. Some of them are painful, especially those about people I loved who are no longer with us. Other memories are embarrassing, including the treatment of our immediate neighbors, all of them black, under societal customs that, as Mama said, were never questioned at the time. No one would want to return to the old days of unchallenged racial segregation, when blacks "knew their place."

But in the dramatic changes we have witnessed, something has been lost as well as gained. My own life was shaped by a degree of personal intimacy between black and white people that is now almost completely unknown and largely forgotten. Except for my own parents, the people who most deeply affected my early life were Bishop Johnson, Rachel Clark, my Uncle Buddy, Julia Coleman, and Willis Wright. Two of them were white.

Recently, a twelve-acre site in Archery including our farmhouse, commissary, barn, blacksmith shop, and the home of Rachel and Jack Clark was designated by the U.S. Congress to be restored and preserved as it was in 1937. Now owned and operated by the Park Service, it is the only historic site in America that will show how rural families lived during the Great Depression.

A good portion of our fields and woodlands still produce cotton, wheat, peanuts, and timber. Rosalynn and I care for the land as best we can, but we don't know what will be done with it after we are no longer active. Our three sons and our daughter live in Atlanta or more distant places, and our ten grandchildren are scattered even more widely. They can't envision my father and me planting young trees, laying off terraces, building hog-farrowing houses, or operating the forge together. It is not easy for them to conceive how my mother nursed families in shacks that are no longer there, or how she harvested nuts from the now sixty-year-old pecan trees and sold them to a Lebanese merchant. As Rosalynn and I stroll down the relatively somnolent Main Street of Plains, it is difficult even for us to remember how packed with excited shoppers and visitors it used to be.

Although they will inherit what we own, none of our children or grandchildren have farming in their blood or any special attachment to the land that will be theirs. I don't know that any of them will ever return to our farms, some of which have been in our family for six generations. Times change, and deeds to the various fields will be held in the future by one family and then another. They may or may not be my descendants, but I am confident that the earth itself will remain basically the same, continuing to shape the lives of its owners, for good or ill, as it has for millennia. After all, the land belonged to the Indians before it was ours.

Acknowledgments

It's not easy to describe my emotions as these memories of my childhood came back to life. I am glad that, since I was born, things haven't changed much around Plains, Georgia. I was able to walk again through Willis Wright's fields, look down through the foot-worn floor of Rachel Clark's house where my pallet used to lie, hoist the hand-operated elevator in my Uncle Buddy's store, worship in Bishop William Johnson's country church, and sit in the same school chapel where Miss Julia Coleman's words helped shape my life. I've wandered from room to room in my boyhood home, savored the ancient but pleasant odors in our commissary store, and visited the barn lot where we caught mules each morning, an hour before daylight.

For seven years, I put these thoughts on paper, and then shared them with my wife, Rosalynn, who was my neighbor from the time of her birth. She corrected and enhanced some of my recollections, and then Nessa Rapaport, Karl Weber, Steve Hochman, and Alice Mayhew helped me improve the text with their incisive editorial suggestions. As usual, my assistant, Faye Perdue, coordinated the entire process.

For me, this has been a labor of love, and I am grateful to all those who made it possible.

Index

Page numbers in *italics* refer to illustrations.

Photo Credits

About the Author

Jimmy Carter, thirty-ninth president of the United States, was born and raised in and near Plains, Georgia, and still resides there. Accomplishments of his administration (1977–1981) include the Camp David Accords and peace between Egypt and Israel, the Panama Canal treaties, the SALT II treaty with the Soviet Union, the creation of the departments of Energy and Education, the deregulation of major industries, the Alaska Lands Act, and the establishment of diplomatic relations with China. His commitment to human rights inspired freedom movements throughout the world.

After leaving the White House, he and his wife, Rosalynn, established the nonprofit Carter Center in Atlanta, and work globally to prevent and resolve conflicts, enhance freedom and democracy, and improve health. They have monitored more than two dozen elections, brokered peace agreements in North Korea, Haiti, the Sudan, and Bosnia, and led worldwide efforts to eradicate debilitating disease.